The White Garden

The

WHITE
GARDEN

Diana Grenfell &
Roger Grounds

The Crowood Press

First published in 1990 by
The Crowood Press
Gipsy Lane
Swindon
Wiltshire SN2 6DQ

British Library Cataloguing in Publication Data

Grenfell, Diana
  The white garden.
  1. Gardens. Planning
  I. Title II. Grounds, Roger
  712.6

ISBN 1 85223 352 4

Dedication
To all the white garden owners who made us so welcome.

Picture Credits

All photographs and plans by the authors.
Flower paintings by Jenny Jowett.

Frontispiece: The White Garden at Hazelby House.

Page 3: Apricot petunias and Lady's mantle combine with verdigrised copper to warm white petunias.

Typeset by Avonset, Midsomer Norton, Bath.
Printed in Great Britain by Richard Clay Ltd, Bungay, Suffolk

Contents

Acknowledgements   6

Part 1 – Concept and Reality

The Concept of White   7
The Concept of Garden   8
Four White Gardens   12

Part 2 – Design and Features

The Genius of the Place   22
Aspirations   23
Organising Space   25
Enclosure   27
Screens and Semi-Screens   28
Articulations   32
Fixed Assets   33
Clipped Greens   36
Reflections on Water   36

Part 3 – Plants and Planting

The Basic Plants   40
Twelve White Flowers of Exceptional Beauty   52
Annuals, Biennials and Bedding   65
Bulbs   74
Perennials   80
White Perennial Foliage   95
Ferns and Grasses   98
Roses   102
Climbers   106
Greys and Silvers   111
Trees and Shrubs   117
Shrubs – Foliage   128
Water Plants   133

Part 4 – Garden Plans and Planning   137

Index   156
White Gardens to Visit   160

Acknowledgements

Many people have helped this book come into being. The original ideas grew out of the writings of Miss Jekyll, although white gardens existed before her time. Our greater debt is to Penelope Hobhouse whose book, *Colour in Your Garden*, contains the clearest possible exposition of colour and how it behaves in the garden. Our greatest inspiration has been the white gardens we have visited and we should in particular like to thank Lyn and Peter Prior, Mr and Mrs Martin Lane Fox, Richard Lyte, Christine Brain (Head Gardener at Barrington Court), Mrs Diany Binny, Lady Boxer, Mrs Sybil Spencer, Mrs Elizabeth MacLeod Matthews, Jane Williams-Thomas, Mrs Hugh Astor, Mr and Mrs Michael Verey who all made us welcome.

We also wish to extend very special thanks to Jenny Jowett whose exquisite paintings adorn this book.

Many people have helped us with advice and information of varying sorts and in particular we should like to thank John Bond VMH, Charles Puddle VMH, Martin Puddle, Graham Thomas VMH, Avon Bulbs, Martin Harwood (Holder of the National Reference Collection of Narcissus), Elizabeth Parker Jervis, the staff at the National Trust's Photographic Library for England and for Scotland, Peter Harkness, Zara McCalmont, Peter Maynard (British Iris Society), Sid Linnegar (British Iris Society), and Alan Page (Holder of the National Reference Collection of Trillium).

Part 1
Concept and Reality

THE CONCEPT OF WHITE

When you enter a well-made white garden your overwhelming impression will be of overall shimmering whiteness. But if afterwards you analyse the components of which that whiteness was made you will find that the eye has been deceived, for whiteness is most intensely white when it is an illusion. White gardens are not made by planting flowers of laundered whiteness everywhere; the impression of whiteness is created out of greens and greys and off-whites that lean towards ivory, pink or gaudy-green. In the

Ice-cool: grey Helichrysum petiolatum *neutralises the warm yellow in the throat of white petunias.*

world of colour nothing is quite what it seems, and no colour is so pure that it cannot be humoured by its neighbour.

To a physicist colour is a matter mainly of light. White light contains all the colours of the spectrum, and when passed through a prism it is split into its component colours, each colour being a different wavelength. A flower that looks red reflects red light but absorbs all other wavelengths; a leaf that looks green reflects green light and absorbs all the other wavelengths. A white flower reflects all wavelengths; a black flower absorbs all wavelengths.

What the eye sees or the brain interprets may not be so simple. Colours are modified by the colour that lies next to them or was seen before them, or by the tint of the ambient light. The eye tends always to supply a residual impression of the opposite colour to the one last perceived, perhaps as part of some neutralising process, as acid is neutralised with an alkali. While this phenomenon is best known as a sequence in time, it also occurs, though less obviously, as a concurrent event where colours lie side by side.

White flowers behave in similar ways. A white rose in front of sable yews will blush with a red counter-image of the green, but against a blue sky, it will take on a jaundiced orange hue. At the same time the white flower gives of itself to its neighbours, showing them in their truest colours: neighbouring blues seem a purer blue, reds purer red. Grey, like white seems to enhance the colours next to it, but in lesser measure. Like white it is itself affected by its neighbours, taking on tints of their after-images.

There are two other dimensions of colour, which bear directly on the nature of white gardens, value and intensity. Value is a measure of the luminosity of colour. The luminosity increases as white is added and diminishes as black is added. Intensity is a measure of the brightness or dullness of a colour. A colour is at its brightest as a pure hue, that is when it is reflecting all the wavelengths of that colour. As light fades, less of that colour is reflected and so it appears duller, greyer or what colour theorists call desaturated. White, which reflects all colour wavelengths and therefore more total light, is always less affected by falls in the level of light than other colours.

In a garden as the light fades on a summer's evening blues and violets, which have little luminosity, disappear first, followed by reds, browns and orange. Greens are next to go, first the dark greens of yew and box, then the lighter green of lawn. Yellows, creams and whites are last to go, lingering even when there seems to be no light left for them to reflect. Many leave a haunting fragrance on the air for they are often pollinated by creatures of the night and are more likely to be fragrant than flowers of any other colour. And at night by moonlight, white flowers gathered together in a white garden can weave a spell of enchantment such as no other kind of garden can.

(In this book, we have drawn heavily on Penelope Hobhouse's *Colour in the Garden*, Collins 1985. Her interpretations of colour theory are the clearest we have found anywhere.)

THE CONCEPT OF GARDEN

When first we come to gardening most of us grow whatever plants come our way or take our fancy, finding them sufficient unto themselves and we take no thought for how they look together or for the overall effect of the garden. Only gradually do we come to see that a garden is more than the sum of its plants and that a garden, at its finest, can be a work of art as perfect in its way as the Sistine Chapel ceiling, the Brandenburg Concertos or the Divine Comedy, and that the concept of garden owes far more to shape and form and structure, to pattern, rhythm and repetition, than it does to flowers.

The garden as art has its origins in the cloister which itself is a development of the peristyle of classical antiquity. The typical cloister is set around a square of grass, sometimes with a fountain at the centre and the cloister itself is a covered, pillared ambulatory. Significantly, cloisters are always inward-looking. Such a square may be created almost anywhere and is virtually independent of site. The simple cloister has evolved into a series of rooms of varying sizes and proportions, each different in character, linked by allees and vistas dependent on site, and as one moves from room to room, there is a sense of development as there is in a sonata or a novel.

Because organisation is fundamental to the idea of garden, a garden, whether formal or informal, may be seen as a series of walks and open spaces, the walks being corridors between rooms or, as at Sissinghurst, allees in their own right. If the walks can be as long as possible, and the rooms as varied in proportion and content as possible these contrasts will be deeply satisfying. Changes of level add another dimension. Gardens are not merely for looking at, they are there to be experienced. The experience of walking down a pleached allee is quite different from that of sitting looking across a wide expanse of lawn.

Gardens need both unity and variety; indeed, the point of the unity is to pull together the diversity of the garden. Pattern, rhythm and repetition can give unity just as in music. A theme once stated needs to be repeated with variations throughout the garden. The theme might be box beehives like those which flank the stone path at Tintinhull that leads from the west front of the house down to the white garden. Those box beehives are about 1.2m (4ft) tall. Variations could be in using beehives 60cm (2ft) tall or 4m (13ft) tall; or shorter, squatter beehives, or taller thinner

ones – the mind would still pick up the essential unity in these variations.

Such pattern, repetition and rhythm should also occur in the planting. The pattern might start with four silver shrubs (*see* page 142), their spacing nearly symmetrical so that their essential rhythm can be seen. To the left of three of these, but to the right of one, might be yellow-leafed perennials keeping the repetition but departing a little from the pattern. A green-leafed small shrub might make the third element of the pattern. Two might be planted close together, yet distant enough to retain their own identities, behind one of the yellow-leafed plants, and the others used one each behind two of the remaining yellow-leafed plants, leaving one yellow-leafed plant without its green-leafed companion, thus keeping the rhythm but breaking the pattern (*see* page 142). Using plants to echo each other gives variety within unity and similarly creates pattern and rhythm. *Viburnum tomentosum* is distinct with its horizontal branches; variations might include *V.t.* 'Nana' a dwarf, 'Mariesii' the most horizontally branched and 'Cascade', lowest growing of all; all placed nearly equidistant apart in the border to point-up their essential similarities.

Another essential quality of a garden is its other-worldliness. A garden is a place to pause and draw strength, a place in which to rest the mind and delight the senses. Such rarefied gardens cannot accommodate the mundane needs of a growing family. There are definite ways in which gardens distance themselves from the commonplace world. They are usually enclosed, which isolates them. The vegetation they contain differs both in kind and in organisation, from that of the natural world beyond them. The more it differs the more distinctly 'garden' it is. A garden once deserted will soon be taken over by the native vegetation and in not so many years will be indistinguishable from it. Every

Rhythm, pattern and repetition give a garden cohesion. Hazelby House.

weed that grows is a step down that road. A wild garden is already half-way there, and a wild flower garden is scarcely a garden at all. It is control that makes a garden a garden, control over which plants grow and which do not, over lawns and edgings, over the growth of hedges and topiary, over pests and diseases. A garden like any other form of art is a discipline not an indulgence, and the greater the discipline the more intense the experience of garden. Gardens also set themselves apart from the natural world by their neatness (another aspect of organisation). The perfect garden should look manicured; the grass for

Artifice, essential to the concept of garden. At Hazelby House terracotta pots of tender plants provide the white in this otherwise grey and green scene.

ever newly cut and the edges always newly trimmed, and never a weed in sight.

A garden is a highly structured entity. The more structured (and therefore the less natural) it is the more intensely it is a garden. The highly structured formal gardens of the Italian renaissance – the Villa Medici at Fiesole, the Villa D'Este at Tivoli – come nearer to the platonic ideal of a garden than do those parklands which a mistaken aesthetic led 'Capability' Brown to design.

A white garden is perhaps best conceived as a single compartment in a garden of compartments. It could also be the entirety of a town garden or a courtyard. Certainly white gardens are usually relatively small.

The final ingredient of all really good gardens is some element of frivolity or fun

Control is the essence. Clipped cypresses seen through a clair voyée *in a yew hedge at Sissinghurst.*

Unity and variety at Barrington Court. This group of white and green is repeated with variations in other parts of the garden.

and this is entirely in keeping with the white garden. Pavilions and arbors should not look like sound, substantial structures designed for a practical function but rather should look like something seen in a fairytale and the statuary should not be solemn but rather the young men and maidens should disport themselves smiling as though Paradise had never been lost. The very essence of a garden is control and it is folly to think that we can control a garden when in the end we must lose all control of it.

FOUR WHITE GARDENS

All white gardens bring together the concept of white and the concept of garden, and yet in each the realisation of these ideas is quite different. For each is a specific solution to the problems of a particular site. The white garden at Sissinghurst is utterly different from the white garden at Hazelby House. The problems of making a white garden at Folly Farm are quite different from those at Lytes Cary. Interestingly, several good white gardens have come about as adaptations of gardens originally intended for other purposes. The white garden at Hidcote was originally the phlox garden, and the one at Sissinghurst was originally a rose garden, with wide lavender walks and an avenue of almonds. The white garden at Chenies Manor started as a herb garden, and the one at Folly Farm originally an ornamental fish pond. To show how diverse white gardens may be we have chosen four that are as different from each other as possible: Tintinhull, Hazelby House, The Little Cottage, and Lytes Cary.

Tintinhull

The white garden at Tintinhull is really called the Fountain Garden, for it is made round a small circular pool at the centre of which there is a fountain. One of its great strengths is that you do not even realise the white garden is there until you reach it. You approach it from the west front of the Ham stone house. Stepping down from the house you see in front of you a stone path laid in an unusual diamond pattern, flanked by large beehives of clipped box at the very furthest end of which is a delicately fashioned seat painted white set against a dark yew hedge. It is that seat that draws you down the vista, passing through the Eagle Court and the Middle Garden, and then down four steps into the Azalea Garden. Only then do you realise that the white garden is there at all.

Miss Jekyll makes the point several times that where gardens of restricted colour are concerned, the approaches are as important as the garden itself because they prepare you for what is to come. Yet the white garden at Tintinhull is not the culmination of the entire garden as it is at Lytes Cary. Rather, being situated in a corner of the garden, it is at the point where two major axes meet. It therefore serves the same function in the garden as does lemon sorbee at a banquet, to clear the palette and leave it receptive to the next experience.

Tintinhull is an ancient house, dating from perhaps 1630, though its present elegant west facade is an eighteenth-century addition. Its gardening history by comparison is relatively recent and began at the turn of the century when the then owner, Dr Price, laid, probably on the advice of Harold Peto, much of the paving which plays so important a part in the white garden and its approaches. The paving in the white garden is of random Ham stone, the same stone as the house. In 1933 the two-acre garden passed to Captain and Mrs Reiss, who set about making the garden we see today. Phyllis Reiss was noted as a garden designer and had an eye for creating borders using a limited palette of strong colours, like the west border in the Cedar Garden which is composed of red flowers and copper and yellow-leafed shrubs. It was Mrs Reiss who first planted the white flowers in the Fountain Garden. After Captain Reiss's death the property passed to the National Trust, though Mrs Reiss continued to live there. Since her death in 1961 the National Trust has continued to nurture the garden. The present inhabitants of Tintinhull are Professor Malins and his wife Penelope Hobhouse.

The white garden consists of a rectangle enclosed by yew hedges, at the junction of two paths and it has a small circular pool at the centre. The planting is therefore almost entirely in the corners. Each of the four beds is in effect a right-angle triangle with a curved hypotenuse. The planting space available is limited, and it has taken great skill to plant so that the visitor is unaware of these problems.

The high points of the borders occur in the corners, and the particular plants that have been used draw the eye: *Salix helvetica*, grown as standards and clipped into formal balls are the only formal element here. The greyness of the leaves as well as the clipped shape stand out distinctly against the dark yew hedges but highlight one of the problems that can beset formal features. Three of the salix grow beautifully and are perfectly matched, but the fourth languishes and is smaller than the others. It grows in the southeast corner where it comes under the aegis of a huge holm oak which deprives it of light and rain, and robs it of nourishment. It is fed more and pampered more than the others, but cannot keep up. These salix are recently planted (within the last five years) and it is worth trying to envisage them in, say, 20 years time, when the balls could be 2m (7ft) in diameter. At that size they would look out of proportion and it may be that the plan is to replace them every few years. Most of the white flowers are provided by rose 'Iceberg', decidedly pink in bud, but *R.* 'Margaret

Merrill' is also used affording a nice contrast, for 'Margaret Merrill' is not quite white. Both are tall roses: 'Margaret Merrill' in particular having a usefully narrow habit which makes it ideal for fitting into confined spaces. The rose 'Snow Carpet' is used at their feet, echoing the theme. It has better flowers than the ubiquitous 'Little White Pet' but is not in flower for so long.

Height is given to the planting by the Arabian thistle, *Onopordum acanthium*, grey and ghostly against the dark hedges. It is allowed to seed itself and selected seedlings are then left to grow on. The tall, slender *Iris orientalis* with its grey leaves and white-cream flowers, links other elements in the garden. It is happy growing up between herbaceous plants. The grey theme is carried on by *Brachyglottis* 'Sunshine', argyranthemums, *Seriphidium tridentatum* (*Artemisia tridentata*), *Santolina pinnata neapolitana*, *Lychnis coronaria* 'Alba' and *Anthemis cupaniana* and *Leptospermum grandiflorum*, big and bushy. The grass *Helictotrichon sempervirens* provides an unexpected glaucous element. Of these elements *Brachyglottis* 'Sunshine' and the santolina have yellow flowers, while the argyranthemums and the anthemis have white daisy flowers with yellow centres. Clumps of tall, bearded, white-flowered irises flank the entrances, dating from Mrs Reiss's time. The tall spires of white foxgloves and *Campanula latifolia album* spear up through other plants, as do *Galtonia candicans* and *Epilobium glabellum* at a different season, and the slender grey stems of *Lychnis coronaria* 'Alba', bearing their small clean white flowers. In shade *Dicentra spectabilis* 'Alba' hangs its little white lockets on arching stems. White, grey-leafed Brompton stocks fill the garden with their scent. Woodruff and white valerian are used to underplant the roses. We were intrigued to find blue-flowered plants, plainly there by design; a pale blue aquilegia, and a blue

At Tintinhull a distant white seat lures the visitor down the pathway to the white garden. Both the box beehives and the pattern of the path establish rhythm through repetition.

The Fountain Garden at Tintinhull. Salix helvetica *grown as a clipped standard gives height in the corner, in company with* Onopordum acanthium.

delphinium, but they are just what is needed to sharpen the planting in a white garden. Besides, the blue is linked through greys to the foliage of rue.

The circular pool at the centre of the garden has a single fountain in the middle which throws up a vertical, pencil-thin column a metre or so high. The planting is simple, leaving plenty of open surface. There is the white, scented water-lily *Nymphaea* 'Odorata Alba' and a clump of the Falkland Island daisy, *Senecio smithii*. By the pool the hardy white agapanthus, *A. campanulatus* 'Albus', grows in a hole in the paving. In winter, when its leaves have disappeared, the bare flower stems remain, topped by the stalks that held the seeds, all radiating from a central point and repeating, but in miniature, the pattern and rhythm of the stems which also seem to radiate from an unseen central point. Across the cold, dark water of the pond the dried heads of a white hortensia hydrangea, all colour gone, play a variation on the same theme.

Lytes Cary

The white garden at Lytes Cary could scarcely be more different from the Fountain Garden at Tintinhull. The greater part of the gardens at Lytes Cary are laid out to formal simplicity, clipped yews and quiet lawns enclosed by hedges. There is an air of antique mellowness which belies the reality for the gardens were laid out in the teens of this century by Sir Walker Jenner, and the present flower gardens are the work jointly of the present inhabitants and Graham Stuart Thomas, a friend of the family. The only splash of real colour is the long border which itself is interestingly devised. The border lies at the foot of a low stone retaining wall and to the left of a path which runs east-west. To the right is mown grass punctuated by hedge buttresses alternating with small stone vases

At Lytes Cary the white garden is reached only by running the gauntlet of the colourful border.

The white garden at Lytes Cary is a secret compartment at the end of the long border.

15

and beyond that, visually balancing the combined effect of the retaining wall and the flowers, is a yew hedge grown to the regulation 2.4m (8ft). The retaining wall faces south and the flowers at its foot are in full sun. Had flowers been planted to the right of the path, they would have been in shade on the north side of the yew hedge, and grown in such conditions the plants would never compare with those in sun. The border is richly planted in strong bright colours. Large-flowered clematis festoon the retaining wall, consorting with warm rich roses, potentillas, *Penstemon* 'Garnet', and pinks. As you walk down this brilliant border, almost dazzled by its brightness, you presume that the next compartment hidden from view by buttressed hedges, will contain more of the same when in fact it is the white garden. Nowhere as you approach it can you foresee this. Yet it is perfect; Miss Jekyll herself would have applauded. The whole scheme seems designed to bring you to the white garden.

Yet the white garden is tiny, a fraction the size of the hot herbaceous border. It is a square, the same width from wall to hedge as the herbaceous border allee but planted on both sides of the path, in spite of the aforementioned problems of shade on one side. At the far end of the white garden is a flight of steps and it is to these that the path has been leading you all along. They take you up on to a long grassed walk and in so doing return you to the clipped greens and lawns and hedges which predominate in the garden as a whole.

The whiteness of the white garden is stunning after the colours of the herbaceous border; it is breathlessly white, the planting composed of *R.* 'Iceberg', philadelphus hybrids, argyranthemums, ox-eye daisies, campanulas, *Malva moschata* 'Alba', *Brachyglottis* 'Sunshine', white aquilegia, *Convolvulus cneorum*, white geraniums, with the white-variegated arabis spilling out on to the path and the white *Viola cornuta* running

about under other plants. We saw it first in June when there were white flowers everywhere, no doubt following the maxim that says that everything that flowers at the same time should be grown in the same place. But in such a small space that leaves very little scope for the garden to be white at other seasons, though many of the plants would remain in flower until the end of October. In the making of every white garden the dilemma has to be faced of whether to have one moment of glorious whiteness or a lesser whiteness for longer. Most people want both and this can be achieved but only by the copious application of bedding in season.

It is curious that whereas the herbaceous border was only to the north of the path (facing south), the white garden is planted on both sides of the path. Presumably the intention was to double the area of border, thereby creating a sense of its being in balance with the length of the herbaceous border. But the left-hand side (the same side as the herbaceous border) grows and flowers far better than the right side, at the foot of the hungry, shade-giving yew hedge. Much the same plants were used left and right, no doubt to give unity.

Hazelby House

Hazelby House has not the venerable antiquity of Tintinhull and Lytes Cary, being Victorian. Nor has the garden the benefit, as had the garden at Tintinhull, of being worked on by a succession of good gardeners over the years. Yet it is on a par with Tintinhull.

When the Lane Foxes bought it in 1974 the garden consisted of a large lawn sloping to the south-west, a few hybrid tea roses, and an overgrown walled vegetable garden. The garden also differs from Lytes Cary and Tintinhull in being situated on acid greensand whereas they are on heavy, sticky, alkaline clay. An overall plan was devised at the outset which involved first creating out of the sloping ground a series of level terraces, and then planting good-quality hedges to create on these terraces a series of self-contained compartments. Now, fifteen years later, this investment has paid off, for the hedges do indeed create self-contained compartments, of which the white garden is one. Like all good gardens, the pieces fit together so naturally that it seems there could be no other way of arranging them.

To reach the white garden from the house you first enter the main axis of the garden, a wide grass path flanked by wide borders on both sides backed by tall hedges. The borders are interrupted with a pattern of alternating brick and stone recesses, each containing a stone urn or a lead and stone statue arising from a plinth of variegated box. The main planting is of shrubs, with white-flowering cherries at the back. One combination we particularly liked in these borders was *Cistus laurifolius* with *Helianthemum* 'The Bride' at its feet spilling out across the stone mowing strip, for their flowers are virtually identical, but larger or smaller, a lovely combination for the white garden. There were also two greys that had unexpectedly been combined and worked beautifully — *Euphorbia characias* with *Salix lanata*. Near the top of these borders there is a turning to the right into the cross axis. Access is through a wide wooden gate with a curved top on to a gravel path flanked with borders and confined within tall beech hedges. At the far end of the path is a gate identical to the one at the entrance. Halfway down the path a white wooden arbor astride the path is laden with the pearly-pink flowers of rose 'The New Dawn'. On the right is a narrow gap in the beech hedge through which can be seen a mound of glaucous hosta leaves and a haze of white flowers. This is the white garden.

Interestingly the white garden at Hazelby thus does not lie on a main axis, but is set aside as though of lesser importance. Nor is its presence announced by gates or pillars. Indeed the gap in the hedge is narrow so that one seems to slip through it almost surreptitiously. No sooner have you entered it than your progress is blocked by one of the beds so that you have to turn aside and find another way foward. This is a most useful device for by slowing one's progress, one is given time to look and enjoy the garden instead of speeding through it. This is, in fact, the route to the swimming pool.

The white garden is contained within hedges, three of them beech, the fourth thuya. Behind the thuya hedge are the white-flowering cherries of the double borders in the main axis of the garden. The beds in the garden are pleasingly asymmetrical. At the foot of the thuya hedge, shaded by the cherries, a border runs the whole width of the white garden, with a sundial, supported by three lead cherubs, at its centre. The rest of the garden is paved with narrow red bricks interrupted by four smaller rectangular beds, each of which contains as its centre-piece a narrow trellis-work pillar inside which is a climbing rose 'Iceberg'. At the feet of the 'Icebergs', lesser white flowers abound in variety: several sorts of white geraniums, white pinks, campanulas, phloxes, white lupins, the white bleeding heart, the Shasta daisy 'Wirral Supreme', *Dicentra spectabilis* 'Alba', white valerian and Japanese anemones for autumn. In the large border at the foot of the thuya hedge larger plants are grown: *Crambe cordifolia*, the rugosa rose 'Blanc Double de Coubert', clumps of rose 'Little White Pet' and drifts of Madonna lilies. At the corners of the gardens white pithoi in black iron stands contain yet more white flowers. There are several hostas: *H. sieboldiana*, a small hosta of the Tardiana group, as well as *H. hyacinthina*. The garden has a decidedly glaucous undercurrent, and is quite distinct from the other white gardens on

17

At Hazelby House a turning off this coloured corridor leads into the white garden.

that account. At Tintinhull the glaucous tones are neutralised by the lime greens. Another option is an undercurrent of lime and gaudy-green, which is the scheme used at The Little Cottage.

The white garden at Hazelby House is ten years old, and yet the search for still more appropriate flowers goes on: for a perennial sweet pea with no hint of pink in its whiteness, for example, and a white pink that will flourish on an acid soil.

The Little Cottage

The Little Cottage is essentially an L-shaped Georgian cottage with Victorian additions. It is built in a warm, mellow brick and is prettily asymmetrical. It lies at the edge of Lymington on the south coast, two miles from the sea, so that the climate though mild is maritime.

When Lyn and Peter Prior moved here in

The white garden at Hazelby House. A beautifully balanced composition to which the enclosing hedge provides the background.

The white garden at The Little Cottage glimpsed through a gateway framed by Victorian ironwork.

The white garden at The Little Cottage leans towards lemon yellows. Robinia pseudoacacia 'Frisia' behind the domed arbor.

1985 they soon evolved a master-plan for the quarter-acre garden which consisted basically of using fences and trellis to divide it into a necklace of compartments each of which will in time contain a garden of a different colour. The first compartment to be made contained the white garden. It lies to the south of the house and is bounded by a trellis-work fence. The reason for having the white garden there, where it is seen from both the sitting room and the dining room, is to avoid the dilemmas created by clashing colours. From the sitting room, which is predominantly pink, you look across the white garden and through an archway into a compartment that will become the pink garden, while from the dining room,

which is a mauve/blue room, you look across the white garden into the compartment that will become a garden of silvers, blues, mauves and turquoise. The white garden itself has a lime-green ambience. The whole area is paved with random Purbeck slabs set in a ground of what look like Purbeck chippings. In fact they come from Ireland, at great expense. Pea-grit was found to be the wrong colour, and grey granite road-chippings, which were also tried, were not right either. The combined effect is of overall off-whiteness, and the idea of this mixed surface is that the Purbeck slabs provide a firm surface to walk on while the chippings provide a soft surface in which occasional plants can grow. *Alchemilla mollis* seeds itself about and excess seedlings are weeded out. Since the chippings are laid on 30cm (12in) of hardcore, the plants are starved and the Lady's mantle remains attractively small. *Sagina glabra* 'Aurea' makes dense moss-like mats of yellow leaves spangled with starry white flowers, and also seeds itself about, the seedlings coming true to leaf colour. There are a few dwarf phloxes and the little variegated arabis. At the centre of the paved area is a small circular pond, less than 2m (7ft) across, beside which long-haired white cats sit watching ghostly white goldfish slip and slide beneath the pads of a dwarf scented white water-lily. Set around the pool are four shallow stone pots in which the dwarf white-variegated ivy 'Little Diamond' used to grow. It thrived not, perhaps because the courtyard is too hot and has now been replaced with Universal white winter pansies, to be followed in summer by white petunias.

There are two arbors in the garden both Victorian in inspiration, one at the east end and one at the west end, each different, yet each made of white iron work and shading a white seat. The one at the east end is an elegantly elaborate rotunda. Behind it is a *Robinia pseudoacacia* 'Frisia', which drapes its branches over the curved roof, raining gold leaflets in the autumn. Over the iron work of the arbor grow *Clematis spooneri*, that less vigorous white *montana*, the double *C.* 'Duchess of Edinburgh' and two plants of the old rose, 'Aimee Vibert', which is such a disappointment, its flowers invariably balling and browning. 'Mme Alfred Carrière' will be planted instead. Another problem has been the perennial white sweet pea, *Lathyrus* 'White Pearl', which could be so valuable as it flowers in July and August, but turns out always to be more or less pink as at Hazelby House. The arbor at the other end stands in front of a mellow brick wall and is square-topped not domed. Behind it, against the

wall, is a white chaenomeles, which was disappointing to begin with as it would not grow flat nor flower properly, but it has now settled down and is both flat on the wall and floriferous. Over the arbor itself grows the white-flowered *Clematis* 'Huldine' whose flowers are always seen at their best from below and the white form of the small-flowered *Wisteria japonica* chosen partly for its lateness of flowering, July and August, when other wisterias in the garden are over and partly because, although the individual flowers are small, the raceme branches and all the flowers on the same raceme are open at the same time. (On *W. floribunda* the first flowers on the raceme are over before the last have opened.)

The trellis that divides the white garden from the gardens beyond is draped with a rich variety of climbers, the intention having been to get an effect quickly and then thin. The golden hop, *Humulus lupulus* 'Aureus', was planted in this spirit and is now due, after four years, to be removed. The large-leafed ivy, *H. colchica* 'Paddy's Pride' ('Sulphur Heart'), was planted at the east end, near the domed arbor. In this north-facing position its leaves are lime-green and dark green, never yellow. The same is true of two *Choisya ternata* 'Sundance', a harsh, gambogeous colour in sun but in shade a subtle lime-green. Through it scrambles the double white *Clematis* 'Sylvia Denny' the two together being most effective. Other clematis grown are *C. armandii*, *C.* 'Mrs George Jackson', *C.* 'John Huxtable' and the double-white 'Jackmanii Alba' as well as all the different sorts of white *montana* that can be traced. Roses also abound. Great reliance is placed on dependable old 'Iceberg' (the climbing form), but other roses have performed with varying success. 'Sanders White' and 'Felicité et Perpetue' grow together and flower together, but each is so different it complements the other. Nearby *R.* 'Nevada' is being trained flat against the trellis. 'White Cockade' and 'Purity' are not a success, suffering badly from blackspot.

The walls of the house itself support the best of the climbers. A great many things were planted with the intention of later thinning some out. In view of its south coast location it was expected that several tender climbers might succeed. *Mandevilla suaveolens*, the Chilean jasmine, raised from seed produced 14 plants, seven of which were planted against the house and seven variously about the garden. The seven against the house flourish and flower well, in spite of two successive severe winters; the others perished in the first cold spell. In spite of this encouragement the white cup-and-saucer vine, *Cobaea scandens* 'Alba' will not survive the winters, and needs to be raised from seed afresh each spring. The deciduous hoya, *Wattakaka sinensis*, thrives, filling the warm air of summer evenings with its fragrance. The short-lived white parrot's beak, *Clianthus puniceus* 'Albus', succeeds admirably and is treasured almost as much for its foliage as for its flowers. Both *Trachelospermum asiaticum* and *T. jasminoides*, as well as *T.j.* 'Variegatum' luxuriate in the warmth of the wall, their flowers filling the air with a scent like that of jasmine. *Solanum crispum* 'Album', usually considered tender, grows like a weed and flowers for ten months of the year, as does *Clematis sieboldii* 'Alba Plena'. The white Passion flower, 'Constance Elliott', has individually the most beautiful flowers of all the climbers on the wall but will one day become too rampant and outgrow its welcome. *Clematis* 'Marie Boisselot' refuses to flourish and has to be renewed each year. *C.* 'White Moth' has repeatedly failed to establish itself and *C.* 'White Swan' is being tried instead. ('White Moth' is known to be difficult though no one seems to know why.) *Abutilon vitifolium* 'Album' was planted as a stop-gap while waiting for *Magnolia grandiflora* 'Exmouth' to come of age. The abutilon now reaches the guttering and covers itself in flower. In its first years it flowered from May till October, but now in its fifth year it has settled down to two good bursts of blossom with a few intermittent flowers at other times.

In spite of the exotic climbers and sophisticated planting the white garden at the Little Cottage is essentially a cottage garden, intimate and informal.

Part 2
Design and Features

THE GENIUS OF THE PLACE

At the Casa dei Vettii in Pompeii there is a famous colonnaded peristyle garden. It is like a small private rectangular cloister at the centre of which plants are grown in pots or small beds around a formal pool or *piscina*. Such a garden, being inward looking and independent of site, could be made almost anywhere, and would always look essentially the same. More usually a garden is a marriage between the mind of its maker and the spirit of the place – the *genius loci*. It arises as a direct response to the problems and assets of a site. The better the marriage the more beautiful and harmonious the garden.

The restfulness of a level site invites the intricacies of formality but they in turn need the counterpoint of smooth grass. Rousham in April.

In an abstract way the genius of the place may be interpreted simply as what a place feels like and this is as important as what it looks like. If a place has the feel of a woodland garden then a woodland garden is probably what will succeed best there; but if it feels like a cloister then an austere, even ascetic, formal garden would be appropriate. It would not be appropriate to impose the formal garden on the woodland setting nor the woodland garden (nor its plants) in the cloister. Similarly certain sorts of plants look right in certain settings and wrong in other settings. Rhododendrons can of course be grown on bare chalk if enough trouble is taken, but they look outlandish in company with the typical chalk garden flora, cistus and helianthemums, lavender, old roses and junipers. Similarly with materials. In a locality where stone occurs, stone is the natural material from which to build both house and garden. On clay, brick will be the local building material, and to use stone might seem odd.

The lie of the land is important. A garden on a hillside feels quite different from a garden in a valley. It has a sense of superiority. It looks down on the valley beneath. The eye is drawn along the silver ribbon of a river or road. It also makes a difference whether the garden is perceived as going up-hill or downhill. Rising ground emphasises the height of things above one, ground that falls away tends to foreshorten them, reducing their significance. A valley garden has a quite different feel, enclosed by hills and often trees; it may have a damp, misty atmosphere.

Level sites have an inherent stability, whereas a garden on a slope seems always to be about to slide away and one needs to create a level area near the house to stabilise it. The levelness of such sites can be emphasised by large lawns and even more by large sheets of water, but such strong horizontal lines need to be counterbalanced by verticals, Italian cypresses, for example.

The most difficult sort of garden to work with is one that seems to have no style or feel, no particular features of ground form or planting to provide a starting point. When a sculptor takes hammer and chisel to a block of stone and chips away, what he is doing is revealing the figure that he sees concealed in the rock, he is not imposing a figure on the rock. We do the same when we make gardens. They are already there. We reveal them.

ASPIRATIONS

Good gardens are always a marriage between the genius of the place and the aspirations of the garden-maker. The scope is infinitely varied. Whiteness need not extend to a whole

The white garden at York Gate, Adel: a connoisseur's collection of white flowers and foliage. Note the detail of the path edging.

garden. It may be just a seasonal incident (snowdrops at the foot of a white-stemmed birch) or a single border. We know of one such border in a garden that runs down to the Solent, its long axis backed by a x *Cupressocyparis leylandii* hedge, bounded at its north by a brick wall and at its southern end by the stems of birches and hawthorns. It is separated by a lawn from the conservatory, and much silver is used (appropriately in a garden so near to the sea). *Artemisia schmidtiana* 'Nana', variegated arabis and white garden pinks spill out into the paved mowing strip. Rose 'Iceberg' provides height, echoed by 'Little White Pet' in a low key. Bushes of Mexican mock orange blossom provide a good glossy mid greenery, jostling with taller artemisias such as 'Lambrook Silver' and 'Powys Castle'. Clearly marked off at each end from the rest of the garden, this makes a satisfying self-contained white border.

Quite different is a white border in a garden that is not so much informal as freehand. The ground rises and falls here and there, and the amoeba-shaped borders are placed with apparent randomness, sometimes astride the ridges and sometimes slouched in the hollows. The white border lies against the boundary and is backed by *Spiraea arguta* and *Exochorda giraldii*, with *Choisya ternata* and *Philadelphus* 'Beauclerk' as neighbours at one end and *Osmanthus delavayi*, and *Escallonia* 'Iveyi' at the other. Right at the front of the border, *Viola cornuta alba* and pansy 'Little David' nestle between *Hebe pinguifolia* 'Pagei' and *H. albicans* 'Prostrata'. *Helianthemum* 'Wisley White' grows next to *Geranium clarkei* 'Kashmir White', while the middle ground is held by *Paeonia potaninii* 'Alba', *Cimicifuga simplex*, *Lysimachia ephemerum*, *Lychnis viscaria*, *Paradisea liliastrum*, *Poterium magnificum*, and *Veronica virginica* 'Alba'. Across the small lawn from this white border is a yellow-green border.

In another garden an area of scrub has been cleared revealing white-stemmed birches. A mown path wends its way through them and in the rough grass grow snowdrops and snowflakes, drifts of white crocus, followed by pheasants' eye narcissus and white snake's head fritillaries, all of which are overtaken in the high summer by waist-high Queen Anne's lace. This glade, sunlit until the birches become heavy with leaf, leads down to damp ground where giant hogweed complements the Queen Anne's lace, and the whole area is bounded by large cherry laurels, which themselves have white flowers. Without this enclosing belt of dark laurels the effect would be dissipated for the enclosure concentrates the effect. This looks the most casual and naturalistic white garden we know, yet it is just as much work and just as artfully contrived as a formal garden, for, left to its own devices, the area would be invaded by cowslips and bluebells, red campion, mauve dentaria and creeping yellow buttercup.

At the other extreme are courtyard gardens, in which artifice is evident everywhere. In courtyards, because of the obtrusiveness of the architecture obviously architectural plants need to be used: *Fatsia japonica* 'Variegata', Mexican mock orange blossom, *Cordyline australis*, *Trachycarpus fortunei*, phormiums and white agapanthus with strap-shaped leaves or the brilliantly variegated *A. africanus* 'Univittata'. The variegated *Alchemilla*, *Hosta plantaginea*, *Hebe andersonii* 'Variegata', *Miscanthus sinensis* 'Variegatus' all make a framework amid which intense whiteness can be provided by bedding in season. Pots and tubs should abound, and stone sinks if the setting is right, with white-painted iron seats and tables to enhance the whiteness.

In town gardens a small terrace can often be treated as a courtyard so that, as at The Little Cottage, you look across the lemon sorbet of the white garden to the colours beyond. Alternatively the whole garden, provided it is

24

not too large, can be white though more usually such gardens are made into a series of rooms one of which is white. We know of one where white cherries seemingly set at random pre-date rectangular box-edged borders which can never remotely approach symmetry because of the cherries. In the dappled shade the usual 'Icebergs' have grown leggy but white columbines and white foxgloves seem at home springing up through the leaves of white primroses and polyanthus and the last white tulips, together with Solomon's seal, woodruff and lily of the valley contrasting with the more substantial mounds of *Hosta undulata* 'Univittata' and *H.* 'Thomas Hogg'.

It is important to set the level of aspiration before embarking on the making of a white garden, for a white garden will always be more work than other sorts of gardens, but also more rewarding.

ORGANISING SPACE

All garden design is about organising space and in a white garden this assumes a particular importance because the amount of whiteness must be set against a sufficiency of some neutral tone, lawn, paving or hedging. Yet space is an odd, elusive element, for in a way it is not really there at all until you put a boundary round it.

The basic space occupied by a garden is defined by its boundaries. Lesser spaces may be defined by creating compartments within that space. Even lesser spaces may be defined as beds or borders. The first paradox of space is that by sub-dividing it you make it larger, just as an empty room looks smaller than a furnished one. Space is as large or small as it is perceived to be. Extremes discomfort. Too large a space will dwarf those within it, too small a space will crowd them. A narrow space hurries people through it, a square or circular space encourages them to pause. How a space

is approached or entered also modifies how it is perceived. Entering a compartment through a narrow gap will make it seem larger, through a wide gap smaller.

Thus a white garden should be entered through a narrow gap, and it should be square or circular to emphasise its serenity.

There are other factors which can affect one's comfort or discomfort in a particular space. If the wall or hedges are too tall in relation to the width of the space it will feel claustrophobic; too low and the space will feel insecure. As a rule of thumb the width of a space should be at the smallest the same as the height of the surrounding boundary, and at the greatest three times its height.

The centre of a defined space has peculiar properties. If there is a depression at the centre of an enclosure it seems to reinforce the feeling of enclosure, as in the Fountain Garden at Tintinhull, where the limpid pool seems as deep as the sky it reflects. Conversely ground that falls away from a central point dissipates the sense of enclosure. If either a hump or hollow is set off-centre in an enclosure, it sets up dynamic tensions which one does not want in a white garden.

Most of us spend more time indoors than out and when we step outside we take with us the scale of the rooms we most inhabit. The scale out of doors is different. Our sense of the size of rooms is determined more by the height of the ceiling than anything else but outside there is only the vast immeasurable distance to the dome of the sky. A sculpture which may dominate an indoor room may seem insignificant in the garden. It is important to remember this when buying sculptures or ornaments for the white garden, or pots and tubs or more importantly when planning a pergola, colonnade or arbor. On the whole it is better to make such objects too big rather than too small. Massive pillars in a pergola suggest strength and permanence; slender ones a sense of insecurity.

Space needs boundaries to define it. The cedar lawn at Hidcote.

ENCLOSURE

Gardens are, almost by definition, enclosed.
The actual material that does the enclosing
exerts a strong influence on the space within
because it presents itself vertically. If the same
surface were seen obliquely, as it would be if
it were laid flat like a path, it would make far
less impact. Similarly, walls, hedges and
·fences present themselves very strongly to the
eye.

The classic setting for white gardens is yew
hedges. Their darkness provides a perfect setting for urns and statuary but is almost too
sharp a contrast for white flowers which need
the foil of grey or light green foliage to bridge
these extremes. There is sometimes the pro-

*(Opposite)   A narrow gap makes the space
beyond seem larger. The entrance to the white
garden at Lytes Cary.*

*Entrances modify the space beyond them and
invite visitors. Oxford Botanic Garden.*

blem with yew that because it grows very little in its first three years a new white garden might have no proper background. The solution is to enclose the white garden with trellis-work, with the yews planted inside it. By the time the yews have reached their regulation 2.4m (8ft), the trellis will be ready to be discarded. Even if it is only a temporary measure the trellis should be properly finished, the panels and the posts capped and the posts finished with ball finials. Tall box hedges, *Buxus sempervirens* or *B. balearica* but not *B.s.* 'Suffruticosa' which is fit only for hedges up to knee height, will do almost as well; they are a whole tone lighter in their green but make up for this by emitting, on warm, still days, a pungent aroma. Beech and hornbeam are also classic hedging plants, but of a yet lighter shade of green, turning rich russet through the winter months. All four have the merit of making formal hedges, with vertical sides and flat tops, and of needing to be cut but once a year. There are other hedging materials but they do not measure up to these strict demands. *Thuja plicata* and *Lonicera nitida* both suffer the defect that when older they will bulge and fall about as though trying to ape storm-driven clouds. Common privet impoverishes the soil for several yards each side and moreover demands to be cut four times a year and laurel is too coarse and too large-leafed to be attractive. The ubiquitous x *Cupressocyparis leylandii* suffers the defect of its macrocarpa parent in that it must always be allowed to make some green; if it is cut back to old wood it will never shoot again.

Walls, like hedges, have a strong architectural geometry. They are more durable than hedges and this makes them more imposing. Walls should always be built of the local material: stone where stone occurs, and brick where brick is usual (and preferably local brick).

Fences are the flimsiest, least imposing and least permanent form of enclosure. Because they are made of materials that are easy to work they offer great scope to those tempted to create original designs, but the more original a fence the more of a distraction it will be. The simpler a fence the more easily it will blend with the plants in front. For this reason simple lap fences are a first choice from a design point of view, with interwoven fencing a poor second because of its impermanence. Fences made of vertical slats nailed alternately each side of central horizontal beams are effective because they filter the wind rather than affronting it. Post and rails are useful for containing animals but not in conjunction with plants.

Softwoods need to be treated against the weather and the darker the colour the less distraction there will be. Paint can be another invitation to distract, but white, dark green, dark blue and muddy turquoise can all be appropriate in a white garden. The choice depends on whether the whiteness of the white garden is to be all in the plants, or in the artefacts – for one could make a stunning white garden simply with grass, green hedges and a single white seat.

SCREENS AND SEMI-SCREENS

In some white gardens lesser partitions may be needed. The classic device for dividing a garden without concealing what lies beyond is the colonnade; a pergola is in effect two colonnades in parallel joined by beams overhead.

The most important decision about structures of this sort is whether the structure is what matters, or the plants. If the aim is an abundance of roses overhead, or wisteria or grapes, then the less one notices the structure supporting the plants the better. A structure of tubular iron finished in matt black would soon be hidden by the plants which then appear to be self-supporting. But if the structure is to be the more important, then care must be taken to ensure that the plants do not take it over.

Pergolas are essentially directional: they usually straddle a path, so there must be a goal at the far end, a seat, perhaps painted white, or a statue. An arbor is in effect a non-directional pergola, a place to sit. At its simplest it may just be four vertical poles linked by swags of rope at the top. A colonnade is a single row of uprights that are linked across the top.

Pleached walks provide another sort of screen. Limes can be grown along tautened wires stretched between sturdy uprights, but to be effective the uprights need to be at least 2.5m (8ft) high, and the wires spaced at foot intervals from the top down over the upper 1.2m (4ft) of the poles. The width of the walk between the lines should be the same as the height of the poles. There is a fine example of a lime walk of this sort at Mottisfont Abbey, near Romsey. The limes are planted in squares of bare earth in a broad, level lawn, and these squares were originally planted with *Chionodoxa luciliae*, but these have now spilled over into the grass and in spring, just as the buds reveal the fresh green of the lime leaves, the ground beneath is a veritable carpet of blue (worn a little thin down the centre, like a corridor carpet). In the white garden one might borrow the idea, and plant a few white scillas, white puschkinia or best of all, white *Chionodoxa luciliae*.

The term stilt-hedge is used of similar hedges when they are made of hornbeam (*Carpinus betulus*). The classic example is in Major Lawrence Johnston's garden at Hidcote Manor, Hidcote Bartrim in Gloucestershire. No doubt he drew his inspiration from earlier models in France, for hornbeam is a classic hedging material. One might also think of beech, which shares with hornbeam the juvenile characteristic of retaining its sere leaves through winter, but it is not so suitable, for it loses this juvenile trait at about 1.2m (4ft).

One merit of such stilt hedges or pleached walks is that because the hedge occurs at eye-level one is constrained to look downwards and the eye is focused on a limited field of vision, which could be filled with white flowers. They are also excellent in adding height to a wall, since the stilts carry the hedge above the wall and do not conceal what may be beautiful old brickwork.

A walk that meets overhead is a tunnel, and tunnels have a fascination of their own. They are most simply made by using flat or tubular steel arches set astride a path and linked by wires set at regular intervals of a foot or so, with the branches trained along them. At Bodnant in North Wales laburnums are trained on low, wide arches so that all the foliage grows upwards and the flowers hang down into the tunnel creating a shimmering haze of gold. For the white garden one could create a similar but more pristine effect using one of the white wisterias, *W. sinensis* 'Alba' for preference, because its flowers are whiter than those of other sorts; though the rare double white wisteria, *W. venusta* 'Alba Plena' has reputedly longer-lasting flowers.

In the construction of pergolas and arbors it is important to get the proportions right. The uprights should always be massive enough to support not only the roof but also the very considerable weight of the plants which will cover it. Brick and stone are the two traditional materials for the uprights, but dressed stone columns can be effective in a suitable setting, or can be imitated by concrete drainpipes as has been done at Kemerton Priory in Worcestershire. The relative proportions of the beams can present problems. The longitudinal beams are usually large and support smaller transverse beams.

Such devices can be used to give height to sites that would otherwise be flat.

Ham stone walls enclose the white garden at Barrington Court. Later in the season lemon-yellows pick up the warm yellowish tones of the stone.

Enclosures within enclosures. The brick walls contain a courtyard; the box-edged beds contain roses.

Apple tunnel at Heale House. Trees are trained on an iron frame. White wisterias could be grown in the same way.

Rose-covered colonnade at Hazelby House.

ARTICULATIONS

Gardens are designed to be experienced rather than just seen, and to experience a garden it is necessary to move through it safely and without hindrance, and that means making paths. In white gardens, which are often formal, particular attention needs to be paid to paving.

A path made of material of a similar tone to its surroundings may be scarcely noticed. Grey stone, for example, differs little tonally from grey-brown earth; but a red brick path through an emerald lawn is visually inescapable.

The formality of a house, with its straight lines and squareness, demands formality in the paving immediately around it. The classic material to use round the house is rectangular stone paving: it has a dignity and quality that no other paving material can approach. It is also, when properly laid, the best walking surface and the ideal material for paths through formal areas.

Further from the house formality decreases. The patterns become less uniform. Slabs may be used in combination with other materials. Lutyens and Miss Jekyll favoured ribbon patterns, herring-bone brick contained between edging bands of stone, as at Folly Farm, Sulhampstead. There is another variation on this theme at Sissinghurst, where regular square stone slabs are laid in a straight line flanked by soldier courses of bricks, their longest axis widening the path.

Brick paths can have a charm all their own, but whether their contribution is quietly formal or oddly cottagey will depend on the pattern in which the bricks are laid. The two classic patterns are herring-bone and basket weave. Both have the advantage of being non-directional. A path, laid in stretcher bond with the stretchers lying along the length of the path, is moving in the same direction as anyone walking along it but if the stretchers are laid across the path from side to side, they are set against the direction of anyone moving along the path and this seems to slow the path down. Such effects can be exploited deliberately.

Crazy paving is also a cottage garden style, no doubt originally created by cottagers from odd bits of stone left over from work done at their master's house. It has obvious overtones of makeshift cheapness. For this reason it is very acceptable in cottage gardens and totally inappropriate anywhere else.

Away from the house itself a well-laid and well-kept gravel path can be one of the best, both pleasing to the eye and pleasant to walk on. Modern weed killers mean that they are no trouble and little expense to keep free of weeds. They need to be properly laid on a deep bed of hard-core, cambered and properly edged with gravel boards.

Paths that are confined, for example, by low box hedges, have a sense of purpose which other paths do not. One cannot simply step aside from such a path: one must go where the path goes, only deviating at predetermined intersections. Where paths meet there is sometimes a conflict of materials, or of directionality. Where paths of differing materials meet the lesser path should give way to the more important. Where paths of the same material meet the intersection can be marked by a change in pattern – concentric rings, for example, or diapers.

When a path encounters any noticeable change of level then it must give way to steps, but the less the steps interrupt the flow of the path the better. In the garden steps should always be as broad and generous as space permits. The ascent or descent should be as gentle as possible, not a challenge to one's strength. A few rules have evolved over the centuries. The treads should never be less than the length of one's foot – about 30cm (12in) – and the risers never more than half the length of the tread – 15cm (6in) –

though 10cm (4in) is more comfortable. Where long flights of steps are needed, as at Dumbarton Oaks or the Villa Tarranto, there should be a landing after every five steps, each landing, though only perhaps a stride long, allowing a moment of rest. If steps are to be safe they must be seen clearly, and the sophisticated way of achieving this is to ensure that the steps have 'noses' – that is that the treads overhang – casting a sharp shadow on the riser. The eye picks up little details like this, just as it picks up the serifs on the type in a printed book.

One does not always want to be on the move in a garden, so places must be provided where one can pause or rest. These are most satisfactory if they have a hard, level surface such as paving, so that a chair or table will be stable and secure. Such terraces should be made of the same material or materials as the path, though perhaps laid in a different pattern. As with paths and steps, terraces should be of generous proportions, with ample room for chairs and tables when required.

FIXED ASSETS

Seats and statuary may seem at first odd subjects to put together, yet both can set the tone of a garden. Statues compel attention; seats invite repose.

Statues elicit responses that are hard to define. They are at their most potent when they are human or nearly human, most effective when a little larger or a little smaller than we are. They can do things we dare not do in our own gardens, kill dragons, go naked, dance in the fountain basins.

They can be used discreetly, perhaps half-hidden among the foliage, as a casual incident encountered in the garden, or they can be used dramatically as a focal point, seen at the end of a vista and compelling closer inspection.

Over the centuries a vast quantity of statuary has been placed in gardens, some of it among the finest ever produced. Yet it can be a problem knowing what style to choose. Greek gods, nymphs and satyrs really belong to a more heroic age and the rustic figures of the eighteenth century often seem out of place. Copies present their problems. A statue only looks right when it expresses some of the genius of place. A statue that has been the genius of the place in one garden cannot play the same role in another. Copies by being copies lose their vitality. The best effects are achieved when a modern sculpture, figurative or non-figurative, is carefully chosen for its particular position. There are several contemporary sculptors producing good garden statuary, Simon Verity, for example, and Wally Cole, Philippa Denby and Marion Smith.

There are other sorts of ornaments of statuesque quality that can serve as well in gardens and which can be more effective than bad statuary. Terms, trapped for ever in their squared plinths, have a quality of stillness that can intrigue. Urns and vases can be found to suit most moods and situations, and there are all sorts of architectural antiques in stone or brick or sometimes iron which, when seen with a designer's eye, can assume an entirely new life in the right garden setting: chimneys, gate-posts, mill-stones, wine and cider presses, and many others.

Seats similarly draw the eye, especially if painted white. They are sculptural in form, inviting the eye to seek out the detail of their structure. Seats should appear to belong, to be permanent, as though they have always been there and have taken root. Stone seats have the advantage of bulk and weight, but it is the setting that most gives a seat a sense of permanence. If it is placed in an alcove in a hedge or wall – as though the alcove had been made for it – or on a plinth of stone or brick, this helps the sense of permanence.

A typical Lutyens path at Folly Farm. The bricks form arrows that are strongly directional.

Sackville's Brighton garden (over lunch on the day he received the commission for the Cenotaph) fits perfectly into its setting as used at Sissinghurst Castle, or at the end of the hosta walk at Hadspen House, though it has now perhaps been used too often.

In the white garden the problem is whether

Steps in the new white garden at The Manor House, Birlingham. The ball finials echo the roundness of the steps.

The scale of seats and sculptures needs to be judged to a nicety. Small individual seats in a small enclosed area give an air of intimacy which would be lacking if grand benches were used. But large benches suit larger gardens. The seat that Lutyens designed for Lady

Seats like this can draw the eye when placed at the end of a vista. The Greenwich seat in the Winterthur Collection.

the whiteness is in the planting or in the structure and framework of the garden. At first it might be thought that a white seat or white statue would be right for the white garden but this is not necessarily the case. A white seat in the wrong place – in front of a white border, to take an absurd example – would detract from both. However, if a white seat were set against a hedge of beech or yew opposite a white border, enabling the visitor to sit and enjoy the plants, then the seat would act as a complement to the border. In a courtyard with white walls there might not be enough room to separate the seat from the planting, and in such a situation it might be better to paint the seat dark green or leaden blue or even leave in its natural state and let it weather to a lichened silvery-grey.

'The Huntress' by Simon Verity. Good modern sculptures are usually more in keeping than copies.

CLIPPED GREENS

Clipped greens have a particular relevance to white gardens for they can be used to create rhythm and pattern. They provide an easy means of creating a framework for the small formal garden or an internal structure to pull a large garden together. This is especially the case when they are used as geometric sculptures, clipped balls on stalks or any other clearly contrived shape, that can be repeated around the garden. Topiary as an art includes not only the clipping of bushes into geometric or figurative shapes, but also the making of perfect hedges, and the deliberate placing of markers. Box and yew, the classic hedging plants, and also the best for holding their shape once clipped, are ideal subjects. Not only are they evergreen, but they are also of a darker colour than most other species (especially in a white garden), and consequently they are always conspicuous and if used in strong designs can enhance the garden in winter as well as in summer.

The essence of box edging is to create a formal pattern of beds which can then be planted informally. In white gardens this technique can be used to reinforce rhythm and repetitious pattern. If, for example, balls of box were taken as a theme they could be used large and small, in green or yellow (a variegated form), at ground level or as finials on top of a hedge, or raised off the ground on a single stem, or as one large ball with a single smaller ball above it on a single stem. Box can also be clipped into spirals, large or small, twisting to the left or to the right.

Topiary pieces need to be positioned carefully, with due regard to how they may develop in the future. They are most effective when used, usually in pairs, as markers, to emphasise something: the top or bottom of a flight of steps; to draw one to a doorway or archway, or simply to draw the eye this way rather than that. The best shapes are simple ones — balls, cones, pyramids. The simpler the shape the more versatile it will be. Simplicity is the keynote of sophistication.

In the modern garden figurative topiary seems to belong rather to the comic and curious than to the realms of serious gardening. Topiarist peacocks are perhaps acceptable for they have become so stylised that they no longer resemble peacocks. But to have the entire hunt, fox, hounds and huntsmen in holly, box or yew for ever charging in static array across one's front lawn (as it does at Ladew in Maryland) can hardly be conducive to resting the mind or pleasing the senses. Such things are much more appropriate in cottage gardens and it is readily observable that those who create such scenes seldom pursue any other sort of gardening.

Producing one's own topiary is not the problem it used to be, nor does it take as long as people expect. It is important to start with the right materials; both box and yew are unbeatable because they hold their shape. Holly, privet, phillyrea and *Lonicera nitida* can all be used though they are less satisfactory – and the last is inclined to fall apart from the middle. Yew, if heavily manured grows surprisingly fast, especially after its first two or three years. In the old days *opera toparii* were shaped by a clipping over long, slow decades; nowadays a topiary frame is used. One merely clips to the shape dictated by the frame. By so doing a passable peacock can be achieved in four or five years.

REFLECTIONS ON WATER

Water has two moods, rest and play. These moods may alternate but can never co-exist. Its restfulness can be emphasised by containing it in a formal pool within a dressed stone edging; its vitality by holding it in an irregular shape, the margins of which are obscured by a mass of vegetation. If you choose formality you cannot hide the edges with plants, but on the other hand if you opt for agitating the water with fountains or cascades you cannot enjoy the calm reflections to be seen on still waters. Running water presents other problems. A stream running through a garden, especially if it runs fast, may be felt to drain away the very soul of that garden. The simplest way to avert this is to slow the stream, to widen it out into a pool, before it moves on again. Planting stream-sides in narrow ribbons seems only to make the stream run faster. To 'slow' the stream down, the planting should be done in triangles, with two 'feet' on the bank and the third protruding into the stream; this planting needs to be dense and bulky.

Slow-moving water needs to be treated differently. The surroundings, grass, trees and perhaps garden buildings, need to be used to accentuate the stillness of still water. The rule of thumb is that the stretch of level ground beyond the water should be twice as wide as the water it is seen across. If there is not space enough for this, then the planting should be of sufficient height and bulk to provide a reflection that halves the water's apparent surface.

Informal waters should lie easily in the landscape, fitting into it as naturally as possible, the most natural position being the lowest. Formal sheets of water – tanks, canals, basins – can be higher in the scheme of the garden, and near to the house.

If the purpose of a pool is to bring light into the garden, then the nearer to the level of one's eyes the surface of the water is, the brighter it will appear. Shadowed water can have its own appeal: provided the surface is at the level of level ground, then by planting on the far side a curtain of dark evergreens, one cuts off the lateral rays of the sun and concentrates the reflection on the deep blue of the sky directly overhead. If, on the other hand, one wants the surface to reflect objects

on the further bank, then one must make calculations in optics. The angle at which the line of sight strikes the water is the same as the angle of reflection. At Vaux-le-Vicomte, Le Notre arranged the levels so that the visitor to the garden cannot see the waters of the canal (a major feature of the garden) from the upper terrace, but only the reflection of the cascades gushing into the raised square fountain on the second terrace. When the viewer looks back from the banks of the canal it is the facade of the chateau that is reflected in this same raised square fountain.

The vertical accent of a few reeds rising through the water's surface enhances the water's calm horizontal accent, and a few white water-lilies floating like bursting stars among their disc-like pads may be appropriate in a white garden, but to so fill a lake or pond with vegetation that its surface can no longer be seen is to totally destroy the purpose of having water at all. The best of both worlds may be achieved if the planting does not obscure more than one-third of the water's surface.

Water at rest invites reflection, but water at play invites one's enjoyment of it. What makes fountains exciting is the interplay of light and water, but in different lights different effects are needed. The fountains that play and sparkle in the sun in Italy or California will not do the same in the dark, grey climate of England. Under the bright blue Italian skies, the fountain basins are made of white marble; in the fountains of the Tivoli Gardens in Copenhagen, under very different skies, the basins are made of wood. Both materials look eminently right in their own setting. There are those who would say that fountains can only be appreciated to the full in a hot country, and indeed the Italians brought endless imagination to their aquatic architecture. The French, under greyer skies, use water differently, concentrating more on large reflective surface areas, though this is

In the white garden at Hidcote topiary birds watch and wait.

Organisation is fundamental to the concept of garden. Sissinghurst: the white garden in winter.

The pool in the white garden (the Fountain Garden) at Tintinhull.

perhaps as much a matter of topography as climate. Under English skies the playing Italian fountains would merely be a depressing reminder of the all too frequent rain, and fountains are better used as bubblers, merely animating the surface of water, or as single playing jets. Water has depth, as well as surface, and its transparency can be exploited. In shallow pools, if the water is clear enough, the bottom can be seen, and fascinating effects can be created by the interplay of a patterned bottom and the reflections on the surface.

Part 3
Plants and Planting

THE BASIC PLANTS

In the making of white gardens certain plants seem almost always to be used. Nor should they be despised for this for they all have proven virtues. Those with flowers are all of an acceptable whiteness, and they are all hardy, reliable and the perennials are soundly perennial. To practised gardeners they may at first seem a mundane selection but paradoxically it is in the most sophisticated and successful white gardens that most reliance is placed on them.

In all the white gardens known to us a white rose is one of the basic plants, perhaps even the basic plant, and always the same white rose, 'Iceberg'. The odd thing about 'Iceberg' is that on its own in isolation, it does not rate very highly. There are other white roses with a better scent, a better habit and with perhaps even whiter flowers yet 'Iceberg''s combination of qualities, its freedom of flower, the size, shape and substance of the flowers, as well as its particular quality of whiteness make it unbeatable in a white garden. Occasional flowers show a faint pinkness at the centre and on the backs of the petals. This usually passes unnoticed amid the general impression of whiteness, but at Folly Farm it is brilliantly exploited. Among the massed 'Icebergs' are grown regal lilies whose white trumpets are striped with exactly the same shade of pink. In other white gardens 'Iceberg' is used in different ways. At Barrington Court it is used as

low bushes but, at Tintinhull, it is pruned to fit quite a narrow space. At Hazelby House it is used in its climbing form, constrained within narrow trellis-work pillars from which it spills out. If 'Iceberg' lets itself down at all it is in October and November when a high proportion of the flowers are strongly flushed with pink, but it is so good at other seasons that it may be forgiven.

In most white gardens more than one white rose is used, and the second choice seems invariably to be 'Little White Pet', a lowly rose, useful for tucking in under 'Iceberg' to hide the latter's knees. It arose as a sport on 'Felicité et Perpetue' in 1879, and it exactly resembles that rose in every way except that it is smaller in all its parts. It grows to no more than 60cm (2ft), and the flowers, produced in small clusters, are borne continuously throughout the summer and autumn. They are perfectly double and milk-white, though they open from decidedly crimson buds. It is an exceedingly hardy rose, and virtually evergreen which is a bonus, for its foliage is glossy and attractive.

Crambe cordifolia, the giant sea-kale, is one of the largest of cultivated perennials, for not only does it have huge floppy, dark green, rather coarse leaves, but it produces the most enormous panicles of strongly-scented, pure white flowers. The individual flowers are quite tiny and shaped like those of the common cabbage, but they are produced in such abundance on stout branching stems 2m (7ft) high that it might pass for a giant gypsophila

– certainly that is the effect. It is a plant that really comes into its own in a white garden, the whiteness of each tiny, individual flower reinforced by and reflected in all the other whites around it. Because of its size *Crambe cordifolia* belongs right at the back of a border or the far corner, not only by reason of its height but because the basal leaves are unattractive and best hidden by the plants in front. In small white gardens it may have to be used as a singleton but, where space permits, it is better used in bold clumps of five or seven or even nine for its tiny flowers are presented very thinly and when massed the slender flowering branches intermingle making a far denser cloud. At Hazelby House several plants are used together in a corner of the white garden and at Barrington Court they are grown in large groups in each corner of the white garden. It is a plant for alkaline soils, where gypsophila can be used to repeat its form and style, but in a lesser way, for neither is a success on acid soils. It looks best grown with other bulky plants, *Rose rugosa* 'Blanc Double de Coubert', for example, and *Fatsia japonica*.

The musk mallow *Malva moschata*, a first cousin of the hollyhock, is one of the most beautiful flowering plants native to Britain. Its white form, *M.m.* 'Alba' is one of the most desirable of all plants for a white garden. It can grow as much as 1m (3ft) tall, but is more usually under 60cm (2ft) and it has deeply cut, dark green leaves, a bit like those of a buttercup. Its white flowers resemble those of the hollyhock; the stamens are exquisitely pink-tinted. Like other perennials with deeply-penetrating, carrot-like tap roots it grows best on well-drained soils. We know one garden where it languishes in the heavy clay borders though self-sown seedlings flourish in the gravel paths. It is a true perennial but tends to be short-lived. It is best used in good clumps or drifts in front of shrubs such as philadelphus and deutzia, with

Alchemilla mollis at its feet and *Nicotiana alata* (*N. affinis*) or *N. langsdorfii* next to it.

Lychnis coronaria 'Alba' might be considered too wispy and insubstantial to be effective, but like the crambe, it accentuates the solidity of more solid plants. The lychnis overwinters as a clump of grey leaves of a flannelly texture, but then in early summer it sends up slender stems bearing pairs of the same silvery-grey flannelly leaves topped by flowers which, individually, resemble single, old-fashioned pinks. In the form 'Alba' it is pure white; in *L.c.* 'Oculata' there is a delightful pink eye and this form would go well in a white garden where the predominating tone is on the pink side of white, and it would associate well with *Geranium renardii*. *Lychnis coronaria* is the perfect white-flowered plant to have thrusting its way up carelessly among more positive and glamorous plants, and to bring an air of casualness to a garden in which formality has become too rigid. It is a weed of poor soils, so is never happy in heavily manured ground.

In the white garden candytuft provides a link between the spring-flowering daffodils and early tulips and the main power-house of flower in high summer. Its tufts of dense evergreen foliage make useful ground-cover and a contrast to other white-flowered plants for the rest of the season. If left to its own devices candytuft will smother the ground for at least 2m (7ft) and so should be kept rigorously in check. There is a dwarf form, *I.s.* 'Little Gem'. It looks especially good in a formal white garden when grown at the front of the border, beside paving, in such a way that roses growing behind it can lean over it when they are heavy with bloom. Although each individual flower is a brilliant, pure white, *en masse* the flowers can appear slightly grey.

Generally the most successful white gardens are those contained within a formal

At Folly Farm 'Iceberg' roses and regal lilies grow together revealing an unexpected undertone of pink.

framework but a feeling of stiffness and rigidity can be avoided if a proportion of the plants included are 'cottagey'. They will create an air of relaxation and profusion. *Achillea ptarmica* adds just this quality. The best form in this context is 'The Pearl' raised by Lemoine in the 1870s, but double forms have been known since the sixteenth century. Although basically a vigorous weed, preferring moist ground, it is very adaptable and flowers for many weeks during the summer. It has sturdy upright stems of well-branched flower-heads carrying many florets of daisy-like, double button flowers 2cm (¾ in) across. The general effect is greyish-white although the individual flowers are pure white. The serrated leaves are dark green. 'Perry's White' and 'Snowball' are less effective since they tend to fall outwards from the middle leaving a bare centre. 'The Pearl' does this least of all.

Continuing the cottage-garden theme, no white garden that can grow them should be without a few garden pinks. Like gypsophila they are often not a success in acid soils. Few other plants can provide at one go blue-grey foliage, white flowers and a heavenly scent. It is not for nothing that they are called Dianthus, the flower of the gods. They are the perfect plant for the front of the border, especially if the border is edged with stone across which they can sprawl. To thrive they need full sun and sharply drained soil; a handful of coarse Cornish grit ,at planting time is a help. They detest peat and leaf-mould which seem to make them rot. They also dislike those cold desiccating east winds that blow in the spring. They are easily propagated from pipings (which are cuttings that are pulled not cut) and should be renewed from time to time, especially as they cannot be cut back to the old wood: they simply won't grow again.

'Mrs Sinkins' is justly famous, an old cottage pink, which more than any other always

Crambe cordifolia: *one of the most spectacular plants in the white garden repertoire.*

seems to feature in white gardens. It has good foliage – although it tends to separate from the centre – and double white, fringed flowers within a split calyx, and a powerful clove scent. Like most cottage pinks it was raised in the nineteenth century — apparently by the Master of the Poor Law Institution (workhouse) at Slough and named for his wife. It is depicted on the coat of arms of that borough. *D.* 'Joy Sinkins' is similar and is named for their daughter. 'White Ladies' has green foliage, whiter flowers, better fragrance and a stronger constitution but is harder to come by.

Sadly these old pinks flower only in June and do not repeat, and their habit of growth is untidy. Modern varieties are more upright and stiffer in habit and flower from early summer right through until the frosts. On the whole they are more effective than the older varieties, but lack the particular clove scent of the old-fashioned sorts. 'Haytor' is probably the best known, its flower opening palest ivory and quickly turning white. They are shaggy and this makes the plants more suited to an informal white border. It grows to 45cm (18in) and has a light clove scent overlaid with that of Euthymol toothpaste. For the more formal white garden, *D.* 'Ballerina', a semi-double with a flatter face, and slightly fringed petals is a perfect choice. It has a glorious clove scent. 'Nan Bailey' has more glaucous foliage and a coronet in the centre of its semi-double, pure white flowers. The petals are barely fringed at all. It, too, has a lovely scent. These two both reach about 30cm (12in). For a white garden on the pink side, *D.* 'Alan Titchmarsh', a semi-double with slightly bloodshot pinky-green eyes and wonderful fragrance, is a winner.

Campanulas are as inseparable from the white garden as they are from the old roses with which they consort so well. They are an enormous group of good, garden-worthy plants with many whites and white-forms among them. Much-loved though they are, they never quite rise to star quality; they never top the bill as do paeonies, or irises or lilies, but are best as companion plants in a supporting role among plants of greater quality. They are mostly of the easiest culture, although susceptible to rust, and they need dividing often to ensure a crop of flowers each year. They do well in any fertile soil, in sun or a little shade, the taller sorts growing through and propping themselves up against more solid neighbours, perhaps roses or philadelphus.

C. latifolia, the giant bellflower, is one of the taller species for the back of the border, reaching 1.2m (4ft) and forming good clumps of oval, toothed leaves with pointed tips. Both leaf and stem are hairy. The long, bell-shaped flowers are upright or pendant, and the form for white gardens is *C.l.* 'Alba' which is pure white. This species prefers a moist soil, and is of most use in the shaded areas of the white garden where it will glow in the dusk if given a dark hedge as a background. *C. alliariifolia* is a species which is naturally white-flowered, though it is a creamy-white. The lovely garden form 'Ivory Bells' is slightly whiter and will associate well with roses 'Margaret Merrill' and 'Pascali' and also with white day lilies which are on the creamy-yellow side of the spectrum. It grows to 60cm (2ft) with heart-shaped basal leaves and large narrow bells 10cm (4in) long, hanging on arching stems.

The white form of *C. pyramidalis* is breathtaking at the back of the border, its whiteness sharpened by a background of sable yews. It begins by building itself up into a great, pyramidal mound of heart-shaped leaves and then from the centre of the mound there arises an erect stem which, with good cultivation, can reach 2m (7ft) and upon whose side branches are borne an abundance of stemless wide-open white flowers. There are few white-flowered plants that can beat it for sheer showiness though it does not succeed in all gardens. Although a perennial forming a great carrot of a root, it is best treated as a biennial, renewed each year from the non-flowering side-shoots which occur right at the bottom of the stem. At the other extreme, *C. glomerata* 'Crown of Snow' is a sturdy front-of-border plant.

The gem of the genus is a form of *C. trachelium* known as 'Alba Flore Plena' with pendant double white bells a full 10cm (4in) long. *C. trachelium* is quite distinct from other campanulas because its leaves resemble those of the stinging nettle. It grows to 60cm (2ft) and increases quite steadily and flowers freely throughout June. It is perfectly suited to a cottagey white border.

C. persicifolia, known as the peach-leafed bellflower grows to about 60cm (2ft) occasionally more, and increases quite rapidly and is happy in sun or shade. There are several white forms: 'Alba' is a single white with wide-open bell-shaped cups, as is 'Snowdrift'; 'Alba flore pleno' is very double with many rows of petals and is thought to be synonymous with 'Boule de Neige'. In fact it is so double that its petals tend to roll up and stick together after rain. For this reason and because it is a martyr to rust it would not be a first choice for the white garden, whereas 'Fleur de Neige' has less rows of petals and is thought to be rust resistant. *C.p.* 'Moorheimii' is a semi-double white. There is also a peach-leafed campanula simply known as 'white cup and saucer'; the name describes the flower which has utter simplicity, rather like a distinguished Canterbury bell. It was apparently found by Marjorie Fish, and may or may not be the same as the plant which won an award from the Royal Horticultural Society under the name 'Hetty'; or again it could be 'Hampstead White'. In any case it wins our award for the best campanula for the white garden.

C. takeshimana is one of those off-white plants which one may or may not like in a white garden. It has rosettes of heart-shaped basal leaves and arching stems, 60cm (2ft) tall, bearing long dangling tubular bells which, from a distance, appear grey but turn out on closer inspection to be palest lilac-white spotted with maroon inside. It is an exquisite plant which may look well in a white garden draping itself like a garland round the neck of small white amorini, the bells dangling above some lowly greyling, *Stachys lanata* 'Silver Carpet' or *Tanacetum densum*. *C. takeshimana* is an invaluable ingredient for the white garden which veers towards the pink tones and would look wonderful planted next to *Berberis thunbergii* 'Atropurpurea Nana'.

There is a small campanula relative that may also have a place in the white garden. This is the balloon flower or Chinese bellflower, *Platycodon grandiflorum*. Balloon flower is most appropriate, for above the campanula-like clumps of leaves arise straight stems beset, in the manner of a campanula, with big, round balloon-like buds. These open to become wide, cup-shaped flowers. There is a white form, 'Alba' which has dark blue veins across its face; and a double white, 'Flore Pleno'. Both produce flower spikes 60–75cm (24–30in) tall. 'Mariesii' is similar but grows to only 45cm (18in) and there is a lovely white form, 'Mariesii Albus'.

A white garden or white border in August is unthinkable without phlox. With their big heads they add large blocks of solid, pure white and have a delicate sweet scent, and as long as they have enough moisture at their roots, they can tolerate full sun although they prefer a little shade. They are an excellent foil for the pompon and cactus varieties of white dahlia which flower at the same time.

The wild phlox is *P. paniculata*, a north American that grows to 1.2m (4ft) and has quite small flowers compared with the

(Overleaf, left) Camellia japonica *'White Swan'*; *(right)* Narcissus *'Thalia'*.

Jenny Jowett

Jenny Jowett

modern sorts. Its form 'Alba Grandiflora' is larger flowered, though only a little larger, and is worth mentioning because it is a plant of redoubtable good health. Not all phloxes are. The problem is eelworm. Stem cuttings and divisions transmit the problem, quickly recognised by swollen shoots and twisted leaves, so plants should only be acquired if they have been propagated from root cuttings which is probably why so few nurseries stock them today. Affected plants must be burned and no more phlox grown in the same area. Their preference is to be grown in greensand but to keep them in good health grow them in humus-rich soil and mulch them every year with more humus for although usually grown in garden borders in full sun they came originally from woodlands. They do not thrive on chalk or heavy clays. The modern sorts grow to 90cm (3ft), some a little more and a few a little less.

Phlox have a fresh, sweet scent when just open but this becomes less pleasant as the flower matures. *P.p.* 'White Admiral' is the white phlox most often encountered. It has huge, domed heads of clear white flowers with the minutest green eye. 'Iceberg' is white shaded violet at the centre; 'Mia Ruys' is a dwarf at 60cm (2ft) with large white flowers and 'September Schnee' extends the flowering period well into September especially in cooler gardens. Phlox show signs of stress from lack of water before almost any other border plant so a frequent ample soaking during periods of dry weather and removal of any weak shoots will prolong the flowering period.

Much stronger and healthier, though less showy, are the forms of *Phlox maculata*: the flowers are cylindrical rather than pyramidal. Of these 'Alpha' is pure white, 'Omega' is white with a lilac eye and would fit in well to a pink-toned white garden. Usually the lower portions of the phlox stems look brown and straggly and are best concealed by the green and white variegated leaves of hostas or bergenias.

The Shasta daisy, *Leuchanthemum maximum*, until recently *Chrysanthemum maximum*, is an indispensable plant in any white garden. Its dark green, toothed leaves have an almost rubbery texture, but its other attributes more than make up for this, for it is extremely hardy and will put up a good show on just about any soil. Most cultivars need some support for though the stems are strong and stiff they tend to keel over from ground level. The modern doubles and semi-doubles are much more attractive than the old singles. *L.* 'Esther Read', is an old variety, fully double and growing to about 45cm (18in), 'Aglaia' is semi-double and does not show its yellow centre but is a little taller, while 'Fiona Coghill' is fully double and 'Wirrall Supreme' has short white petals at its centre; both are taller still at 75cm (30in). 'Cobham Gold' is fully double and similar to 'Esther Read' but the petals at the centre are gold which may be useful in some white gardens. 'W.L. Harkness', 'Phyllis Smith' and 'Bishopstone' are virtually singles with fringed petals giving the flowers a pleasingly shaggy appearance. All have a prominent yellow eye but, again, this may be a benefit in white gardens when creamy tones and acid yellows are introduced. 'Snowcap' is semi-double and, at 30cm (12in) is a dwarf for the front of the border. 'September Snow' usually gives a second crop of double white flowers in early autumn, thus extending the flowering season. By choosing varieties with care it is possible to have essentially similar sorts of daisies in flower from early July through August right into October, closing the season with the tall Hungarian daisy *Leucanthamella serotina* (*Chrysanthemum uliginosum*) and with *Nipponanthemum nipponicum* (*Chrysanthemum nipponicum*), a dwarf species with big white flowers with an acid greenish-yellow eye.

In the more shaded parts of the white garden white violas are indispensable. Supreme amongst these is *Viola cornuta* 'Alba', a hummock-forming heartsease with rich green leaves and two seasons of flower if the spent stems are clipped over and there is plenty of moisture at its roots. It produces a dense matt of smaller leaves and flowers in early summer. When happy it will seed itself around making an attractive carpet beneath shrubs and roses. There is a form known as V.c. 'Alba Minor' but this is probably too fiddly for our purpose. There are many pure white violas and pansies, and some with creamy tones like 'Little David', which has a minute yellow eye, but a second choice has to be *V. septentrionalis* which is large and scentless but has delightfully fashioned white flowers with just a hint of greyish-mauve. It too will seed itself around.

The basic tree in most white gardens is the weeping silver pear, *Pyrus salicifolia* 'Pendula'. It somehow has just the right qualities for a white garden; it is also the perfect small tree for courtyards and enclosed spaces – and most white gardens are enclosed. A circle of 3m (10ft) across should be allowed to give it sufficient space when fully grown. While this tree makes a lovely single specimen, it is also often used in twos and fours, and though it is usually very difficult to produce matching pairs of trees, weeping silver pears grow more uniformly than most, providing that each one has the same amount of nutrients and moisture available and that different planting sites are correctly catered for. It is, however, a tree that needs a little attention if it is to delight. What is usually available is a young tree that has been grafted at ground level. If left to its own devices it will slowly grow into a tangled and untidy mess – a great heap of grey foliage trailing over the ground. It needs to be trained up with a leader and the lower branches gradually pruned away so that the lowest twigs are well clear of the ground.

Training is simply a matter of staking the tree, tying a tall cane to the stake and tying a leading shoot to the cane. The leader should be trained up to 2.5 or 2.8m (8–9ft). The trees will look much more effective if treated in this manner. But do not remove too many of the lower branches too soon or the tree may sucker. Occasionally one comes across top-worked trees (in which the graft is 2m (7ft) above ground level) and these are much to be preferred if they can be found.

For those who like to be a little different there are a number of other silver pears. *Pyrus salicifolia* is always a weeping tree, the form 'Pendula' being only marginally more pendulous than the typical plant. *P. eleagrifolia* is, in effect, a non-weeping version. It makes a tree to about 10m (33ft), and it is every bit as silver but definitely needs more space than the familiar weeping silver pear. *P. nivalis* is similar, but its leaves are almost white in spring, fading through silver to grey and nearly green by late summer. In *P.* x *canescens*, a hybrid between *nivalis* and *salicifolia*, the leaves end the summer a shining dark green.

The basic grey shrub for all white gardens and filling many roles, is *Brachyglottis*, formerly *Senecio*, 'Sunshine', previously *S. laxifolius* or *S. greyi*. It has oval, grey, felted leaves and gnarled stems. If its harsh yellow daisy-like flowers are clipped away each summer, together with stems which have grown out of shape, it will soon become a shapely mound 1m (3ft) tall and 2m (7ft) wide. It is a veritable evergrey and associates well with the glossy foliage of camellias, choisya and the ribbed leaves of *Viburnum davidii* which will give shape and structure to the white garden in winter. Add *Euonymus* 'Emerald Gaiety' to this grouping and snowdrops and crocuses with white flowers and a most satisfying winter white group will be created. The leaves of the senecio becomes more silver towards summer and make perfect partners for the

Basic plants producing brilliant and reliable whiteness at Lytes Cary: 'Iceberg' roses, Leucanthemum *'Esther Read' and tall campanulas.*

white roses, phlox and agapanthus and contrast well with the flimsiness of some of the white-flowered campanulas. *B. munroi* is in effect a dwarf version with smaller, oval toothed leaves. It is smaller in stature and less hardy.

Choisya ternata, the Mexican orange blossom, has so many virtues that it has become a basic component of most white gardens. It forms a dense rounded bush of 1 to 1.5m (3–5ft) tall with highly polished mid-green trifoliate leaves (like those of a clover) which, like the stems, emit a strong and pleasing fragrance when crushed. It produces flat heads of sweetly-scented starry-white flowers, mainly in the early summer,

but intermittently right through until the frosts. Happy in sun or some shade, and any soil, it dislikes cold winds. It is often bleached by frosts.

The most basic foliage plant for the white garden is *Hosta sieboldiana* in its form 'Elegans'. It is suitable for every sort of white garden, provided that it has dappled shade for much of the day, and adequate moisture at its roots. It is grown for its enormous heart-shaped glaucous, grey-blue leaves, which are puckered and ribbed like seersucker. An established plant, at five years old, can be up to 2.5m (8ft) across, with a leaf mound 1m (3ft)

(Opposite) Trillium grandiflorum.

50

Jenny Jowett

tall. The flowers, which are crowded into a dense, one-sided spike, are palest mauvey-grey, fading to off-white if grown in sun, in perfect harmony with the leaves. The flowers scarcely rise above the leaf mound. There is a form called var. *hypophyllum* which is said to be non-flowering because the flowers are never seen above the leaves, and this form is even more useful in a white garden. There are many named forms of *H. sieboldiana* available now and of these 'Big Daddy' and 'Blue Mammoth' are two of the bluest. There is also a form with virtually white flowers, *H. sieboldiana* 'Elegans Alba'. *H. tokudama* is, in effect, a smaller version of *H. sieboldiana* but its leaves are blue not grey. It is very slow growing. A cross between *H. sieboldiana* and *H. tardiflora* has produced a race of small-leafed hostas with leaves in a variety of shapes and shades of blue to greyish-green. Of these *H.* 'Halcyon', 'Hadspen Blue' and 'Blue Moon' are some of the bluest. Those with the most pronounced shade of blue in their leaves will not fit into a white garden which is made up of creamy-yellow tones. *H.* 'Snowden', a much more greenish-grey-leafed hybrid of *H. sieboldiana* is a better bet where a very large specimen is needed and 'Blue Skies' and 'Dorset Charm' would add the complementary small-leafed greenish-grey. All these hostas lose their intense blueness if grown in full sun all day, but some stay bluer than others.

These hostas look marvellous in the white garden planted in association with *Alchemilla mollis*, Lady's mantle, a plant which to the untutored eye can scarcely be seen from its showers of tiny, acid, limey-green flowers to be a lowly relative of the lovely rose. It is one of the indispensable ingredients of most white gardens, only perhaps out of place in white gardens wholly on the pink side of the spectrum. It tones exactly with the lime green *Nicotiana alata* and *N. langsdorfii* and makes all the whites look whiter. Its leaves are like those of no other plant, limp, umbrella-shaped greyish-green with a soft downy texture and are covered in fine silky hairs which trap raindrops which themselves capture a microimage of the sun. It is at its loveliest when its showers of tiny flowers on lax stems tumble out of a border on to paving. If not cut down after flowering, it will seed prolifically and though the seedlings look particularly charming when allowed to grow randomly in cracks in stone paving an excess of them can be a problem. Add tubs of white petunias in unpainted wooden barrels for an air of informality. There is also a form known as 'Robusta' or 'Robustica' with larger greyer leaves and bigger heads of flowers and another called 'Variegata' whose leaves are splashed with radial wedges of creamy-white, which is appropriate for the white garden, though much less vigorous than the typical plant. *Alchemilla mollis* associates well with the hybrid tea rose 'Pascali' and with the blue rue, *Ruta graveolens* 'Jackman's Blue', which should have its harsh yellow flowers removed for the sake of the colour scheme. Lady's mantle grows very quickly and so adds an air of maturity to a newly-planted white garden when not much else has fully developed.

TWELVE WHITE FLOWERS OF EXCEPTIONAL BEAUTY

Beautiful flowers do not a beautiful garden make. What makes a garden beautiful is its overall effect and in this the beauty of individual flowers is merely a detail, but a vital one. Beautiful flowers gain in loveliness when they are grown among more ordinary floral furnishings.

Camellia japonica was introduced to Europe at the beginning of the eighteenth century and by the middle of the nineteenth century, it had become the most popular greenhouse flower of all: its stiffness, the polished opulence of its leaves and its rather formal flowers which seem to combine showiness with a certain reticence were almost emblematic of the age of Victoria. At the end of the nineteenth century its popularity waned and it became the most despised of plants. No doubt many fine specimens were physically ejected from greenhouses and conservatories. And then came the surprise. They turned out to be hardy, indeed one of the hardiest of all evergreens. The problem is that the flowers are vulnerable to frosts which leaves them bruised and brown-edged. This problem can be overcome in most gardens, for it is not so much the frost that does the damage as the thaw, especially if thawing is rapid. The ideal place for a camellia is at the foot of a west-facing wall, with some overhead shelter from trees. In such a position the sun will not reach the flowers till noon or later, and frozen flowers will thaw slowly as the air warms.

Perhaps we garden to tempt fate or defy nature, for white camellias are now more popular than ever. Hillier's *Manual* lists over 20 white varieties of *Camellia japonica*, and Trehanes, the camellia specialists, list nearly 30. They range in form from singles and semi-doubles to formal doubles and blowsy paeony forms, and from ancient camellias brought back from Japan by earnest Victorian seamen to the latest hybrids raised in Australia or America. On the whole the older varieties have the merit of being tried and tested, their performance proven. Generally it is best to match the formality or informality of the flower to the formality or informality of the garden. It is also important to study the habit of growth, for some camellias make very dense, compact bushes, some are narrowly upright while others sprawl untidily on the ground.

'White Swan' is perhaps the most beautiful white camellia for general planting. Its large semi-double flowers are of classic simplicity, opening to a wide, saucer-shape and containing at their centre a trumpet-shaped boss of rich golden stamens rather like those of the Higo camellias. Had it only one row of petals the flowers would be stiffly formal, like those of *C.j.* 'Alba Simplex', but the second row of petals softens the formality and gives the flower greater interest. The foliage is dark green and not excessively polished, and the leaves are somewhat recurved, with the veins deeply impressed. It forms a rounded, well-furnished bush and flowers in mid-season, late March and April. It prefers some shade from early sun. It has been known and grown in Britain since about 1920 and should not be confused with an American camellia of the same name but of later date whose flowers are pink.

We would rate *C.j.* 'Haku-rakuten' next for effectiveness, its flowers being just about as weather-proof as those of 'White Swan'. It is variable in flower from semi-double (revealing its golden stamens) to paeony-formed (and hiding them), with fluted petals. It overlaps the flowering season of 'White Swan' and extends beyond it into May. Of the singles 'Henry Turnbull' has, by contrast, an open and gracefully relaxed habit of growth, 'Lily Pons' has long, fluted, pointed petals round a good column of stamens and tends to semi-doubleness – a rather formal flower – while 'Yuki-Botan' has a distinct twist to each petal and 'Charlotte de Rothschild' has flowers that open flat, the central mass of stamens being pale gold; it forms a neat, rounded bush and is quite slow growing.

Of the semi-doubles 'Lotus' (which is also known as 'Gauntlettii' and 'Sode-gashuki') has flowers that resemble a water-lily. 'Swan Lake' is an informal double with rather untidy almost shaggy flowers presented with

(Overleaf, left) Iris *'Cliffs of Dover'*;
(right) Wisteria sinensis *'Alba'*.

53

Jenny Jowett

Jenny Jowett

great freedom on a gracefully relaxed bush. 'Matterhorn' is, by contrast, the most formal double of all, the petals pointed and overlapping symmetrically, the bush compact and upright with downward sweeping branches and long, tapered leaves. It is the most popular white camellia for town gardens.

The one disadvantage of *Camellia japonica* and its forms is that the flowers remain on the branches when they are over, marring the appearance, especially of the white flowered sorts. In a courtyard garden one can pluck these off by hand but in a large garden this is scarcely practical. *Camellia saluenensis*, on the other hand, drops its flowers as soon as they are over. It is just as hardy as *C. japonica* except that it detests cold winds. The foliage is not glossy, as in *C. japonica* nor so dark, but midgreen, matt and reticulated, and the flowers have great refinement of form, being single, trumpet-shaped and usually borne in great profusion. A form with a pure white flower does exist, though it is fabulously rare, but its hybrid 'Francis Hanger' produces its single flowers in great profusion, and sheds them as soon as they are over, as does 'China Clay', a semi-double whose white flowers open flat.

There are other white camellias for those who can accommodate them or have a taste for something a little different. *Camellia sasanqua* is the autumn camellia, flowering in October and November, and it too needs a sunny south wall to flower freely. 'Snowflake' is a single white with well-rounded petals and a boss of yellow stamens; 'Blanchette' and 'Duff Alan' are other single whites, while 'Mine-no-yuki' is a double white and 'Fuji-no-mine' has paeony-form flowers of rich creamy-white. *C. oleifera* is the hardiest of all camellias and opens its flowers in mild spells from November till February. The flowers are single, cup-shaped and small compared with modern hybrids.

Camellias present problems of placement and association in the white garden. They are very powerful plants. They draw the eye very

strongly. Their leaves are almost too polished and their flowers have dramatic size and substance. These qualities make camellias difficult to associate with other plants. They go better with a conservatory or a town garden than they do with a country garden, and they are set off to perfection by trellis work. They are most at home when stood out in front of a house or in a courtyard, as orange trees once were in white-painted Versailles tubs. They look ill at ease against yew hedges and in company with Shasta daisies, rose 'Iceberg' and the old garden pink 'Mrs Sinkins'. The answer is to grow *Camellia japonica* in association with ferns such as the winter-green *Cyrtomium falcatum*, or the more delicate forms of *Polystichum setiferum*, with glaucous hostas such as *H. sieboldiana* 'Elegans' and perhaps a white-variegated grass nearby. Another possibility is to use it as a background to the flowers of white hostas, *H.* 'Freising' or *H.* 'Wiehenstephan', or for such subjects as *Galtonia candicans*.

Two of the most beautiful daffodils ever raised happen to be white. Both have *Narcissus triandrus* 'Albus', popularly known as the angels tears daffodil, as one parent. 'Thalia' is the more beautiful of the two, growing 35–40cm (14–16in) tall and carrying heads of one to three beautifully formed flowers on each stem, the flowers 2.5–3cm (1–1¼in) across, of a glistening, almost opalescent whiteness. It flowers in mid-season. In the paved garden at Knightshayes Court, surrounded by sombre yew hedges, 'Thalia' is used in drifts and bold clumps beneath ancient apples. The theme is repeated in the woodland garden, where 'Thalia' is used beneath white flowering cherries, white magnolias and among the white form of *Rhododendron schlippenbachii*. In both, on a misty March morning the effect is haunting. 'Silver Chimes' is its sister *triandrus* hybrid, but the other parent is *Narcissus tazetta* from which it inherits more flowers to each head – up to seven – and a delicate scent. Some prefer it to 'Thalia' but it is not so white. Of similarly delicate appearance are three earlier-flowering white *cyclamineus* hybrids. They have reflexed petals – folded back away from the trumpet like an egret in flight. 'February Silver' grows up to 20cm (8in) and has milk-white reflexed petals and a trumpet of palest lemon; the flower is exceptionally long-lasting. 'Dove Wings' is similar, with ivory-white wings and a pale yellow trumpet, while 'Jenny' produces the whitest flowers of the three, the trumpet opening cream but fading white.

For those who find these daffodils too fey there is 'Mount Hood', which is in effect a white 'King Alfred' – a true large-flowered trumpet daffodil. Big and blowsy, it lacks the grace and refinement of the smaller hybrids. Also large, but long-lasting and valuable for its later flowering and of venerable antiquity, is the double form of the pheasant's eye or poet's narcissus, *N. poeticus flore-pleno*. The flower is pure white, very double and superbly scented. Both grow to about 45cm (18in) tall.

In flower at about the same time as the pheasant's eye is the *Trillium grandiflorum*, a North American woodlander. All the trilliums have poise and style and are most aristocratic plants but what makes *T. grandiflorum* especially beautiful is its simplicity and the harmony of all its parts. Each rounded tuber sends up a single stem, bronze to begin with when it first shows itself above ground in March, but green by the time the leaves, usually three, sometimes four, rarely five, have unfolded, revealing the soft yellow flower bud at the tip of the same stalk. The flower opens in mid-April and is composed of three broad, pure white petals that open horizontally, their tips curled downwards towards the ground. In flower they stand about 30cm (12in) tall. There is a pink form, to be avoided, and, choicest and rarest of all,

a double form, 'Flore Pleno', of unsurpassed beauty and exceeding rarity. They need cool, damp conditions in the garden, preferably a corner where the soil has been well-enriched with leaf mould and look lovely planted in drifts among hostas, erythroniums and ferns.

The tall bearded iris is one of the four sorts of plant without which no flower garden can rightly be called a flower garden (the other three are roses, lilies and paeonies). The archetypal bearded iris is *I. germanica*, a stately plant with stiff 75–100cm (30–40in) stems bearing well-formed, scented flowers of lavender-purple with deep, violet-purple falls, a common denizen of town and cottage gardens. It is not, though, the parent of the modern hybrids, for it is sterile, as is *I. florentina*, which is perhaps only a selected form of *I. germanica*, but of enduring value in the cottage garden because its dried rhizomes yield the fragrant orris root, the base of pot-pourris and many toiletries. *I. florentina* is a lovely flower for the white garden, with greyish leaves and sweetly scented flowers of ghostly greyish-white. There is a supposedly pure white form, 'Albicans', but it seems not to differ from the typical plant. The most beautiful generally-available white, tall bearded iris is 'Cliffs of Dover' raised in Northbrook, Illinois, USA in 1952 by Orville W. Fay. It grows 90cm (35in) tall and bears large flowers of ruffled pure white with a yellow beard. The American Iris Society gave it an an Award of Merit in 1953, and the Royal Horticultural Society gave it Award of Merit in 1959 after trials at Wisley. It is outstanding. 'Henry Shaw' is another classic white though a little shorter in the stems and bearing a small orange dot on the haft. 'Cup Race' is a newer American variety, with very large flowers, ruffled round the edges. For

(Overleaf, left) Paeonia *'White Wings'*;
(right) Rose *'Margaret Merrill'*.

57

Jenny Jowett

Jenny Jowett

smaller white gardens there is the Intermediate bearded iris, 'Just Jennifer', which grows to about 60cm (2ft) or, even smaller-growing to less than 40cm (16in), the standard dwarf bearded, of which 'Lilli White' is outstanding, with beautifully shaped flowers of purest white with ruffled falls. 'Irish Doll' is more intriguing, the standards pure white and the falls marked with green. Miniature beardeds are irises which grow to less than 20cm (8in), and the only white we know is 'Moonlight' which has large, snow-white standards with rather small falls of the palest green.

The foliage of irises draws the eye strongly and for this reason irises are most useful at the front of a border as one of the elements used to give a garden rhythm and pattern. They look particularly good grown next to and between low spreading plants such as the perennial candytufts, *Geranium sanguineum* 'Album' or *Artemisia schimdtiana* 'Nana'. They also look good with *Lavendula spica* 'Alba', white rosemary or *Ballota pseudodictamnus*, and contrast well with the round leaves of bergenias.

Wisterias exercise a fascination in a way that no other climbers do, perhaps because of the way they twist and twine like lianas in some primaeval jungle. There are several white-flowered forms and species, and from a garden point of view *Wisteria sinensis* is one of the most beautiful. It is the most vigorous of all, capable not merely of climbing but of covering the most lofty trees. It climbs by twining (anticlockwise in this species, clockwise in *W. floribunda*) and so needs suitable wires or rods to twine round. If grown on a wall or up a house it can extend more than 6m (20ft) each side of its main stem. The racemes are borne in May, and there is often a second, if inferior, flowering in August, each raceme being about 30cm (12in) long. The white form is called 'Alba'. *W. floribunda* is less suited to walls, really needing a pergola to

show off its racemes; but it is also suitable for growing as a free-standing bush, and two plants grown in this way at Kew are now no more than 2.5m (8ft) tall after more than a century. The bush form is achieved by pruning back to the flowering spurs every winter. The white form is *W.f.* 'Alba'. It is this species that has been trained to such good effect over the arbor in the white garden at Folly Farm. Through it has been trained an inconspicuous honeysuckle which perfumes the air unseen at a later season.

W. venusta is a white-flowered species, particularly useful in the white garden because it can be kept permanently shrubby simply by pruning back the long growths once or twice in the course of the summer, and then again to within a couple or five centimetres of the base in winter. It is a most beautiful wisteria, the individual flowers larger than those of the other species and of greater substance. The racemes, though scarcely 30cm (12in) long, have the virtue of opening all their flowers at the same time, thus making a far greater display. There is a rare double white form more curious than beautiful, known as *W.v.* 'Alba Plena' – though it has previously and confusingly been known as *W. sinensis* 'Alba Plena'. After flowering the long shoots need to be tied in to the wall or frame, and in winter shortened back, leaving only a couple of buds at the base of each shoot.

Paeonies are superlative plants for white gardens, for not only do they have flowers of great beauty, but they also have good foliage. The single-flowered sorts are the most beautiful, though the double-flowered sorts are longer-lasting. 'White Wings' is the loveliest of the whites. It has very large flowers, shallowly cup-shaped, with long, elegant petals that part as the flower ages and a jewel-like boss of golden stamens at the centre; its foliage is dark green, and colours briefly as it dies. 'Whitleyi major', a selected form of *Paeonia lactiflora* (from which the so-called Chinese paeonies were bred), is similar but slightly smaller in flower, the petals more rounded. Of the double Chinese paeonies, 'Duchesse de Nemours' and 'Kelways Glorious' are unsurpassed. Both have huge globe-shaped flowers with abundant petals, purest white with a hint of cream at the centre but, 'Duchesse de Nemours' errs rather more on the creamy side, and is very fragrant. Of the species, *Paeonia obovata* 'Alba' is outstanding, each stem producing but a single cup-shaped, pure white flower with a touch of crimson at the centre and a boss of pure gold stamens. It is particularly useful as it will take shade.

One of the useful things about paeonies is that their cycle of growth fits well with that of bulbs. In the white garden paeonies may be under-planted with snowdrops, white scillas, pushkinia, and white chionodoxa to flower as the foliage is emerging, or late white gladioli, acidanthera or galtonias, to flower as the foliage begins to fade away. They also associate well with border phloxes which may be grown behind them.

It would be unthinkable to make a white garden without white roses, but the choice is so great that it is easier to hesitate, embarrassed by the riches in prospect, than it is to decide which is most beautiful. 'Mme Hardy' seems an obvious choice. Many people consider it the most beautiful rose ever raised. It is a hybrid Damask, and was bred by Eugene Hardy who took charge, after Du Pont, of Josephine Bonaparte's garden at La Malmaison, famous for its roses, and he named it for his wife. It forms a bush about 1.5m (5ft) tall with matt, mid-green leaves (inclined to mildew). Its buds have long, elegant calyces and the flower, when fully open, is symmetrically quartered, of the purest white, with the central petals folded inwards to reveal a green eye, sweetly scented. But in places with high rainfall, the rain causes the flowers that are open to turn brown, and

those that are not to ball, making it quite hideous in nine years out of ten. 'Iceberg', though probably the most popular white rose ever raised, has rather floppy flowers so is scarcely a contender.

It is 'Margaret Merrill' that we consider of outstanding beauty. Like 'Iceberg' it is a cluster rose (a floribunda). It comes from the Harkness stable and was sired by 'Rudolph Timm' out of a seedling of 'Dedication' crossed with 'Pascali', itself a lovely white rose variously regarded as a cluster rose or as a large-flowered rose (a hybrid tea). It has long buds and as it unfurls it becomes for a moment the most perfect 'rosebud' shape. When wide open the flower is of ivory whiteness, with a boss of golden stamens at the centre. It grows a little shorter than 'Iceberg' and has a rather upright habit which it inherits from 'Pascali' and which makes it the ideal rose in small white gardens.

The regal lily was first discovered by E.H. Wilson in Szechwan in 1903, and he described it growing 'in narrow semi-arid valleys . . . encompassed by mountains . . . whose peaks are clothed with snow eternal . . . There, in June, by the wayside, this lily in full bloom, greets the weary wayfarer. Not in twos and threes but in hundreds, in thousands, aye, in tens of thousands.' In the wild it grows in rough grass, the stems concealed by grass, the flowers seemingly floating on top of the grass. Each flower is trumpet-shaped, of marble whiteness with pinker claret-coloured stripes on the outside, the inside purest white with a canary-yellow throat, and richly, spicely scented. The flowers are usually held facing slightly upwards on the tops of stems 1 to 1.25m (3–4ft) tall, usually three or five together, sometimes as many as eight. It is easily grown in well-drained soil, alkaline or

(Overleaf, left) Lilium regale;
(right) Clematis florida *'Plena'*.

61

Jenny Jowett

Jenny Jowett

acid, and is happiest with its feet in the shade and its head in the sun. In other white gardens the pure white form, *L. regale* 'Album', might fit better, especially if the garden leans towards chartreuse. Regal lilies are best planted behind low, rounded shrubs such as skimmias or lavender, or grown up through lesser artemisias, *A. canescens*, for example, or *A. stelleriana*, or through *Anthemis cretica* ssp. *carpatica* (*A. cupaniana* of old). They are at their most effective used in bold drifts of tens, twenties or fifties.

Several other lilies also have divinely scented white trumpet-shaped flowers more or less marked pink on the outside: *brownii*, *phillipense*, *wallichianum*, *formosanum* and *lencanthenum* var. *centifolium*, for example; but they are all more tender or more temperamental – or both. *Lilium pricei* is sometimes billed as a dwarf equivalent of *L. regale* but the similarity ends at white trumpets with pink pyjama stripes on the outside. *L. pricei* is one of those plants that are ugly because out of proportion, a huge trumpet on a tiny stalk, the tube too long for the mouth.

Clematis florida is a plant to be avoided by the faint-hearted in spite of being one of the most beautiful of clematis, for what emerges from the ground is a thread-like stem of such seeming delicacy that one would suppose the merest breath of wind would break it. Its performance usually but not always belies its delicate appearance, for it will climb to 2.5m (8ft), branch repeatedly and produce an abundance of its fascinating flowers. These are sometimes likened to and even mistaken for, those of the Passion flower, though really they are quite different. *C. florida* has six normal, white sepals but the stamens at the centre of the flower have been transformed into bright purple petaloids stamens, giving it a double appearance. As with so many doubles, its flowers are long lasting, the central mass of petaloids usually remaining well after the petals have fallen. It starts flowering in June and goes

on through July into August. All the flowering occurs on the last yard or so of the current season's growth, and so can be cut back quite hard in winter. It is an ancient variety, long-cultivated in Japanese gardens. It was brought back to Europe by Siebold and introduced to England from his nursery in 1836. It is notoriously difficult to please, and in some gardens simply fades away without a hint of an explanation. *C.f.* 'Plena' ('Alba Plena') has its stamens similarly metamorphosed into petaloides, but they are white and undifferentiated from the petals. It might seem that this all-white flower would be better suited to the white garden but this is a matter of taste. It is, in fact, decidedly greenish-white, very cool and sophisticated. The group of large flowered hybrids known as the Florida group are not in fact bred from *C. florida*. The nearest most of them come to it is having a touch of *C.f.* 'Fortunei', as is the case with 'Duchess of Edinburgh', and the once almost defunct 'Belle of Woking'. 'Duchess of Edinburgh' has double white, scented flowers shaded with green while 'Belle of Woking' is palest amethystine mauve. These clematis need no pruning beyond the removal of their old flowering wood.

Most hostas, by contrast, enjoy such rude good health as to be almost indestructible – a major contributory factor in their increasing popularity. However, the one species that we include among our twelve most beautiful white-flowered plants, *Hosta plantaginea*, though the first hosta to reach Europe and a great favourite of the Miss Jekyll, is now scarcely known in British gardens due mainly to a misapprehension of its needs. Hostas, as everyone knows, are shade-loving plants, all except *H. plantanginea*, which needs the hottest, sunniest place in the garden and an abundance of moisture. In shade it never flowers and its foliage is dull and disappointing. Moreover, with the low light intensities that go with shade it soon dwindles away. To flower at all in cool temperate countries it needs either to be grown at the foot of a south wall or in tubs and over-wintered under glass. When it does flower it is the most spectacular of all the hostas, producing, above rich, shining green leaves, spikes of flowers of the purest glistening whiteness, long-tubed and with a widely flaring mouth, the individual flowers as much as 15cm (6in) long and 10cm (4in) across. Moreover, the flower, which opens in the evening and closes again at dawn, possesses a fragrance as strong as any in the garden, spicy and redolent of the Orient.

Crinum x powellii 'Album' also produces flowers of exquisite beauty, comparable with those of the loveliest lilies. The crinums, which are sometimes called Paradise lilies, grow from bulbs the size of footballs, with roots as thick as a finger. The tops of the bulbs are elongated into curious necks known as 'chimneys' which remain above ground even when the foliage has died away in winter. The bulb throws up long green strap-shaped leaves as much as 15cm (6in) wide and 1.5m (5ft) long, and produces its flowers in a cluster at the top of a tall, stout stem. The sweetly scented flowers open in succession, giving a long season from mid to late summer. *Crinum x powellii* is a hybrid between two South African species, the cross having been first made in England by a Mr Powell. They are perfectly hardy in all but the coldest gardens, though they flower most freely in a warm position, at the foot of a wall, for instance, and they need a deep, moist soil and plenty of feeding.

The last in season of our white plants of exceptional beauty is *Colchicum speciosum* 'Album'. The colchicums are often mistakenly called autumn crocuses, though the true autumn crocuses are really quite different, not only in flower but also in the size and shape of the leaves. Indeed the two are not related, even distantly, for the colchicum is first cousin to a lily, while the crocus is first cousin to a daffodil. The two are easily told apart: the colchicum has a huge, unsymmetrical tuber, while the crocus has a small, neat, symmetrical corm; the colchicum has very large, broad, strap-shaped leaves, while those of the crocus are narrow and grass-like. The largeness of the leaves rather governs where one grows them, for the leaves can soon crowd out lesser subjects. They really need space to themselves, at the edge of a shrubbery, tucked in behind the box edging at the front of a border, for they enjoy semi-shade.

C. speciosum 'Album' is one of the finest flowers there is. It is tulip-shaped and as large as a good tulip flower, but without the long stem, of an exceptionally pure white with only the faintest tinge of green at the base. A patch of these colchicums, their clear white goblets gleaming against the bare earth in the September sun, is one of the glories of autumn.

ANNUALS, BIENNIALS AND BEDDING

In the white garden it is the effect that matters rather than the means used to achieve it. Most white gardens need annuals and bedding plants to boost their whiteness in high summer. In this, as in other aspects of the white garden, there are certain basic ingredients. Most white gardens have white petunias, white busy lizzies, white cosmos and white argyranthemums (as standards), to name but a few.

White petunias have a glistening crumpled elegance. The largest-flowered sort is *Petunia hybrida grandiflora*, of which there are two white strains. 'White Magic' has flowers 9cm (3½in) across, pure white: 'White Swan' has double-white flowers with frilly edges. Both grow to 25–30cm (10–12in). *P. h. multiflora* has slightly smaller flowers, but produces more of them. 'White Cloud' and 'Prio

At Chenies Manor argyranthemums and white dahlias are set out in season.

White' are also good whites. They are at their most effective when used in bold drifts rather than when merely dotted around here and there. Much the same goes for the busy lizzies, *Impatiens hybrida*, of which there are at least two good white strains, 'Futura White' and 'Super Elfin White', both making dense bushy plants with large flat white flowers with a green eye. The marriage of green and white is particularly pleasing in these, the green eye being the same green as the leaves. The white cosmos, *C. bipinnatus* 'Purity', by contrast, is a plant one can use on its own, dotted amongst other plants. It has deep green foliage as finely cut as fennal and

beautiful white flowers with yellow centres, like single dahlias. It grows to about 75cm (30in). It can look lovely used so that its simple single flowers contrast with more complex flowers such as the roses, 'Pascali' or 'Margaret Merrill', the yellow centre of the cosmos flower seeming to draw out the yellow tints in the rose flowers.

Dahlias are used to great advantage in the white garden at Chenies Manor near Amersham. There is a great variety of sizes, shapes and flower forms and it is important to choose those that fit in one's overall scheme. Among

(Opposite) Hosta plantaginea.

Jenny Jowett

the best are 'White Moonlight'; which is a cactus and grows to 1.5m (5ft) and 'Peace Pact', which is a water lily and grows to 1.2m (4ft). 'Nicola' is single and smaller.

Almost as frequently used are the fibrous begonias, lavatera and the various nicotianas. The fibrous begonias are *B. semperflorens*, and the best strain is 'Viva', which grows to 20cm (8in) and has green leaves and rather translucent white flowers. It can be used for edging and massing and is one of the few annuals that is as happy in shade as in sun. Tuberous begonias might also be used, but as specimens in pots or urns, never massed. The lavatera 'Mont Blanc' is one of the showiest white annuals, growing to 60cm (2ft) and hides its lobed leaves beneath an abundance of pure white mallow-like flowers. If they have a fault it is that the flowers are too white and therefore uninteresting. The nicotianas have flowers whose shape is intrinsically more interesting, long-tubed with a flaring mouth. Several sorts are useful in white gardens, and for different reasons. *N. affinis* is the tobacco plant, with intensely fragrant, pure white flowers, which open in the evening. It grows to 90cm (35in) and like many nicotianas the coarse leaves are covered with clammy hairs. 'Dwarf White Bedder' is a recent introduction, and generally a great improvement, being not only half the height but bushy and compact, and, moreover, opening its flowers all day instead of only in the evening. *N. sylvestris* is a woodlander from Argentina where it is a short-lived perennial but in this country it is best treated as an annual and grown in the sun. It grows 110–120cm (43–47in) tall and produces big clusters of fragrant pendulous, long-tubed white flowers. Because the leaves of these nicotianas are unattractive they are best grown behind a bush of lavender or a low rosemary, or planted where *Lavatera* 'Mont Blanc' can be grown in front of them. *N.* 'Lime Green' is a bedding nicotiana with

gaudy-green flowers much the same size and shape as those of 'Dwarf White Bedder'. *N. alata* is similar. Far more interesting, but probably best as a foil to 'Lime Green', is *N. langsdorfii*, which produces diffuse heads of small, pendent lime-green flowers. Like *N. sylvestris*, it is a short-lived perennial though it will usually perpetuate itself by self-sown seedlings.

There is a third tier of white-flowered annuals which may be used to add a little extra interest and individuality. The white sweet pea, *Laythrus odoratus*, is most useful for running up and over early-flowering shrubs such as deutzias and philadelphus or over the panicles of *Crambe cordifolia*. They are used quite differently at Barrington Court where they are trained up tripods of canes. 'Royal Wedding' has long stems and large pure white flowers with a first-rate perfume; 'Snowdonia Park' is smaller flowered and less scented; 'White Leamington' has frilly white flowers. 'Jilly' is virtually odourless (which is no recommendation). They do best in a slightly alkaline soil; daily deadheading keeps them flowering for longer. *Cobaea scandens*, the cup-and-saucer vine, is a tender tendril climber from Mexico. Its form 'Alba' produces sumptuous greeny-white bells, each 7.5cm (3in) across and each set in its own inverted saucer, of great substance and produced throughout the second half of the summer. It is not a plant to grow around your bedroom window, or next to the tea-room; its flowers are scented but the scent is of carrion. There are also white ipomoeas, those tropical bindweeds most often grown for their vivid blue flowers. If seed is sown in late winter the plants will begin flowering almost as soon as set out and will go on until winter.

Nigella damascena, an annual cornflower popularly known as 'love-in-a-mist' was one of Miss Jekyll's favourite annuals and it is fitting that the white form should bear her name. 'Miss Jekyll Alba' grows 45cm (18in) tall and has thin, filigree green leaves and double flowers which are pure white, with green shadows. The flowers are followed by big inflated seedheads, also green. It is useful because it can contribute a light, airy quality to counterbalance the heaviness and solidity of some other white flowers. *Clarkia elegans* always seem to be in much the same category of wispiness, though the modern 'Albatross' has double white flowers packed in a short but dense spike. It grows to 60cm (2ft) and is useful as an inconsequential white-flowered filler. More impressive is the white opium poppy, *Papaver somniferum* 'White Cloud', which has enormous very double pure white poppy flowers borne on slender stems above grey-green leaves. The flowers, in spite of their doubleness, are followed by the typical 'pepper-pot' seed heads. It is a lovely plant to allow to seed itself among white roses and lesser green-leafed plants so that while one has a concentrated group of it somewhere, scattered seedlings appear here and there creating an air of relaxed enchantment.

The bedding lobelia is *L. erinus* and it is useful, both in its ordinary and in its trailing form, as a filler of small gaps in one's planting. 'Snowball' is a tiny, bushy variety with good white flowers, and 'White Cascade' is a good white trailing sort.

Omphalodes linifolia is so unlike the perennial navelworts that one might not connect the two at first sight, though they are merely different species in the same genus. *O. linifolia* has willowy grey leaves and produces from June till August showers of gypsophila-like flowers. It grows to about 30cm (12in), and needs to be replaced once it is over. The modern antirrhinums, developments of the Mediterranean *A. majus*, are large flowered and faintly scented. Flowering from June till the frosts, they might be suitable plants to replace the omphalodes. One might even inter-crop them, having the snap-dragons coming up among the omphalodes and tak-

ing over once they have finished flowering. 'White Wonder' has good white flowers and grows to 45cm (18in). 'White Spire' has flowers of an equally attractive white but grows to 90cm (35in), which is too tall for many gardens. 'Taff's Pride' is a variegated white-flowered antirrhinum with leaves half the normal size and edged creamy-white. It is tender and has to be perpetuated by cuttings.

Wallflowers are often lumped together in the mind with antirrhinums, perhaps because both are old stalwarts of cottage gardens. 'Ivory White' and 'White Dame' are both creamy–white, but 'Ivory White' is the whiter of the two. It is used at Sissinghurst in the box-edged beds with *Helichrysum petiolatum* and the white form of *Thunbergia alata* (black-eyed Susan). Both these wallflowers grow to about 40cm (16in) and flower in spring. They prefer an alkaline soil.

Three other first-rate plants for white gardens are also biennials and also cottagey. The white foxglove is *Digitalis purpurea* 'Alba', and it is one of the coolest, serenest and most dignified of plants for shade or semi-shade. It is lovely used sparingly at Tintinhull beneath dark yews, but it can look just as good at the back of a rose border or in a shaded courtyard. It grows 110–180cm (43–71ins). Occasional seedlings will produce purple flowers. The verbascums like the foxgloves, throw a tall flowering spike from a rosette of coarse basal leaves, but in the mullein the leaves are grey, like felt, and the flower spike branches into lesser spikes. In *V.* x *hybridum* 'Mont Blanc' the flowers are white. It grows 100 to 120cm (40–47in). Honesty is *Lunaria annua* which, like the foxglove is typically green in leaf and purple in flower; there is also a form with white flowers and green leaves, 'Alba', one with white vari-

(Overleaf, left) Crinum x powellii *'Album'*;
(right) Colchicum speciosum *'Album'*.

Jenny Jowett

Jenny Jowett

gated leaves and purple flowers, called 'Variegata' and one with white variegated leaves and white flowers called 'Alba-Variegata'. This last is lovely in a white garden, and like the other biennials looks best when it is allowed to grow where it seeds itself, with only a little judicious weeding out. It sometimes produces seedlings with green leaves or purple flowers, which need to be rogued. It looks well in the white garden at York Gate, and is particularly effective fluttering its pearly iridescent seed heads in sunlight against the backdrop of beech and copper beech hedges.

Two unexpectedly desirable annuals for the white garden are white verbena and a gaudy-green zinnia. The verbena is *V.* x *hybrida* 'Marbella'. It is compact, low-growing and produces its pure white, ragged robin flowers endlessly all summer; it needs a good hot, sunny position, but likes a little extra peat in the soil. It survives occasional winters out of doors, but cannot be relied upon. Zinnias are all too often used like guardsmen on parade and obviously lend themselves to such treatment, but the aptly-named 'Envy' is so unexpected that one can dot it about the garden among smaller white annuals. There are also two good white zinnias, 'Carved Ivory' and 'Big Snowman'.

The osteospermums, which used to be dimorphothecas, are indispensable white garden plants especially in formal white gardens, town gardens and courtyards, and lovely in pots and tubs. All have daisy flowers, gleaming white inside, but have variously coloured backs to the petals. *O.* 'Blue Streak' is blue-backed, and grows only 23cm (9in); *O. ecklonis* 'Prostrata' grows to only 15cm (6in) and has a blue instead of yellow disc at the centre of the flower; *O.e.* 'Weetwood' has a grey reverse to its flowers, and 'Tauranga' ('Whirligig') has curious waisted flowers, with a blue reverse. All need sun and sharp drainage and are easy to grow

from cuttings rooted and overwintered under glass.

Just as indispensable, especially in courtyards and town gardens, are the various pelargoniums. The zonal pelargonium is the sort most usually used, with rounded, slightly scalloped leaves and a characteristic radial band on the leaf (usually absent in the white varieties). 'White Orbit', a good, compact single white is an exception, having some banding. 'Avalon' is dwarf, at scarcely 15cm (6in), and 'White Century' is a first-rate single. 'Hermione' and 'Snow Queen' are both doubles, but the latter is rather pink in the centre. Most grow to about 25cm (10in). The regal pelargoniums are *P.* x *domesticum*, and they have much larger flowers as much as 5cm (2in) across and leaves that are more palmate than round. 'White Glory' is pure white, 'Nomad' white with crimson spots. *P. peltatum* is the ivy-leafed pelargonium, the species often used in hanging baskets but also useful as a trailer. It has rubbery leaves, brittle stems and a longer flowering season than the others, starting earlier and going on till the frosts. 'Snowdrift' has white flowers and green leaves, 'L'Elegante' white-edged leaves that flush lilac late in the season and flowers of a lilac tint so pale they appear white. There are also several sorts of variegated pelargoniums that may be useful, but most have mauve flowers.

Marguerites or Paris daisies have changed their name from *Chrysanthemum frutescens* to *Argyranthemum frutescens* and are back in fashion. All have white daisy flowers with yellow centres, produced all summer long and most have an abundance of attractively cut blue-grey leaves. They can all be trained up into small standards by the simple expedient of tying the leader to a cane and removing the side shoots. As standards they are extremely useful in white gardens, giving height where it might otherwise be lacking. The leafy heads of the marguerites can also be clipped into rounded heads in winter, making the plants quite formal in appearance. 'Snowflake' and 'Powder Puff' are good double white varieties.

Fuchsias have a whole range of uses, from bedding to pots and tubs and hanging baskets or as standards. The hardy sorts are very limited as to whites but there are several good tender sorts. 'Ting-a-ling' seems to be the best known; it is very free-flowering producing classically-shaped fuchsia flowers of pure white with protruding pink-tipped stamens. 'White Fairy' is double white, but the flowers are very heavy; 'F.M. Abbot' has a compact habit and slender single white flowers; 'Constellation' is double and cream rather than white, and 'Annabelle' is a blowsy over-double with pink stamens. 'This England' is a discomforting combination of golden foliage and white flowers with pink stamens.

The daturas have huge pendent white trumpets 15cm (6in) long which echo the shape of the fuchsia flowers, so that both together in the same garden re-inforce the idea of a single flower form, flaring, trumpet-shaped and pendent. The typical datura is *D. cornigera*, which grows to 2.5cm (8ft) with love and care. It is semi-evergreen. 'Knightii' is a lovely double form. *D. suaveolens* is similar but more compact. They are seen to best advantage when grown in Versailles tubs and stood out in niches in the planting scheme, but they are really only for the most sheltered white gardens. They have coarse leaves like those of the nicotianas (to which they are closely related) and are prone to red spider mite and white fly, against which precautions should be taken.

The oleanders are Mediterranean shrubs with a predilection for sunny climes, and they seldom flower in temperate climates as freely as they do in their own. They do best in sun-baked town gardens and courtyards, and fit in well with such gardens, especially as they are usually grown in decorative tubs or pots.

'Soeur Agnes' is a single, pure white; 'Alba' is semi-double and 'Alba Plena', fully double with large flowers. All these varieties are scented. They can be used as bushes or trained up as standards.

Finally there are some indispensable grey-leafed plants for bedding. The best of these is *Helichrysum petiolatum*, which is grey-woolly all over, with wiry stems and round grey leaves. It is a charming plant that weaves its way in and out of other plants. *H. microphyllum* is in effect a small-leafed version of the same thing. Sometimes it is useful to use both together so that the relationship of leaf-shape and plant style can be appreciated. There is also a most useful yellow-leafed form of *H. petiolatum*, its great merit being that the leaves are of a pleasantly subdued yellow. A further variant has leaves with a yellow splash at the centre – rather like *Brachyglottis* x. 'Aunt May'. In the same line of tender greys are two centaureas with leaves that are silvery-white. *Centaurea gymnocarpa* makes fountain-like mounds of bi-pinnate and very fine cut leaves that are so silvery people seem to need to touch them to see what they are made of. It grows about 30cm (12in) tall. *C. candidissima* (*C. rutifolia*) is smaller, with less finely divided leaves: it looks rather like a silver-leafed dandelion. Leaves so intensely silver-white need to be set among solid greens to show to best advantage.

There are two biennial thistles which are indispensable in white gardens. *Silybum marianum*, the milk thistle, is the larger of the two. It has large, dark green glossy leaves, lobed and spined, with the veins marked in white, which gives it a marbled effect. It has purple thistle heads borne on branching stems, in late summer and these will reach 120cm (47in) or more. *Galactites tomentosum* has similarly decorated leaves, though they are narrow in proportion to their length and more intensely white. It grows to 45cm

73

Beautifully blended container planting in the white garden at the Manor House, Birlingham.

(18in). Both seed themselves around. *Euphorbia marginata* is also grown in white gardens for its foliage not its flowers, though its foliage could scarcely be more different from that of the thistles. *E. marginata*'s white-margined leaves are limp, flaccid, borne in four ranks up the stem. The green in them is the colour of a fresh lettuce. The flowers are insignificant, yellowish but are surrounded by leaf-like bracts which are variegated in just the same way as the leaves. It is a long-season annual and needs to be sown as early as possible out of doors if it is to reach full size and flower. In soils that suit *Euphorbia marginata*, self-sown seedlings will appear.

BULBS

Bulbs have an economy of performance that is an absolute boon in the white garden. They spring up, flower and disappear often in a few short weeks, and that is invaluable in an area as concentrated as the white garden.

Among the first flowers of the year are the crocuses. They are natives of the Mediterranean, where they enjoy long hot summers and they should always be planted in full sun. Most will naturalize when suited. The earliest of the whites, appearing in early January, is 'Snow Bunting', a selected form of *Crocus chrysanthus*: the flower is pure white inside, the outer petals being creamy and feathered with dark lilac. 'Warley White' is another selection, with large, creamy-white petals but heavily suffused with bluish-purple. Next in season, flowering in early February, is *C. sieberi* 'Bowles's White', which has a pure white flower with a yellow base. Mr Bowles, who was the expert on crocuses in his day, considered this his best white, spring-flowering crocus. Of the large-flowered garden varieties, which bloom in late February and March, 'Kathleen Parlow' has lovely large, goblet-shaped flowers of pure white with prominent orange stigmata, 'Snowstorm' has very large flowers, also of pure white, while 'Joan of Arc' has enormous flowers, white but tinged with violet towards the outside, and with orange stigmata.

If crocuses are among the first flowers of the year, they are also among the last. *C. vallicola* flowers in September, its creamy-white flowers veined with pale lilac, with two gold spots at the base of each petal. It comes from high alpine moorland in the Pontic mountains in Turkey, and so needs less of a summer baking than other species. *C. ochroleucus* flowers in October and though pure white forms exist it is usually creamy-white with yellow blotches at the centre of the flower. Mr Bowles considered *C. niveus* the most beautiful white autumn crocus, though flowering in November the flowers are apt to suffer if the weather is inclement. The most reliable of the autumn crocuses is *C. speciosus*, which flowers in September and October, the flowers are goblet-shaped, and as much as 10cm (4in) tall. Though no selected white form has been named, white forms are common and are offered from time to time by bulb merchants. They increase readily.

It is unthinkable to have a white garden without snowdrops. Unlike the crocuses, which are sun-lovers, snowdrops are plants of damp woodlands and happy in shade, under shrubs or trees, and lovely among wintergreen ferns with *Arum italicum* 'Pictum'. The earliest snowdrops to flower are *Galanthus nivalis* and its forms in January and February. The wild single form has a remarkable elegance, but the common double form, 'Flore-pleno', is far showier and perhaps surprisingly, seems to multiply as fast. 'Atkinsii' is a tall, vigorous form, which flowers in mid-January, but it is sterile and can only be increased by division. In spite of this, it is one of the finest, showiest snowdrops. Usually one of the floral segments is misshapen. 'Sam Arnott', 'Arnott's Seedling' or 'Arnottii' (they are all the same), is also tall and vigorous, but has perfectly formed flowers, and does set seed. It is regarded by many people as the best of all snowdrops. All those mentioned so far have grey-green leaves. *G. elwesii* has broad leaves of an extra good grey and large flowers – especially large in the var. *whittallii* and in 'Merlin'. In *G. latifolius* the leaves are bright, shining green; *G. ikariae* is similar but with larger flowers.

In February the chionodoxa start their season. They are one of the best of all spring bulbs, easy to grow, rapid of increase and unfailing in flower. The commonest, and (as is often the way) best species is *C. luciliae*, of which there is a lovely white form, sold simply as *C.l.* 'Alba'. It produces a flowering stem 15cm (6in) tall, and each stem carries as many as ten starry flowers of the purest white. Once established it will seed itself around happily. Easy in most soils, in sun or shade.

Equally easy are the grape hyacinths, one of which might be included in the white garden – *Muscari botryoides* 'Alba'. It grows less than 15cm (6in) and bears dense spikes of milky white flowers. It is happy in most soils, in sun, and does not increase excessively fast. It is stiff and unfriendly, but some like it. Its season overlaps the chionodoxa.

In flower at the same time, though flowering for much longer, is the spring star flower, *Ipheion uniflorum*, which produces from rapidly-multiplying bulbs tufts of mid-green strap-shaped leaves, like those of a minuscule agapanthus, from the midst of which arises a 15cm (6in) flower stem bearing a single starry flower 3–4cm (1–1½in) across. The whole plant smells of onions. A form with glistening, pure white flowers is called *I.u.* 'Albus', an excellent plant for a white garden. It needs sun and reasonable drainage and will spread into good clumps that produce a succession of flowers for weeks on end.

By mid March other things are coming on course, bergenia, camellias, chaenomeles and *Magnolia stellata*, to name but a few, as well as the Lenten lilies (of which there are some lovely white forms) and polyanthus. Among the finest of the bulbs at this season are the dog's tooth violets – Erythronium – dog's tooth because the tubers are shaped like a dog's tooth, and violet because of the way the flowers are reflexed. Two American species native of acid woodland, *E. californicum* and *E. oregonum,* both have creamy-white flowers, but 'White Beauty', an oregonum hybrid is finer than either, with white flowers, each 7.5cm (3in) across produced at the tips of long, dropping peduncles at the tops of stems which can be as much as 60cm (2ft) tall. It is easy to establish and multiplies freely. It looks lovely grown in drifts among white-edged hostas whose leaves will just be emerging, and finely divided ferns, occupying the same ground as the snowdrops.

Flowering at the same season and enjoying similar conditions – though not necessarily on that account the best of companions since one is a native of acid soils the other of chalklands, are the wind flowers, one species of which, *Anemone nemorosa*, is a British wildling, often seen carpeting the woodland floor in March with its many petalled white flowers. There are finer, selected forms. 'Vestal' is pure white, both inside and out, while 'Leeds Variety' has larger petals that overlap, though it is not of such a pure white. 'Flore-pleno' is a double form, whose flowers

last longer. *A. blanda* which comes from the mountains of Greece, is similar but has larger flowers, 'White Beauty' being most apposite for our purpose. The poppy-flowered anemones are quite different, growing from 15 to 45cm (6–18in) tall and bearing large, showy flowers in a wide range of colours. Famous named strains are the St Brigid, mostly semi-doubles, and the du Caen or French Giant, which are mostly singles. 'The Bride' is a fine single white, but whites of any of these strains, single or double, will be an adornment in a white garden.

There are certain plants that are so strongly associated in our minds with a particular colour that it is almost unthinkable that they should come in any other colour. Scillas, one would have thought, are indelibly blue. But there is a pure white form of *Scilla sibirica* 'Alba' which is lovely in the white garden, thriving in sun or shade. Less familiar is the summer squill, *Scilla peruviana*, a far larger plant which produces in May and June broad, conical heads of squill flowers, as many as a hundred in each head, on a stem 22.5cm (9in) tall. The white form is very showy.

Puschkina is closely related to both scilla and chionodoxa, but most resembles the first. It is typically of the palest imaginable blue, but there is a pure white form as well. It flowers in March, and should be treated much as a scilla.

By April other plants have started to take over the main burden of flowering: *Magnolia* x *soulangiana* is in full bloom, chaenomeles, *Prunus* 'Tai-Haku', and *Cytisus praecox* are all at their peak and bulbs take on a lesser role. A few lowly species tulips flower at this season. They have more refined flowers than the blowsy bedding tulips that follow in May. *Tulipa turkestanica* is one of the best for the white garden with grey leaves and an upright stem 30cm (12in) tall bearing up to nine flowers, each white with a yellow centre, opening from greenish buds. The flowers start goblet-shaped, but open wide to become starry. *T. biflora* and *T. polychroma* are both closely related to it and very similar but lower growing so that their flowers seem to hover just above the ground. *Tulipa tarda* has even more star-shaped flowers, and is of similar colouring. So long as these tulips are planted in a sunny, well-drained site they can be left in the ground from year to year, flowering and increasing well. Not so the large-flowered hybrids which need to be lifted, dried and stored each summer. The classic white bedding tulip is 'White Triumphator', a lily-flowered sort growing to 50cm (20in) and producing long, elegant pure white flowers with reflexing petals. Almost as classic and every bit as useful in the white garden is 'White Parrot', a pure white parrot tulip with large petals fringed at the tips. The viridiflora tulips can look cool and exciting in the white garden, the green streaks on the petals making the white seem whiter. One of the best is 'Angel', which has flowers of white and apple-green. 'Spring Green' is similar, but the tips of the petals are yellowish.

Arum italicum 'Pictum' is usually rated as a spring bulb, because it flowers in early summer, though it is not for its flowers that it is grown but for the leaves. The flowers are just like those of our native lords and ladies or cuckoo-pint, as are the seeds, which are bright orange-red. The leaves are also the same shape as those of lords and ladies, but of a firmer texture and decorated with a distinctive white marbling. The leaves are produced in the autumn and in sheltered places will last right through until early summer. They enjoy a damp, shaded position and relish all the feeding you can give them. When happy they will produce leaves 30cm (12in) long, and form large patches. There is a rare dwarf form, 'Tiny', which grows to 6cm (2½in) tall.

By June the alliums or flowering onions come into their own. *Allium* is a huge genus – 500 species or more – but only a few are useful in the white garden. White chives, *Allium schoenoprasum* 'Album', can be used to make an edging. *A. neaoplitanum* has similar but much larger flowers in much larger heads, from March till May and is more tender than most. *A. tuberosum* is known as Chinese chives and produces its rounded heads of green-eyed white flowers on foot high stems through August and September. *A. beesianum* is usually grown for its intense cobalt blue flowers, carried on 20cm (8in) stems in late summer but there is a white form of great beauty. *A. nigrum* is a tall species, growing up to 1m (3ft) and with usually only two very broad basal leaves. It produces heads as much as 10cm (4in) across of flowers each 1.5–2cm (½ – ¾in) across, in some forms a good white. *A. triquetrum* deserves a mention, if only as a warning, for it has beautiful white flowers, but seeds itself so freely that it is more of a menace than a blessing.

The hardy cyclamen are delightful, often grown as much for their foliage as for their flowers, and ideal for growing beneath shrubs in the white garden, where they will often naturalise and make useful ground cover. *C. neapolitanum* begins to flower in August. It is in leaf for about nine months of the year, and flowers for about six weeks. The flowers are carried singly on slender stems, only 6 or 10cm (2½ or 4in) above the ground, each flower about 1.5cm (½in) long, with reflexed petals with a slight twist to them, like miniature rabbit's ears. Established corms may be the size of dinner plates and produce as many as 50 flowers each. The white form has flowers of startling whiteness. The leaves, which follow the flowers, can vary in shape from almost round to an elongated shield-shape, their edges smooth, toothed or scalloped, and almost infinitely varied in their markings from almost plain green to the most generous marbling and grey and white. *C. europaeum* is similar, but with almost invariably round leaves, with minimal marbling; the flowers are fragrant and there is a beautiful white form. *C. coum* is the winter-flowering cyclamen, producing its dumpy flowers from December till March; the leaves are round or at least roundish, always deep crimson underneath, and appear as early as August, lasting through till April. The white form is lovely in front of Christmas or Lenten roses. *C. repandum* flowers in spring from March till May and is known as the ivy-leafed cyclamen from a fancied resemblance of the leaves to those of the ivy. Its flowers are up to 2.5cm (1 in) long and the petals beautifully twisted. There is a fine white form. I have never managed to get it to establish satisfactorily, but know that others have. All the cyclamen prefer a well-drained soil in semi-shade, and all are happier on alkaline soils than on acid sands. A handful of bone-meal when they are dormant seems to be appreciated.

The gladioli have a flowering season that extends from early April through till the end of August, and range in size from 45cm (18in) to 1.4m (5ft). The best of the small ones are the progeny mainly of crosses between *tristis* and *cardinalis* on the one hand (the Colvillei hybrids) and more recently *nanus* and *tubergenii*. These flower from April through till early June. The best for white gardens is 'The Bride' – one of the original varieties – with pure white flowers. 'Nymph' is white with crimson flakes, and 'Blushing Bride' has carmine flaking. The miniature and small-flowered hybrids flower later – June till August. There is no pure white, but 'Antoinette' is just as useful in a white garden, with greenish-cream flowers, the colouring deeper in the throat and with a crimson blotch. Equally exciting are the chartreuse hybrids which afford an excellent contrast to the whites. 'Green Bird' is greenish, sulphur-yellow, with slightly crinkled edges, and 'Green Woodpecker' is even sharper gaudy-green with a crimson blotch. In general these sharp limey colours are best used with the white-flowered gladioli and with green foliage: they look bilious when used among grey and silver foliage. Of the large-flowered hybrids, 'White Friendship' is white, with flowers 13cm (5in) across; 'Snow Princess' is milk-white with a green throat and equally large flowers, while 'Antarctic' is a tall white with a pale cream throat and a touch of purple at the base.

It is difficult to imagine a flower more different in form from a gladiolus than an arum lily, and yet both hail from South Africa. The white arums are tuberous plants which produce large, arrow-shaped leaves (like those of our native lords and ladies but much larger) and tall stems at the top of which are insignificant, minute, petalless flowers surrounded by a single, large, very showy bract. Botanically these arums are *Zantedeschia* (an awkward mouthful) *aethiopica*. This species grows to about 120cm (47in) and produces a pure white spathe about 30cm (12in) long, with a gold spadix at the centre. It is quite hardy in warm gardens, but the form 'Crowborough' is very much hardier and quite reliable once established. A little straw over the crowns for the first few winters will help. It looks lovely grown beside big drifts of *Sisyrinchium striatum*, whose erect stems and whorls of lemon-yellow flowers afford a perfect contrast. 'Little Gem' is a dwarf, the flowering stem no more than 60cm (2ft) tall, and there is an even smaller one, growing to only 30cm (12in), which I found in an abandoned greenhouse in Farnham Royal many years ago and which we call 'Apple Court'. Both these dwarfs seem perfectly hardy in warm gardens. There is also a legendary giant which we have never managed to track down: 'White Sails' which grows to 1.75m (5½ft) and has huge white flowers. Perhaps it would be tender. All of these can be grown in shallow water. If covered by 10cm (4in) of water they should survive winters of normal severity.

White tulips at Hidcote.

William Robinson, the irascible master of Gravetye Manor, arch-enemy of regimented Victorian bedding and author of *The English Flower Garden*, described anthericums as 'among the most beautiful of hardy flowers'. The species usually grown is the St Bernard lily, *A. liliago* which produces, from amidst tufts of green and grassy leaves, erect wiry stems bearing, in June or early July, several snow-white, lily-like flowers, 3.5cm (1¼ in) wide. When happy it will seed itself about. *A. algeriense* is almost as good, though its flowers open flat and are therefore less charming. The St Bruno lily is in the same idiom though relegated to the genus *Paradisea*. *P. liliastrum* is larger flowered, each flower 5cm

(2in) across, funnel-shaped and of translucent whiteness, but in spite of this it is a less showy garden plant than the St Bernard lily. Reginald Farrer described it as an 'understudy for the Madonna lily'.

Camassias have something in common with the St Bernard and St Bruno lilies, but are used far too seldom in gardens, for they are generally easy to grow and splendidly showy in flower. The finest species is *C. leitchlinii* which throws up from among clumps of lax bent leaves, glaucous beneath, tall slender spires 1–1.2m (3–4ft) of narrow-petalled, star-shaped flowers. In the wild it varies in colour from dark violet through blues to whites; there is also a useful cream-coloured

79

double. *C. quamash* is the common camass of western North America – and it too varies through a similar range of colours and also produces good whites.

The fox-tail lilies, eremurus, are not only the tallest but probably also the most magnificent of bulbous plants. What arrives from the bulb merchant looks rather like a desiccated starfish, as much as 30cm (12in) across. It is necessary to take out quite a large hole to plant this, for its fingers must be laid out horizontally and the whole thing encased in sand. In the spring a shoot will arise from the centre of this starfish: it looks just like a bullet coming out of the ground and is much loved by slugs. This turns into a lax clump of strap-shaped, bent leaves. From the centre of this arises the flowering stem, stiff and straight, surrounded on all sides with starry flowers. The finest for white gardens is the white form of *E. elwesii* which can grow as much as 1.8m (6ft) tall, the whole of the upper half of the flower spike packed with white flowers of glistening beauty. *E. himalaicus* flowers a little earlier, and is also pure white, but only half the size of the former. After some years the roots tend to work themselves up and out of the ground, when this happens they should be lifted, the crowns teased apart and replanted. The fox-tail lilies enjoy the same conditions as the tall bearded irises; to fill the gap they leave when their leaves die away it is a good idea to grow *Gypsophila paniculata* alongside.

Far less spectacular, but quietly magnificent and indispensable in the white garden is the so-called summer hyacinth, *Galtonia candicans*, which produces, from the midst of low tufts of somewhat glaucous leaves, tall stately spires of big white drooping fragrant bells. It is a plant of particular value for planting amongst things which flower earlier; paeonies, for example, or tall bearded irises. It is also useful among agapanthus which flower at the same time.

The flowers of the bulbous irises are similar to but more refined than those of the bearded irises and the English, Dutch and Spanish irises are all potentially useful in the white garden. All three are very like each other, and all have been derived from *I. xiphium*, *I. xiphioides* and *I. tingitana*. The Dutch irises grow to 45cm (18in) with rather rush-like leaves, and flower in June and into July after the bearded irises and about a fortnight earlier than the Spanish irises. 'White Pearl' is a good white, while 'Jeanne d'Arc' and 'Princess Irene' are rather creamy-white, which may be better in some white gardens. There are several good whites among the Spanish irises and not much to choose between them: 'Queen Wilhelmina' is the earliest to flower, and 'L'Innocence' the last. Of the English irises, which flower after the Dutch irises, 'Mont Blanc' is the best white, though new named sorts are being added all the time. All these irises can be left in the ground from year to year, and will increase steadily.

The last bulb of the season is *Zephyranthes candida* which is usually mistaken for a crocus. It produces tufts, of dark green, rush-like leaves, up to 30cm (12in) long, and a succession of pure white, crocus-like flowers, each about 5cm (2in) long, flowering all through September and October. It is surprisingly hardy in a sunny place in warmer gardens, where it increases rapidly and flowers freely.

PERENNIALS

In a white garden it is the perennial flowers that provide most of the whiteness but there is such an abundance of them that we can only mention a few that are particularly useful. The first white perennial of the year is the Christmas rose, *Helleborus niger*, a plant of venerable antiquity known to the Greeks and cultivated by the Romans, not for the white flowers produced in the darkest days of winter, but rather for the black roots for which it is named and which the apothecaries ground up to sell as snuff, long before tobacco was discovered. The typical plant has dark, leathery leaves and sumptuous nodding white flowers, pink-tinged on the outside, held well above the leaves. 'Potter's Wheel' is a famous clone, with extra large flowers, as is the now rare 'Ladham's Variety'. It grows best in shade, in a clayey soil that never dries out, though it appreciates a handful of lime rubble beneath it at planting time, and a good mulch of manure every autumn.

The Lenten roses, perhaps surprisingly, have a flowering season that overlaps that of the Christmas rose. They are similar in flower but more refined, with more beautifully sculptured petals, sometimes delicately freckled or marked inside, the flowers held above the foliage on stems 45cm (18in) tall. The persistent, evergreen leaves are beautiful in their own right, made up of several finger-like segments radiating from a central point at the top of the leaf-stalk. The flowers can vary in colour from palest creamy-white, plain or speckled, through pinks to dark plum-black. There are also some so-called yellows – though they are really of that shade of greeny-creamy-yellow that is such an ideal foil to white in the white garden. Various named white forms exist including 'Prince Rupert' and 'Bowles White'. Hellebores are lovely with snowdrops and ferns such as *Polystichum setiferum*, beneath deciduous shrubs, *Abeliophyllum distichum*, for example, or *Lonicera* x *purpusii*, which flowers at the same time, and they make a good ground cover. They are used extensively at Dartington Hall near Totnes in Devon in this way.

Omphalodes verna, blue-eyed Mary, flowers at the same time and enjoys the same conditions. It produces good green, heart-shaped leaves on long stalks and spreads into large clumps. 'Alba' is a lovely white form, ideal under deciduous shrubs in the white garden.

By March the bergenias are coming into flower. They are in the first rank of white garden plants, their bold, rounded, glossy, leathery leaves making not only a good, dense ground cover but also an excellent foil to plants with strap-shaped leaves, crinums for instance. *B. stracheyi* is the smallest species, with leaves no more than 10cm (4in) long: *B.s.* 'Alba' is a good white form for the very front of the border. *B. ligulata* has tongue-shaped rather than round leaves, edged with hairs and produces clusters of white flowers with contrasting red calyces. 'Silberlicht' is the classic white, with round leaves that stay green all winter. 'Bressingham White' has good white flowers, but odd, rather long, narrow leaves. 'Apple Court White' is a branch sport from *B. cordata* and also has good white flowers and leaves that remain green all winter.

The almost shrubby *H. corsicus* (still often called *argutifolius* or *lividus*) is a much larger plant than other hellebores, growing 60cm (2ft) tall and a full 1m (3ft) across, with three-fingered leaves of a beautifully marked metallic greyish-green and large bunches of little cup-shaped flowers of palest acid green. The whole plant is a symphony of greens. It is lovely with drifts of the white-flowered *Pulmonaria* 'Sissinghurst White', with dark shrubs behind it, *Viburnum tinus* in one of its whiter forms, 'French White' perhaps, or the much smaller Christmas box, *Sarcococca confusa*. It is also attractive with lilies planted in the shade of its leaves, providing a second season of flower from the same piece of ground.

The pulmonarias are really thugs, for while their leaves may be perfectly in proportion to the flowers at flowering time, they continue to grow once the flowers are over, doubling or even trebling in size. Because of this they

need to be grown beside other robust plants, bergenias for example. *P. rubra* is always the first to flower, often as early as January, producing, above its velvety, light-green leaves, bunches of dangling little bells which are clear white in the form 'Albocorollata'. *P. angustifolia* has narrower, more bristly leaves, and white flowers in the form 'Alba'. *P. officinalis* was the apothecaries lungwort, its white-blotched leaves suggesting, to those who adhered to the Doctrine of Signatures, an affinity with lungs and leading to its use for curing pulmonary complaints. There is a lovely white form known, appropriately as 'Sissinghurst White', which is still grown in the white garden at Sissinghurst. 'White Wings' is another white but with brown anthers.

The first of the primulas to flower in the white garden will usually be *P. denticulata*, the drumstick primula. It has typical primrose foliage from the centre of which it thrusts up its round heads of flowers, white in the form 'Alba'. It looks best in clumps of several to many, and is at its happiest on moist alkaline soils. If it seems inclined to fade away on acid soils the cure is to mulch it with bonfire ash. *P. sieboldii* 'Alba' is much more beautiful. Its leaves begin to show in February, at first a bright, yellowish-green quickly turning plain, pale green, serrated and looking almost fern-like. The flowers, which come in April, on 20cm (8in) stems, individually resemble phloxes and are pure, almost glowing white. It naturally forms drifts and clumps, but is not always easy to establish. It likes dappled shade and a peaty or leafy soil, and is often happy in town gardens. The true primroses, *Primula vulgaris*, start to flower a little later, usually in March. They enjoy a position which is in full sun when they flower but in shade for the rest of the year – a south-facing bank

(Opposite) Delphiniums, roses, onopordum and Salix helvetica *in the Fountain Garden at Tintinhull.*

under deciduous shrubs, for example. In the white garden one may have to lift the primroses after flowering and move them to a suitable place, though they always look best when allowed to naturalise. There are white forms of the primrose itself, but also white doubles, hose-in-hose and Jack-in-the-Green. The outer flower is really the calyx. In some forms the calyces are striped, red, green or yellow, and are known as Pantaloon Primroses. Jack-in-the-Greens have the flower surrounded by leaf-like bracts – and this greenery can be particularly attractive behind a white flower. 'Dawn Ansell' is a robust double white, with a hint of Jack-in-the-Green. 'Kiss of Snow' is a mistranslation of 'Schneekissen', which really should be 'Snow Cushion'. It forms a small, neat plant which clumps up well and has pure white flowers that are perfectly round. 'Kiss of Snow Improved' is supposed to be even better. The white polyanthus need the same treatment as primroses.

Dicentras are, perhaps surprisingly, members of the poppy family. They have brittle, fleshy roots and finely-cut fern-like foliage, with flowers that hang down from delicate arching stems. The finest for white gardens is *D. spectabilis alba*, a lovely cottagey, old-fashioned plant growing to about 60cm (2ft) and bearing in May and June white locket-shaped flowers all along the lower side of arching stems. It is happiest in a shaded or semi-shaded place, and lovely in front of dark yews, and with green ferns, such as *Dryopteris affinis cristata* 'The King'. The smaller-growing grey-leafed white-flowered *D. formosa* 'Langtrees' has leaf stalks the colour of rhubarb, a colour which also suffuses the leaves, detracting from their greyness.

The columbines, aquilegia, start to flower in May, overlapping the last of the daffodils. Most are of the easiest cultivation, seeding themselves freely. *A. vulgaris* is the common columbine, with short-spurred flowers produced in abundance. *A.v. nivea* is the

'Munstead White' columbine beloved of Miss Jekyll. It has the greyest leaves of any columbine, and exquisite jade-green stems and buds. The flowers are pure white. Miss Jekyll used to use it in combination with white foxgloves and the white form of the peach-leafed campanula. If grown on its own in the white garden the seedlings will come fairly true. *A. flabellata*, with rounded glaucous leaves and dumpy white, blue-tinged, flowers has a dwarf form, 'Nana Alba' with much whiter flowers. There are several hybrid strains which produce whites, but 'Schneekoningen' ('Snow Queen') is itself a white strain. Their cut leaves and delicate flowers make a lovely contrast with such bulky plants as paeonies, bearded irises and lupins; they are also lovely with *Polystichum setiferum* forms and lily of the valley.

Mugget (from the French Muguet) is more familiar as lily of the valley, an indispensable plant in the white garden, treasured as much for its white flowers as for its fragrance – known and revered by our rude forefathers who called it 'Aqua Aurea' and kept it in sealed gold or silver phials. *Convallaria majalis* is the wild form; 'Fortin's Giant' is larger in all its parts; *flore pleno* or 'Prolificans' is double, with much longer-lasting flowers, and there are two variegated forms, 'Variegata' which has white tips to the leaves, as though they have been dipped in white paint, and 'Lineata' which has longitudinal gold stripes. It needs more sun than the other sorts, to prevent it from reverting. Mugget is one of those plants that grows where it chooses rather than where you choose, so it is best to try it in several places, and encourage it in the one it likes best. Its leaves have an elusive glaucousness, and in the autumn the flower spikes produce surprisingly large orange berries (which are exceedingly poisonous).

The ideal companions for lily of the valley are the Solomon's seals, the mind's eye readily making the association between the arching flowering stems and pendent flowers of both, their similarities enhancing their differences. The Solomon's seal most usually grown is a *Polygonatum* x *hybridum*, which is also known as *P. multiflorum*, although *P. multiflorum* is in fact a quite distinct species in its own right. *Hybridum* is a typical Solomon's seal, producing tall stems straight out of the ground bearing its numerous oval leaves in opposing pairs (the leaves, as in most species, turn butter-yellow in autumn) above which, are borne on the arching top of the stem, pairs of pendent, greeny-white bells. It grows about 30cm (12in) tall. *P. commutatum* (*P. giganteum*) is much taller, up to 2m (7ft) but otherwise similar. The lesser Solomon's seal, *P. odoratum*, is the gem of the genus, a connoisseur's plant, perfect for the white garden, similar to *hybridum* but producing its flowers in ones or twos, rather than threes and fives and straight-sided, those of the other species being waisted. Its greatest virtue is its fragrance, delicate but delicious. There is a double form in cultivation. There are several other species, including some good dwarfs, and also some variegated forms, discussed below. They all enjoy cool, moist shade, and look lovely growing up through a carpet of lily of the valley and backed by the coarser leaves and the more solid spires of foxgloves, together with white-variegated hostas, *H. undulata*, or *crispula* or both, and ferns of great refinement such as *Polystichum aculeatum* 'Pulcherrimum'. Best kept away from dicentras, which are plants of a very different style.

The epimediums are renowned as ground covers, but only one or two have good enough flowers to be admitted into the white garden. *E.* x *youngianum* 'Niveum' is a small-growing species, only 10cm (4in) tall with unexpectedly large, pure white flowers. *E. grandiflorum* is a larger species, to 30cm (12in), variable in its flower colour – but a good white is 'White Queen'. *E. pubigerum* has the smallest flowers in the genus, but in some forms they are of a good white and produced in sprays well above the evergreen foliage. The first two species are deciduous and their flowers are seen best if the leaf remains are cleared away in the winter.

There are several sorts of iris that impress themselves on the mind first and foremost as good border plants. In the front rank of these are the sibiricas (*I. sibirica*), the finest of the beardless irises. They produce tufts of rich green grassy leaves 96cm (38in) tall and slender stems bearing really quite large flowers. 'Snow Queen' (*alba*) is an old variety with rather yellow-ish white flowers; both 'Wisley White' and 'White Swirl' are touched with yellow on the falls, as is 'Snow Princess'. 'Limeheart' is touched with green instead of yellow, which makes it seem whiter. Other tall-growing irises which will succeed in moisture-retentive borders are: *I. orientalis* (of Miller, which used to be *ochroleuca* and not the *orientalis* of Thunberg, which is *sanguinea*) which is lovely in bold groups, has stiff, sword-like foliage 1.2m (4ft) tall and beautifully shaped flowers of white, with yellow falls – 'Alba' is pure white; *I. ensata* (which used to be *I. kaempferi* and is the only iris to hate lime) is the most sumptuous of all, with huge flowers in many shades, including white – 'Alba' is white with a little yellow, but 'Moonlight Waves' is touched with green, as is 'White Swan'; *I. laevigata* which is similar to *I. ensata*, has an 'Alba' form with enormous flowers of pure white; 'Snowdrift' is similar – but *laevigata* needs the ground really too wet for a border.

Ideal companions for irises of all sorts are the day lilies, *Hemerocallis*. Their tufts of grassy leaves often fold, as though broken, in contrast to the stiff leaves of irises. White day lilies are something very new. They are really not white at all but the very palest of creams and so are only suitable for white gardens that lean towards yellow; they would look frightful in a white garden where greys and silvers were used, or whose harmonies are all in pinks. 'Joan Senior' is the best-known white which has a rather flat flower 10cm (4in) across of a good creamy-white with a chartreuse-yellow eye and golden stamens. The flowers are produced on well-branched stems with a lot of buds producing a good succession of flowers. It was given an Award of Merit by the RHS after trials at Wisley. 'Iron Gate Iceberg' is even whiter with a more trumpet-shaped flower of good substance with slightly frilled edges. The flower is 18cm (7in) across, has a cream base, a yellow eye and orange stamens. 'Loving Memories' is cream-coloured but interesting because it has a tendency to doubleness. It is not as vigorous as the other two. 'Serene Madonna' was top of the German day lily popularity poll in 1986, and is a favourite in America. It is quite different in style from the other whites, having narrow leaves and dark flower stems and large round flowers – but still of the same pale cream colour. These white day lilies should be planted where they get as much heat and sun as possible; in shade their flowers are yellower.

The oriental poppy, *Papaver orientale* is, by comparison, big, blowsy and vulgar – yet indispensable in any but the smallest white garden for its flowers are about the largest of any perennial, often 20cm (8in) across, and seemingly made of crumpled silk. 'Perry's White' is the only white commonly available. It has maroon-purple blotches at the base of each petal. The whiteness of the flowers is enhanced by the coarsely hairy silvery foliage. 'Barr's White', which is similar to if not the same as 'Black and White', has even darker blotches. Both grow to about 1m (3ft) tall, with a spread of some 1.2m (4ft), but they are floppy plants and need supporting, either with pea sticks or hoops. The foliage dies away in July, and Miss Jekyll used to plant

Hemerocallis *'Joan Senior', one of the new generation of white day lilies.*

gypsophila or *Artemisia lactiflora* to grow up and fall forward to fill the vacant space.

Gypsophila itself is a chalk-loving plant, as its name suggests, though it will actually grow well in any good soil so long as there is a sufficient depth, for it likes to put its roots down deep, preferably with a handful of good limey rubble beneath it. Its real needs are for sunshine and good drainage. In cold, damp positions it fades away fast. The species usually grown is *G. paniculata* which produces frothy clouds of tiny white flowers totally hiding the foliage in mid-summer. The typical plant has grey-white flowers, while 'Bristol Fairy' has double pure white flowers but tends to be short-lived; 'Compacta-plena' is more reliable.

G.p. 'Nana-alba' is the dwarf gypsophila, and grows to only 20–30cm (8–12in) as against 90–100cm (35–40in). *Galtonia candicans* can fill the gap when the gypsophila dies down in July.

The genus veronica, in spite of being first cousins with the showy foxglove, lacks the obvious glamour of the campanulas. One comes to it later in life, when one's taste has had time to mature. The genus used to include shrubs as well as perennials, but the shrubs are now gathered together in hebe, leaving veronica with the border plants. Several are useful in the white garden. The tallest is *V. virginica*, which grows to 1.2m (4ft) and forms good dense clumps. It is one of those fascinating plants that might have been dreamt up by a designer with an eye to structure, for the leaves are held horizontally out from the stiffly erect stems, and are produced in whorls so that from a distance one sees equidistant bands of leaves up the stem, topped by a slender spike of flowers which in the form 'Alba' are a good white, produced in late summer. The whole plant achieves a satisfying balance in its dynamics, the verticals in harmony with the horizontals. *V. spicata* is only half as tall, and not designed along such clean-cut lines, being more tussock-forming. It, too, produces narrow spikes densely packed with flowers which in 'Alba' are white. 'Icicle' is a superlative form from America, with showier flowers of a better white. *V. gentianoides* is a mat-forming plant with rounded dark, more or less evergreen leaves and 30cm (1ft) high spikes of flowers of the palest slate blue. There is a white form, and also a form 'Variegata' whose leaves are splashed creamy-white. Both may contribute something at the front of the border.

The mallow family forms a distinctive group with a cohesive identity. We have suggested that *Malva moschata* 'Alba' should be rated as one of the basic plants of the white garden, and undoubtedly *Abutilon* 'Tennant's White' is ideal for tall walls. *Lavatera olbia* 'Ice Cool' is intermediate in size though of rapid growth, reaching perhaps 2m × 2m

The opulent flowers of Papaver orientale *'Perry's White' at Tintinhull.*

(7ft × 7ft). At first sight it is thus a plant only for large white gardens, but it may also be used rapidly to furnish a new white garden, being discarded once more refined plants get themselves established. Its flowers are like those of a hollyhock, pure white with a green eye. The leaves are like those of a vine, but smaller. It needs full sun and a rich but well-drained soil.

Quite different in style from anything else in the white garden are lupins, one of the glories of the garden in June. The original garden lupin was the North American *Lupinus polyphyllus* which produced its flowers in widely spaced whorls up a central stem, in blues and purples, mauves and whites, but this was superceded in the 1930s and later by the Russell lupins, bred by George Russell of York. However, the showier flowers were achieved only at the cost of shortening the life span, and named sorts had to be perpetuated by basal cuttings taken in spring. More recently strains have been produced which breed true. 'Noble Maiden' opens white from cream buds; 'Blushing Bride' is a little on the pink side. There are also white strains and dwarf strains. Lupins look best planted in groups and make a lovely contrast with the fine showers of gypsophila flowers, as a footstool to rose 'Iceberg' or in company with the grey biennial thistle, *Onopordum acanthium*.

There was a time when it would have been true to say that the genus chrysanthemum contained more good plants for the white garden than any other genus, but most of the plants once known as chrysanthemums have now been hived-off into other genera, no doubt for good reasons. *Chrysanthemum coccineum* (*Pyrethrum roseum*) has now been transmogrified into *Tanacetum roseum*. It is, or was, the source of the insecticide pyrethrum. It has the most finely-cut leaves of the cultivated chrysanthemums, the segments as thin as threads, bright green, the yellow-centred daisy flowers borne above them on slender stems mostly in May and June, but sometimes again in September. Much breeding was done on the continent in the early part of this century, and the whole group much enhanced by further breeding and selection by James Kelway of Langport, still a major grower. 'Avalanche' is reputed to be the best single white; 'Carl Vogt', 'Mont Blanc' and 'Silver Challenger' being good double whites. They all grow 60–90cm (2–3ft) tall, and flourish in well-drained soils in sun. They go beautifully with white lupins and white tall bearded irises, the contrast in foliage as well as flower form being effective. *Chrysanthemum hosmariense* became *Leucanthemum hosmariense* but is now *Chrysanthemopsis hosmariense*. Under whatever name it is a lovely plant for a white garden, with single, yellow-eyed daisies produced above a dense cushion of rather stiff finely-cut silver foliage. It grows about 30cm (12in) high. Feverfew, whose leaves are supposed to relieve migraines, was once *Chrysanthemum parthenium*, has been *Pyrethrum parthenium* and *Parthenium matricaria* and is now *Tanacetum parthenium*. It forms a small, dense bun of small leaves with deeply cut edges, usually dark green but bright chartreuse in the form 'Aureum'. We know one white garden where this yellow form is used as the dominant foil to greens and whites, no greys being used at all. 'Aureum' has single white flowers with a yellow eye, as has the typical plant. 'Plenum' ('Flore Pleno') is a double with ragged petals. 'White Bonnet' is a good double variety found by Graham Stuart Thomas in a Reading garden and named by him; 'Sissinghurst' is also double white, and a larger grower than most. 'Snowball' is presumably double though we have not seen it. All grow 45–60cm (18–24in) tall, enjoy sun and seed themselves about freely, coming true to type.

Chrysanthemum uliginosum was so called

because it is (or was thought to be) a bog-dweller; it has now become *Leucanthamella serotina* alluding to its lateness of flowering, usually October. It is also the tallest of chrysanthemums, capable of reaching 2.2m (7ft) in damp soils, making it the perfect plant for the back of a white border (perhaps in company with *Cimicifuga ramosa* or *C. simplex* and *Eupatorium cannabium* 'Album'). Its refined yellow-eyed daisy-flowers are produced in big sprays. Plant it where the flowers can see the sun, for they always turn towards it. *Chrysanthemum nipponicum* is the last of these daisies to flower, usually well into November, a fact to which its new name, *Nipponanthemum nipponicum*, makes no reference. It is low-growing, no more than 60cm (2ft) tall, with thick, dark leaves and produces flowers of a stunning whiteness. It is happiest at the foot of a warm wall, in full sun, in well-drained soil, and so lovely it is worth rooting cuttings in the autumn in case the winter carries it off.

Anthemis cupaniana (*A. cretica* var. *cupiana*) is not a chrysanthemum, though to a gardener's eye it ought to be. It is a low plant of soft, floppy growth and inclined to sprawl (a clip with the shears soon remedies this). Its leaves are grey (though not so grey as those of *Chrysanthemopsis hosmariense*). It produces pure white daisies with a yellow eye on slender stems well clear of the foliage, and it flowers from June right through till September. *A. tinctoria* is roughly speaking a green-leafed version of the same thing, the leaves being rich, parsley green. The typical form has yellow flowers, but 'Powys Castle' has flowers of a good white with yellow centres. It grows about 90cm (3ft) tall and tends to need support. *A. cretica*, which used to be *A. montana*, and before that *A. macedonia*, is camomile, once used for lawns. It is a low plant, only growing 7 or 8cm (2¾–3in) tall and the double form, *plena*, can be useful at the front of a white border.

The astilbes contribute to the garden over a long season, but are all too often rejected in the belief that they need their feet at the water's edge. Certainly they will flourish at the water's edge, but they will grow in any ground that is a bit on the damp side, and borders often are, especially if they are in shade. They dislike very chalky soils. Of the white-flowered species *A. rivularis* is the largest-growing. It makes a bold clump of handsome foliage overtopped by arching plumes of greenish-white flowers, the whole plant growing to 1.8m (6ft) the flower head alone 90cm (3ft) long. The flowers when they fade give way to rusty-brown seed-heads which may be out of place in the white garden, but most astilbes do the same. It is appropriate to remove them if they offend, for white gardens need to be better groomed than other gardens. *A. grandis* grows to only 1.5m (5ft) in height and has less handsome foliage but if anything better flowers of a good whiteness. The earliest to flower is *A. thunbergii* in May. It has dense, crowded heads and grows to 45cm (18in). *A. japonica* takes over in late May and into June, when the hybrids start. It reaches 60cm (2ft) and it also has very dense plumes. In addition to the species there are numerous hybrids raised mainly by Lemoine of Nancy (also famed for lilacs and tree paeonies) and taken over by George Arends of Ronsdorf, in Germany, after whom these hybrids are called x *arendsii*. By a careful choice of early, mid and late varieties one can obtain a long season of flower, from May through till August. The tallest hybrid white is 'Professor van der Wielen' at 1.5m (5ft), with big arching plumes; 'Bergkrystall' grows to only 120cm (47in), and its flowers open after those of 'Bridal Veil', which grows to 75cm (30in) 'White Gloria' grows to 60cm (2ft) and flowers earlier. 'Avalanche' is a late white, at 90cm (3ft), and 'Irrlicht' at 45cm (18in) is pure white and very free-flowering. 'Praecox

Alba' grows to only 30cm (12in). They all associate beautifully with primulas, irises such as *kaempferi* and *sibirica*, and ferns such as *Polystichum setiferum*.

Aruncus dioicus is astilbe-like, but of shrub-like proportions. Its feathery 24cm (10in) plumes produced in the very middle of the old rose season, are cream, not white, and soon turn a rusty shade of brown.

In leaf *Lysimachia ephemerum* could almost pass for a phlox though its value in the white garden is quite different. It is grown neither for its leaves nor yet for its flowers but rather for both together, for the long, grey rather leathery leaves are the perfect foil for the narrow spires of grey-white flowers. It grows to 90cm (3ft), forms good, tight clumps and needs no staking. It flowers in the same season as the phloxes. Similar only in so much as that it also produces tall spires of white flowers above long, narrow leaves is *Chamaenerion angustifolium* 'Album', which everyone still calls epilobium. *Epilobium hirsutum* is rose-bay willow herb, that invasive British native seen at its best clothing mountain sides in Scotland and *Chamaenerion angustifolium* is only a little less invasive, so it needs to be planted where it can be kept under control. Its tall spires can reach 1.2m (4ft) and bear flowers of a cool, greenish white. It thrives in damp ground.

Delphiniums are the most magnificent of all the plants which present their flowers in tapering spires. The taller sorts which can reach 2.4m (8ft) are perfect at the back of the border, in front of a hedge or wall, and some of the newer hybrids, being shorter, can be used in the middle ground. They all do best on well-fed, moisture-retentive and preferably limey soils in full sun. The traditional delphinium, the one that is one of the glories of the July border, was originally developed by the firm of Kelways at Langport in Somerset in the 1870s and 80s, but was subsequently taken over by Blackmore and Langdon of Bath, and

has more recently been further developed in America. Of the large-flowered sorts 'Damavand' (so named for a mountain in Iran) is perhaps the best for the white garden. It is a strong grower reaching 1.5m (5ft), of exquisite colouring, greyish-white, with a pure white eye. 'Rona' also grows to 1.5m (5ft) and is also exquisitely coloured, being greenish-white with a white eye. 'Mary Loake' was raised and named by Richard Loake, a vice-president of the Delphinium Society. It is a little taller, near 1.8m (6ft), off-white with a bright, white eye. All three flowers are of such quality and beauty that they evoke *frissons* of delight every time one sees them. Miss Jekyll recommends growing white-striped maize in front of delphiniums to take over once their flowers are finished but this maize seems to have disappeared since her day. A suitable substitute would be *Miscanthus sinensis* 'Variegatus'. Another possibility would be to drop into place pots of *Plumbago capensis* 'Alba' whose flowers are of ravishing whiteness.

Masterwort, astrantia, is a plant whose flowers are not only effective at a distance but fascinating at close quarters. It is not a British native but comes from sub-alpine woodlands in Europe, and was probably introduced by mistake, by apothecaries or by plant-touts acting on their behalf, who thought it was hellebore, for though astrantia and hellebore may be as unlike as chalk and cheese in leaf and flower, both have black roots. The astrantias produce good clumps of finely-divided foliage from which they throw up in July and August 60cm (2ft) stems which branch at the top, each branch bearing a single flower head, each head composed of a posy of tiny florets surrounded by a collar of bracts. In *A. major* the flowers are greenish-white with a pale green collar and a touch of pink at the centre of the. flower; 'Shaggy' is a selection with a larger and ruffled collar. Astrantia is, as Sir J.E. Smith remarked in his *Exotic Botany*,

Astrantia *'Shaggy', tolerant of some shade.*

'not found in every flaunting flower-garden but is rather a favourite of the more refined admirers of nature'.

Some plants look best when jostling cheek by jowl with their companions but others look better grown as clumps on their own and allowed enough space to reveal their shape and form. *Dictamnus albus*, the burning bush or dittany, is one of these. It is known in America as the gas plant, which falls oddly on English ears. The art is not to grow it on its own in isolation. It is a slow starter, and it may take several years to produce a bloom, but once it does it can remain in the same place for decades without seeming to tire or decline. Its leaves are light green, shaped like those of a refined ash-tree and emit a lemony smell. Its flowers are large and white, with many stamens at the centre, borne in tall spikes. The typical plant is white-flowered and comes true from seed. It is the pink and mauve forms that are selections.

Agapanthus or love-lilies (their name is derived from agape and anthos) have, thanks to the Hon. Lewis Palmer and the years he spent selecting them in his cold chalk garden at Headbourne Worthy, become common-place garden plants, when before they were regarded as tender rarities to be over-wintered in the greenhouse. There are several good, hardy whites. 'Alice Gloucester' flowers earlier than the others, and has big heads of white flowers, though the flower-stalks (pedicels) and the buds have a purplish stain; 'Victoria', also one of Lewis Palmer's original plants, has creamy-white flowers and very little of the purplish tint. 'Ardernei Hybrid', which is sometimes sold as *A. orientalis albus* (which is really a very different plant) has too much purple staining for the white garden. 'Lady Moore' has soft white flowers with chocolate anthers and is the best of the bunch. *A. inapertus* is a tall species producing stems 1.5m (5ft) tall bearing heads of long, dangling bell-shaped flowers. There are white

forms which though seldom seen are highly desirable in the white garden, to be used in the middle of the border, in counterpoint to those aforementioned. These white agapanthus flower at the same seasons as the Shasta daisy, though they do not associate well and are better kept apart. Plant bold drifts of *Sisyrinchium striatum* in between, or clumps of silvery-leafed *Achillea* 'Moonshine', whose flowers, though over, will still be contributing a touch of biscuity ochre.

The true aconites, monkshood or wolf's bane, are among the earliest of perennials to emerge from the ground as spring approaches, often as early as February and ahead of the herbaceous paeonies. They are all poisonous in all their parts and should be treated with respect. They enjoy deep, rich moist woodsy soils in semi-shade. *A. septentionale* 'Ivorine' has deeply incised foliage and produces its 60cm (2ft) spires of hooded ivory-white flowers earlier than the others, in May. *A. cammarum* 'Grandiflorum Album' is far showier at 100cm (40in) tall, and flowers into July, while *A. napellus* 'Album' is off-white and not particularly worthwhile in a white garden.

White polemoniums are more like symbols of peace than war, yet the name comes from the Greek 'polemos', meaning war. The story according to Pliny is that two kings discovered the virtues of the plant at the same time and went to war to determine who should take the credit. Sadly we have forgotten who they were. *P. caeruleum*, known as Greek valerian, has a fine white form 'Alba'. From tufts of finely, pinnately divided leaves it sends up leafy stems producing masses of cup-shaped flowers. It reaches 30cm (12in) and flowers in June and July. *P. foliosissimum* 'Album' is similar but much taller, 90cm (3ft) and flowers two weeks later.

Hostas are, in the main, shade lovers. Though usually grown for their foliage there are several good sorts with white flowers. One of the most widely-grown is *H. sieboldii alba*, still often incorrectly known as *H. minor alba*. It produces 20cm (8in) tufts of elliptical, elm-green leaves, glossy beneath, and bears erect stems of white, trumpet-shaped flowers of good size and substance. It forms dense clumps and if grown away from other hostas the seedlings will come fairly true. It is a cool and lovely plant for a white garden. *H.* 'Weihenstephan' is in effect a larger-flowered form, but it must be propagated vegetatively. 'Louisa' is an American selection or hybrid. It was the first white-flowered, white-margined hosta, and it is lovely in bold drifts backed by dark evergreens. It does not thrive in all gardens. *H.* 'Freising' is a selection of the larger-leafed *H. fortunei*. It has stiff, leathery, slightly glaucous, sage green leaves with the suggestion of an undulate margin. It is the only *H. fortunei* form with white flowers and these are borne in July on tall stems. Although little known it can be seen growing in bold drifts in the Savill garden. We use it with *H.* 'Snowden' which has huge glaucous greeny-grey leaves and nearly white flowers. *H. plantaginea* is the most notable exception to the generality that hostas are shade lovers. It is an exceptionally beautiful flower and is described on page 64. Anyone with an eye for hybridising would soon see that a cross between *H. sieboldii alba* and *H. plantaginea* might produce a good, hardy, large flowered hosta of easy culture. *H.* 'Royal Standard' is just such a cross. It is a first rate garden plant with crisp, apple-green, slightly puckered leaves and tall spikes of good white, well-scented flowers produced a month or six weeks earlier than those of *H. plantaginea*, making it a more useful plant. It flowers best in a sunny position. *H.* 'Honeybells' is progeny of the same cross but has by contrast coarse, splayed, unattractive leaves and pale mauvish flowers of no particular merit. It is a rampant grower, fit only for use by landscapers.

The autumn-flowering anemones, *Anemone* x *hybrida*, and *Anemone japonica* are also rudely invasive, for all their charms. They have the reputation of being shade lovers though this is only in part true for once established they will usually migrate to a position where they will flower more freely. They prefer a heavy clay soil that does not dry out too quickly, and will run about underground thrusting their way up through neighbouring shrubs. 'White Giant' ('Geante des Blanches') is tall-growing, up to 90cm (3ft), and produces sumptuous semi-double white flowers with slightly ruffled petals; 'Honorine Jobert' is a single white of the same height, with smooth rounded petals. 'Whirlwind', which was raised in America more than a hundred years ago, is shorter, 60–75cm (24–30in), semi-double with crumpled petals. All are lovely and truly white.

The anemones flower in September and October, a season when there is a wide choice of companions to set them off. Far taller and ideal to put behind them are the Hungarian daisies *Leucanthamella serotina* (*Chrysanthemum uliginosum*) and the white form of Joe Pye weed, *Eupatorium purpureum*, at 2.4m (8ft) a plant so tall that it is suitable only for the back of a very wide border, but when so placed it is most imposing. Its pointed leaves are produced in whorls round the stems and the flowers are produced at the tops of the stems in huge fuzzy plate-like heads. It needs rich soil to flourish, and shade on its roots. *E. weinmannianum* is even larger. *Lysimachia clethroides* is another good companion, particularly useful where the eupatorium is being grown since the arrangement of its leaves echoes that of the eupatorium. Its flowers, however, are tall, narrow spires, a theme which could be picked up at the front of the border by drifts of the white Kaffir lily, *Schizostylis coccinea* 'Albiflora' ('Alba'), a plant which is once again to be seen in gardens and nursery lists and which is being greeted as though it were something new when in fact it was being offered in the 1950s by Nancy Lindsay. It is desirable in the front of the white border, its tufts of grassy leaves spreading to form veritable mats, its flower spikes resembling those of dwarf gladioli, though the flowers open wide and flat. To flourish it should be grown in good fertile soil, in full sun, and it should be lifted, divided and replanted every few years, otherwise it loses vigour. It flowers most freely where the air is damp. Quite different, but echoing at the front of the border the big, flat powder-puffs of the eupatoriums, is the white form of *Sedum spectabile* known as 'Iceberg'. It forms a rounded clump of fleshy glaucous green leaves above which large heads of white flowers appear in September, lasting well through into October. Watch out for any reverting shoots, though.

Miss Jekyll used yuccas in herbaceous borders and that seems reason enough to include them here. They are one of the great glories of the garden in late summer, flowering in August and September, and sometimes into October. Their great, branching candelabras bear flowers that are more cream than white and the buds and backs of the flowers are red or reddish. All have clumps of sword-shaped leaves. In *Y. filamentosa* and *flaccida* the leaves are always and only basal, but in *Y. gloriosa* and *Y. recurvifolia* they are borne atop a short trunk so scarred with leaf-bases as to look positively reptilian. *Y. gloriosa* is a caulescent species with stiff dark green, spine-tipped leaves and huge candelabras of flowers; the spines are lethal and the plant is not to be grown by those who fear for their eyes. *Y. recurvifolia* has leaves that are bent or broken half-way along their length and are, therefore, far less dangerous, though they are also less spectacular. It too, is caulescent, and its flower spikes magnificent. *Y. filamentosa* has greyish leaves whose

margins are edged with white threads; *Y. flaccida* has similar leaves but they are bent or broken half way up, which those of *Y. filamentosa* are not. Both are spectacular in flower, the flowers of *filamentosa* being very fragrant, those of *flaccida* being displayed better. 'Ivory' is a clone of *flaccida* selected by Jackmans of Woking, and is notably free-flowering.

The daisy-flowers of *Leucanthamella serotina* can be echoed by those of the true Michaelmas daisy, *Aster tradescantii*. This was brought over from North America in 1633 by John Tradescant, gardener to Charles I, and it was the first of these useful, late-flowering daisies to arrive. It grows up to 2.4m (8ft) tall and produces erect, wiry stems with small narrow, pointed leaves and branching heads beset with veritable showers of 1cm (¼in) daisy flowers – white rays with yellow centres which create a gypsophila-like effect. *A. divaricatus* always attracts comment because of its shiny black, wiry stems. Its leaves are broad and beset with teeth, confusingly un-aster-like, but the flowers are unmistakably daisy-like, the rays white from a distance but quite creamy on closer inspection, the discs brown rather than yellow. It is an awkward plant, for it flops and therefore needs staking, but looks an absolute fright when it is staked. Miss Jekyll, who called it *A. corymbosus*, used to like it to flop forward over her megaseas (*Bergenia*), and perhaps that is the way to use it. *A. umbellatus* is useful, because it is the last to flower, its flowers dying in October. It grows to 2.4m (8ft) and forms round-topped bushes of yellow-eyed white daisies. At an earlier season it might be overlooked, but it holds its own as one of the last flowers of the year.

The hybrid asters are coarse, unlovely plants by comparison, but they are highly effective, and that is what counts in the white garden. The New England asters, *A. novae-angliae*, are easily distinguished from the

94

New York asters by their rough leaves and the greater number of rays in the flower. The only good white among them is 'Snow Queen', which grows to 2.4m (8ft) and flowers through August till the end of September. The New York asters, many of the best sorts of which were raised by Ernest Ballard at the nursery that still bears his name in Colwall on the far side of the Malvern Hills, come in a far wider range of colours, and include two good whites: 'Alaska', which reaches 75cm (30in) and has pure white flowers, and 'Choristers', which grows a little taller and has starry white flowers. Both flower in September and October. 'White Swan' is earlier flowering, and 'White Ladies' a good 90cm (3ft) plant. 'Snow Sprite' is a dwarf, at a mere 25cm (10in), but is of a quaintly greyish-white; 'Niobe' is similar but whiter.

Geraniums, like campanulas are in the first rank of fillers. There is just one geranium that deserves to be regarded more highly and given a place of proper prominence and that is *Geranium sanguineum* 'Album', the white form of the bloody cranesbill. It is a low-growing plant 15cm (6in) suitable for the front of the border, where perhaps it may stretch itself out across the mowing strip. Its foliage is dark and divided into seven slender segments and the quite large flowers show up as of brilliant whiteness against the leaves. It is noted for its long period of flowering, from early June through till the last days of August. It prefers a sunnier rather than a shadier position.

Two white globe thistles worthy of space in larger white gardens are *Echinops tournefortii* and *E.* 'Nivalis', growing to 1.5m (5ft) and 1.8m (6ft) respectively. Both need well-drained soil and a sunny site.

Finally, if a border of old roses is unthinkable without catmint sprawling at its feet, is a garden of white roses unthinkable without white catmint? There is such a thing as *Nepeta faassenii* 'Alba', although we have not seen it flower.

WHITE PERENNIAL FOLIAGE

White variegated leaves can contribute as much to the white garden as white flowers, but there are other factors to consider. *Polygonatum* x *hybridum* 'Variegatum' has white variegated leaves, as well as white flowers but *Phlox* 'Nora Leigh', in spite of its lovely leaves can be a bit of a shock when it bursts into flower in the midst of a white garden. By and large one can select white plants whose flowers come in restrained pastel tones and can be overlooked (for the eye only sees what the mind wants it to).

The Solomon's seals are woodlanders, and there are two white-variegated forms in general circulation each quite different from the other. The one usually considered most desirable is *Polygonatum hybridum* (*multiflorum*) 'Variegatum', which has its paired leaves heavily striped creamy-white. The other is *P. falcatum* 'Variegatum' which is a smaller grower with rather rounded leaves thinly margined ivory-white. No doubt seeing the two side by side in pots in a garden centre most people would pick the first, but it is the second that is the better garden plant. Both have little white pendent bells hanging from the lower side of their arching stems.

Some of the hostas are also woodlanders and associate well with the Solomon's seals. They are very much a part of the white garden repertoire. 'Louisa', named by its raiser Mrs Frances Williams for her daughter, is a white-variegated, white-flowered selection of *H. sieboldii*, itself a low-growing hosta, reaching only 15 or 20cm (6–8in) in leaf, but spreading by stolons into weed-suppressing clumps. Its leaves are elliptic, about 4cm (1½in) broad, mid-green with a narrow white margin. The flowers on tall stems are a good deep violet, beautifully marked inside; they could easily be removed if they give offence. 'Ginko Craig' is similar but has smaller narrower leaves with more pointed tips, and deeper purple flowers. Quite different and one size up is *H. undulata* 'Unvittata' which has broad but pointed leaves of a lovely rich olive green with a variable amount of white at the centre which undulate at the margin or may even be spirally twisted. *H.u.* has leaves which in their first flush in spring are almost entirely creamy-white and so twisted as to be almost distorted. The white leaves are gradually superseded by green as the season advances. The whole plant is very unstable and the amount of variegation is inconsistent. At its best it is the finest white-variegated hosta for a white garden. Its flowers are violet. 'See-Saw' is a development from it, with boat-shaped elliptic leaves margined and streaked white, with grey and green markings, conspicuous because it suffers from a phenomenon which American hostaphiles call 'the draw-string effect', that is, the margin of the leaf appears too small for the blade. It also has violet flowers.

One of the largest, and loveliest, white-variegated hosta is *H. crispula*, a most distinctive plant with long, broad, olive green leaves – drawn out to a tapering point – whose white margins undulate. The outer leaves are held almost horizontal, the inner leaves being piled up on top of them to make a sumptuous mound of foliage. The carriage of the leaves, and their rippling undulations, make this hosta quite distinct from all others. It needs good cultivation, shade and shelter from wind to look good. *H.* 'Thomas Hogg' (named for an Englishman who established a nursery in New York, or for his son, also Thomas Hogg, who collected hostas in Japan, or for their nursery, also 'Thomas Hogg') is often sold in its stead, but then the name 'Thomas Hogg' is applied by the unwary to almost any white-edged hosta. The true 'Thomas Hogg' (*H. undulata* 'Albo-marginata') has a cream rather than a white variegation and its petioles are flat and winged, those of *crispula* being U-shaped in

section and clean, not winged; it has light lilac flowers. *H. fortunei* 'Albo-marginata' is a plant of much the same size, but it holds its leaves up, rather than piling them up in a mound. Its leaves are dark green and greyish beneath, with broad margins. It grows to about 75cm (30in) and is always interesting because the variegation is unstable and no two leaves are ever quite alike. It needs deep shade to do well.

Also big and bold in foliage, and needing similar conditions of shade and shelter, but otherwise utterly different is *Brunnera macrophylla*, several forms of which might be grown in the white garden. All have big, rough, roundly heart-shaped leaves held aloft on tall petioles and all produce showers of forget-me-not-like flowers. 'Variegata' has leaves richly margined and marked creamy-white; 'Dawson's White' is similar but whiter; 'Langtrees' (syn. 'Aluminium Spot') has leaves spotted with silver. Symphytum is a closely related genus with similarly rough leaves that are equally easily bruised or scorched by the elements. In *S.* x *uplandicum* the leaves are oval and pointed, up to 30cm (1ft) long, greyish-green and in the form 'Variegatum' broadly margined creamy-white. The flowers are a nondescript lilac-pink. It is a bold and beautiful plant but one needs to beware of it for it can easily steal the show at the expense of the overall effect.

As a contrast to plants with such opulent foliage something is needed that has as strong a presence or personality but in a quite different way, grasses for example, or *Iris foetidissima* 'Variegata', whose leaves not only afford the contrast of being narrow and sword-like, but also differ in their poise, for they are held fairly erect in sharp contradistinction to the leaves of the brunnera or the symphytum. It is a typical iris producing fans of leaves, margined and striped and splashed creamy-white at first, the white becoming purer as the season advances. It rarely flowers, which makes it even more use in the white garden. It is a shade-lover, and it will grow well even in very dry conditions.

There are several other irises of varying degrees of usefulness in the white garden. The variegated forms of *Iris pallida* are what pass for variegated bearded irises, for their flowers are of the same form but of a singularly undistinguished mauve. The leaves, however, are strikingly variegated, the white-variegated one being known properly as *I.p.* 'Argenta Variegata', though the variegation is distinctly creamy at first, the yellow variegated form being known simply as 'Variegata' though it fades to nearly white as the leaves mature. Both need full sun and flourish most vigorously when lifted and divided every few years. They are lovely plants near the front of the border where their flowers can easily be removed.

Sisyrinchium striatum is often mistaken for an iris, and the variegated form even more often, but the leaves are presented in bunches rather than in fans. The variegated form has greyish leaves striped creamy-white, and these are topped by spikes of chartreuse flowers, which fade at tea-time. Its proper name is 'Aunt May' after Mrs May Amory, the owner of Chevithorn Barton, Tiverton, Devon, the garden where it originated. Each spike of flowers spells the death of the fan of leaves that produce it, though other fans in the clump should live on. It is not happy in all gardens, and likes to be well fed and grown in full sun.

The variegated strawberry *Fragraria vesca* 'Variegata' is another of those unconsidered trifles that is amusing to have running about beneath the showier things, for it never becomes a nuisance yet is pretty enough in its way, the typical strawberry leaves irregularly splashed clean white, the flowers also white. Similar, in that it spreads above the ground rather than below it, is the variegated ground ivy, *Glechoma hederacea* 'Variegata',

nowadays more usually sold as a house plant, although perfectly hardy. It has long, sinuous stems at the sides of which are little round leaves, about 2cm (1 in) across, prettily edged with clean white. Happy among shrubs, in shade. Far more effective as ground cover if ground cover is needed is *Aegopodium podagraria* 'Variegatum'. One hesitates to state in plain English that this is the variegated ground elder, since ground elder is such a bogey word to so many gardeners, but it is so heavily variegated that it scarcely has the energy to be invasive. The variegation is cream at first quickly turning white, and the flowers are also white, in cymes, typical umbellifers, like Queen Ann's lace, in miniature. The heads should be removed when flowering is over because the old stems look untidy, but the theory is that the flowers are sterile and that the seed, therefore, cannot give rise to the green-leafed menace. The periwinkles are even better ground covers, at least *Vinca minor* is for as it grows its stems criss and cross every which way so that in time it builds up into a thick pile carpet through which no weeds can grow. *V.m.* 'Argentea Variegata' has leaves cleanly variegated grey and white, but the flowers are lavenderish. *V. major* is more diffuse in growth, with long intervals between the leaves. *V.m.* 'Elegantissima' has its leaves margined and splashed creamy-white. It is enchanting running about at the back of a border, trailing through other plants.

Scrophularia aquatica 'Variegata' is a brilliantly variegated form of what is otherwise just a British weed. Its narrow leaves are splashed and striped cream rather than white, which makes it fine in white gardens which lean towards chartreuse. The flowers are small, brown and unattractive, and best cut off. It is winter green.

The variegated form of masterwort, *Astrantia major*, is called 'Sunningdale Variegated' for the nursery which introduced

Foliage group at Chenies Manor: Hosta undulata *'Univittata' and* Artemisia *'Powys Castle'.*

it. Its leaves are splashed yellow and cream – quite strongly yellow, and are most brightly coloured early in the season, fading to a blotchy, discoloured green later. The variegation is brightest in sun but lasts longer in a little shade. The flowers are as for the typical plant, but should be removed as soon as they are over to prevent seeding.

Heuchera brizoides 'Taff's Joy' is a plant for a white garden with a leaning towards pink. It is a variegated London pride but so variegated as to be scarcely recognisable. The almost round leaves are so densely speckled and spotted with cream, white and pink on a grey ground as to appear wholly white from a distance. The petioles and leaf margins are pink, the colour becoming more intense in winter and suffusing the whole leaf. The flowers are typical London pride and may not give offence. It is not so easy to grow as ordinary London pride, needing good moisture-retentive woodsy soil and at least dappled shade.

FERNS AND GRASSES

Ferns have about them an air of quiet restraint and elegance that is wholly in keeping with the idea of white gardens. They are especially useful where one is creating a white garden in the shade, particularly a town garden, and they associate well with snowdrops, hellebores, *Arum italicum* 'Pictum', foxgloves, aquilegias and the late-flowering *Saxifraga fortunei*.

There is only one hardy white-variegated fern, *Arachnoides aristata* 'Variegata', though even that is more likely to be encountered in the house plant section of a garden centre than in their hardy fern section. *A. aristata* itself is one of those lovely Eastern ferns with very shiny rich green fronds, the fronds being broadly triangular, never more than 15cm (6in) long, with narrowly triangular pinnae, which in 'Variegata' are painted white down the centre. The stipes are twice as long as the fronds, and the plant grows from a slowly creeping rhizome. It is an enchanting fern and a delightful plant for the white garden. While like most ferns it does best in shade and damp soil, it will actually survive in dry soil and in more sun than most ferns will tolerate.

The Japanese painted fern, *Athyrium goeringianum* 'Pictum', is well-established in cultivation and is valuable as being one of only quite a small number of grey plants that will tolerate shade. What is not perhaps so generally realised is the extent to which it varies when raised from spores, some plants being quite a dark, charcoal grey, others quite silvery and almost white at the centre of the frond, the latter perhaps being more desirable in the white garden. The damson-coloured veins seem to be a fixed character. There is now a crested form which is even more desirable. The painted fern needs good cultivation, rich, damp, woodsy soil and shade and shelter from wind. *A. otophorum* 'Okonum' is even finer but a little tender. It forms a single crown and throws its beautiful fronds upwards like a shuttlecock to about 45cm (18in). The fronds are palest creamy-

Snowdrops with Polystichum aculeatum, *quietly enchanting in earliest spring.*

greyish green with claret-coloured stipes and veins, and the centre of the frond is stained with the same colouring. Sporelings vary greatly in their colour, though the claret veins seem constant; some have fronds that are palest cream colour all over.

Of the more robust ferns *Polystichum setiferum* is undoubtedly the most useful, in one or other of its many forms. The most generally useful in the white garden are forms of *P.s.* 'Divisilobum' and *P.s.* 'Acutilobum' with very finely-cut soft fronds of a mat mid green, their stipes encased in pale brownish scales. They tend to throw fronds up in the air at 45° from the vertical, which makes them very distinct. *P.s.* 'Divisilobum-densum' (or 'Plumoso-densum', or even 'Plumoso-divisilobum-densum', for these are Victorian names and in urgent need of authoritative re-definition) has far more finely-cut foliage and tends to build itself up into a bird's nest of dead fronds with a few green fronds on top, but in spite of that, is most worthwhile. All of these will grow in full sun though they prefer dappled shade. *P.s.* 'Proliferum' is similar, and all three produce little plantlets in the axils of their pinnae which, if the frond is anchored to the ground with a rock, will grow into new plants. *P.s.* 'Divisilobum Mrs Goffrey' is quite different, with big fronds so dissected that they appear as a haze of greenery. *P. aculeatum* is the hard shield fern (as opposed to *P. setiferum* which is the soft shield fern), and two of its forms are among the most desirable of garden ferns. These are *P.a.* 'Pulcherrimum Bevis' and *P.a.* 'Pulcherrimum Druery'. These are tall, elegant ferns of great refinement, that hold their finely-cut fronds up like plumes. They are quite distinct from other ferns in their poise, and are best in groups or drifts of several to many, among lowly subjects like lily of the valley or hardy cyclamen. *P.a.* 'Pulcherrimum Druery Superbum' is lovelier and rarer, the fronds so finely-cut that they are just a cloud of fine

greenery, very like *P.s.* 'Divisilobum Mrs Goffrey'.

There are a couple of ferns that are useful as underlings in the white garden. The daintiest of these is *Adiantum venustum*, the hardy maidenhair fern, which has broadly triangular fronds composed of masses of tiny, triangular leaflets held airily on wiry black stems. It travels by underground stems and makes a useful understorey to shrubs and white bluebells. The other is *Hypolepis millefolium* which has bright green, scabrid fronds and chocolate brown stipes. It runs around like the hardy maidenhair fern, but is quite different in appearance.

While the ferns are suggested mainly as a foil to other plants in the white garden, there are many grasses (in the horticultural sense) that can contribute positive whiteness. Indeed, gardener's garters, *Phalaris arundinacea* 'Picta', is one of the first plants most people acquire when they come to gardening, because it is so brightly white-variegated and one of the first they discard because it tends to run at the root and look untidy in midsummer. In spite of this, it has a place in the white garden, among other robust perennials, provided that one is prepared to pluck out the errant tufts that come up in the wrong place. Left to its own devices it looks pretty drab by June, but if cut to the ground will throw new shoots with lovely clean, bright new leaves which will see the summer out. It normally grows to 90cm (35in) but in moist ground will run up to 1.5m (5ft).

There are three white-variegated grasses we consider indispensable in our own white garden. The first of these is the variegated Yorkshire fog, *Holcus mollis* 'Albo-variegatus', which only grows about 10cm (6in) tall. Its small leaves are broadly margined bright white, as are the culms. It can be used at the front of the border, where it will form groups of tufts rather than a dense clump but is perhaps better used between paving slabs, as at York Gate, or allowed to run about at the foot of box edging, as at Hazelby House. Like most white variegated grasses its foliage deteriorates in mid-summer and it needs to be cut hard back to make it produce a new crop of leaves. This idea can be taken to extremes with *Holcus mollis* 'Albo-variegatus', for, providing it is growing in damp soil in shade, it can actually be mown, like a lawn.

The second, *Arrhenatherum elatius bulbosum* 'Variegatum', is probably the most brilliantly white-variegated grass of all. It is clump-forming, and though popularly known as the onion couch does not run at all; instead the lower joints, which are swollen, become bulbous and can be used to increase this plant but normally the bulbs fall back into the clump, so it only increases in size rather slowly. It grows about 30cm (12in) tall, and its bluish-green leaves are edged with a clean white margin. Like the variegated Yorkshire fog, it tends to look drab by mid-summer and needs cutting down to induce new growth. If this is done three or four times in the season it can look as bright in October as it did in May. The flowers are unexciting and should be cut when they start to emerge.

The third is the white-variegated Chinese eulalia grass, *Miscanthus sinensis* 'Variegata'. It is a strong-growing, clump-forming grass producing long, narrow arching leaves dramatically longitudinally variegated with a clean, bright white. The leaf mound reaches about 1.5m (5ft) in height and the flowers overtop this. *M.s.* 'Cabaret', a plant that originated in Germany, is in the same style but even more dramatically variegated. Both are very architectural and as such associate well with phormiums and yuccas and with plants with bold foliage such as bergenias, *Fatsia japonica*, hostas such as *H. sieboldiana elegans* and *Lysimachia ephemerum* with its exquisite balance of vertical and horizontal axes.

Of the white-variegated sedges *C. siderostica* 'Variegata' is one of the most suitable for the white garden. It has broad, plantain-like leaves, margined and striped white, pink at first, emerging from red sheaths. It needs shade and damp soil. *C. saxatilis* 'Variegata' has a bright white central variegation and always attracts the eye as its leaves twist and curl in an unusual manner. It is one of the sedges that increases by means of underground runners but never enough to be a menace. It comes from acid bogs in Scotland and in cultivation needs damp, peaty soil in shade.

There are very few grasses that could be described as grey, though many are glaucous. Probably the most useful is *Helictotrichon sempervirens* (*Avena candida*), and even that really is nearly blue. It forms a large cushion of narrow, grey-blue leaves, each 30cm (12in) or so long, above which the open heads of flowers are borne on corn-coloured stems. It looks spiky and interestingly architectural. *Elymus arenarius* is blue lyme grass, Miss Jekyll's favourite and intensely electric blue. It produces a diffuse clump of spiky blue leaves about 60 or 75cm (24–30in) tall, and runs with great vigour and determination in all directions. Because of this we grow it in terracotta pots (a colour which shows it off to perfection). If planted out in the garden it needs to be vigorously controlled. Miss Jekyll recommended cutting it down to ground level (like the white variegated grasses) once the flower spike starts to appear. *E. hispidus* (*Agropyron glaucum*) is in effect a dwarf non-running version of blue lyme grass. It grows about 30cm (12in) tall and has narrow, erect, longitudinally ribbed leaves of the same intense blue; even the flowers and flower stalks are the same blue. *E. magellanicum* (*Agropyron magellanicum*, *A. pubiflorum*) has leaves of a similar intensity of blue but makes lax clumps, the leaves sprawling on the ground. It is not soundly perennial.

Lovely though these blue grasses are they need to be used with discretion in a white garden. *Elymus arenarius* needs to be grown with other strong-growing plants, at the feet of *Crambe cordifolia* for example, or next to *Echinops* 'Nivalis' or one of the giant eupatoriums. The lesser species of elymus go well with small hostas, *H.* 'Freising' for example.

ROSES

If the rose is the fairest flower of all, then a white rose must be fairer than fair, the perfect adornment to the white garden. But there is a worm in the bud, for the flowers of most white roses attain unblemished whiteness only briefly, being ochrous-creamy-yellow on opening, and pink on fading, which is inconvenient, to say the least. One could ameliorate the undesirableness of the yellow tones by planting roses with this tendency only in white gardens in which creamy-yellows are incorporated; or one could make the pink tints less glaring by using such roses only in white gardens where a hint of pink is admitted; but then the prevailing ochrous tones would make the pinkiness more deplorable or the prevailing pinks would make the yellows look out of key. So far as we can see all white roses suffer these defects, differing only in degree: none is of absolute whiteness.

There is no doubt that 'Iceberg' is the most popular white rose in gardens today, and that, at least in part, is because it suffers the foregoing defects in lesser measure than most white roses. It gives the general impression of pristine whiteness, even though the centres of the flowers contain yellow shadows and the

At Sissinghurst hazel rods are used to create an annual framework on which to train the roses.

White roses at Hazelby House.

backs of the petals are often stained blush pink. It is discussed more fully in 'The Basic Plants' (page 40). 'White Spray' is the result of a deliberate cross between 'Iceberg' and an unnamed seedling raised by Le Grice in 1974. It is said by those who grow it to be even better than 'Iceberg' with whiter flowers of a better shape produced in larger clusters. It is shorter than 'Iceberg'.

'Pascali' has exquisitely shaped flowers, a character it has passed on to 'Margaret Merrill', but it is not white; it is decidedly creamy-green at the centre. In spite of that it is probably the best large-flowered rose (hybrid tea) for a white garden, for the overall effect is of whiteness. The shapely flowers are produced on long stems and set against dark, glossy foliage. One of its merits is that it is less susceptible to damage by wind and weather than many other whites. All too often white petals produce pink bruise marks where raindrops touch them, but 'Pascali' is fairly free from this defect. Its only real failing is a lack of scent. It has passed all its good qualities on to 'Margaret Merrill', which is a taller, narrower rose.

Two other large-flowered roses in the same class as 'Pascali' and 'Margaret Merrill' are 'Pristine' and 'Polar Star'. 'Pristine' is unusual in that it is an American raised rose that seems to be perfectly suited to the British climate. It was raised by Bill Warriner of

Jackson & Perkins and introduced in 1978. It won the Henry Edland Memorial Medal for its fragrance in 1979. It is broadly similar to 'Pascali' but with larger flowers, not of pure white but blushing slightly. 'Polar Star' is intriguing because the unfurling buds are tinged with green. The open flower has a shadow of yellow across it – a mere yellow blush. The flowers are beautifully formed, and very fragrant. It was raised by Tantau in Germany in 1982, and won the Royal National Rose Society's Certificate of Merit in 1985; it was also 'Rose of the Year' in 1985 and was the first large-flowered rose to win this award.

'The Nun' which is one of the new English roses from David Austin is, by contrast, much more like 'Iceberg' in habit, making a rounded open bush as wide as high. It produces goblet-shaped, semi-double flowers of great quality and substance, the centre of each flower revealing a boss of yellow stamens. It grows to 1.2 by 1.2m (4ft × 4ft). The flowers have little scent. If it has any failing it is that it has too little foliage. In 'Proud Titania' this failing has become a positive fault, for the rather balled white flowers hang desolately at the ends of naked, thorny branches. 'Winchester Cathedral' promises to be by far the best of the bunch for, although only introduced in 1988, it is a sport of 'Mary Rose', which itself has been tried and tested in gardens and has proved to be a good doer. The flowers are large, double, loosely-petalled – rather like those of the old Damask roses – and very fragrant. It makes a well-furnished, rounded bush that flowers from the beginning of the season right through till the end. 'Fair Bianca' is similar but smaller – growing to only 1m (3ft) at most. Growing a little larger than 'Fair Bianca' is 'Anna Zinkeisen', a superb modern shrub rose producing clusters of fully double white flowers with yellowish tones at the base. It has a strong and most distinct fragrance.

Three of Pemberton's hybrid musk roses may be treasured in white gardens for their relaxed and informal way of growing. These are 'Pax' and 'Prosperity' and 'Moonlight'. All three have a vigorous, arching habit of growth, their flowers produced in such abundance they weigh the branches down. Of the three 'Pax' is the whitest, producing very large semi-double flowers. It will grow to nearly 1m (3ft) tall. 'Prosperity' has large double flowers, creamy white, and is not so tall growing. 'Moonlight' is the yellowest of the three, but ideal for the white garden that leans towards yellow. The flowers are nearly single with pronounced stamens. All three have good fragrance and flower all summer.

Of the smaller roses – those that grow knee-high or less – 'Little White Pet' is probably the best-known. It is discussed on page 40. 'Ice Fairy' looks set to steal the stage. It is a pure white version of 'The Fairy' and arose as a branch sport. It was spotted by John Sanday of Bristol in his rose fields in 1984. He budded the original branch and, as it remained stable, started propagating it. It is a most desirable little white rose with flowers just like those of 'The Fairy' but of a good whiteness with only an occasional hint of pink. It goes well with 'Iceberg' which leans towards pink, but not with 'Margaret Merrill', whose leanings are towards warm ivory.

Another rose of the same size is 'Swany' which also produces very double, pure white, cupped flowers with beautifully shaped petals. It has masses of glossy foliage, deep green but bronzy at first and is altogether a more classy rose than 'Little White Pet' which is perhaps more at home in a cottage garden. 'Francine Austin', a relative newcomer, may prove even better. It was raised by David Austin and is a cross between 'Ballerina' and a Noisette rose – and it is quite different from the new English roses, producing sprays of small, glistening white flowers, each held on a wire-thin stalk. It has dark, healthy foliage and makes a dense bush about 90cm (3ft) tall and 1.2m (4ft) across. In its own way it is as effective as 'Iceberg', but in quite a different style.

It is paradoxical that roses, which on the whole have such lovely flowers should, also on the whole, bear them on bushes that are half lame and ungainly. The clever gardener can turn this to advantage. At Hazelby House, for example, climbing 'Iceberg' is trained up inside square treillage pillars to give them height; but such training also gives them shapeliness. Other roses might be contained in cradles or trained up stripped poles, or tied to swags of rope as at Roseraie de l'Hay. Other possibilities are to train white roses up through four-cornered wooden trellis pyramids, or iron cones again as at Roseraie de l'Hay, or over arches – but for these one needs true climbers – though relatively few of the white gardens known to us actually use climbing roses at all.

In one white garden, the whole of a wall is covered with a white-flowered rose trained flat against it. This is 'Mrs Herbert Stevens', a rose first raised as a bush by McGredy in 1910, and then re-launched in this climbing form by Pernet-Ducha in France in 1922. It has typical hybrid tea foliage – coarse, dark green and glossy, and shapely white flowers (with just a hint of green) that emerge from beautiful, long, scrolled buds. It has a strong tea scent and is, all in all, probably the very best white climber. It will attain 6m (20ft), and seems to tolerate difficult conditions, for the windowless wall upon which it is trained faces east and the rose receives no sun on its roots because of the shadow of an adjoining wall.

Three rather smaller climbing roses, better suited to poles and pillars, are 'Purity', 'Swan Lake', and 'White Cockade'. 'Purity' has the best flowers of the three: loosely double, with long rolled buds opening to reveal golden stamens at the centre. It has a strong and pleasing fragrance, but it seldom repeats and

has the worst foliage of the three. 'White Cockade' is so named from the shape of its flowers, which are rather triangular. They are fully double, pure white, but not notably fragrant. Again the bush is very thorny and bears plenty of good dark green foliage. Although a climber, it grows to only 2.5m (8ft) a little less than 'Mrs Herbert Stevens'. 'Swan Lake' grows to much the same size, and has beautifully shaped flowers, large and fully double opening all summer. The foliage is dark and round, and the bush of tidy habit. This rose's virtue is marred only by the suggestion of a blush at the centre of the flower.

The synstylae roses, roses *filipes*, *longicuspis*, *brunonii*, *moschata* and the like, raise fundamental questions of intention in the white garden. They are all large plants, capable of swamping an apple tree, and they produce their flowers in enormous vigorous trusses, practically hiding their foliage so that in full bloom they are incomparably floriferous. But they flower for only a fortnight: for 50 weeks of the year they contribute no whiteness at all. For this reason one might reject the idea of growing a synstylae rose in a white garden, although just such a rose is the centrepiece of the white garden at Sissinghurst.

'Kiftsgate' is the most famous of these large, tree-climbing roses, though it is also the one least often grown, for few gardens are big enough to accommodate it. The plant at Kiftsgate was bought by Mrs Muir (as *Rosa moschata*) in about 1938 from the rose nursery of E.A. Bunyard, but history does not relate where he obtained it. It is a very superior form and the name 'Kiftsgate' was adopted, by Bunyard, to distinguish Mrs Muir's rose from inferior forms of *R. filipes*. It is a lovely rose of great vigour, making new growths 10m (32ft) long in a season. The flowers are borne in huge trusses, each of a hundred flowers or more, each flower cupped, creamy-white, with yellow stamens at the centre. It flowers from mid-June well into

July in mild areas – as does *R. longicuspis*, rather later than other similar roses. 'Kiftsgate' is a rose for the patient; *R. longicuspis* for the impatient, for it flowers much younger. It is also less vigorous. 'Bobbie James' is similar, also lovely and also very vigorous, capable of growing to 10m (32ft).

Kiftsgate was one of the first well known gardens to have a white garden. It was created by Mrs Diany Binney for her mother, Mrs Heather Muir, in 1938. The intention was to plant a garden using only dark greens and whites as one of a number of gardens of different colours. The first plant Mrs Binney put in it was *Osmanthus armatus*, a real plantsman's choice. More recently Mrs Binney has created a white and silver border at the foot of a north wall in a bed dug out of intractable yellow clay. There is, appropriately, a rose called 'Heather Muir'. It was so named by Graham Stuart Thomas and is a hybrid of *Rosa sericea* (the only rose to have four-petalled flowers) with pure white single flowers and ferny foliage (as in *sericea*) but unexpectedly grey which much extends its season of interest in the white garden. It grows 2.4m (8ft) tall, though it has a narrow habit, and the shoots bear an abundance of strong, triangular thorns.

Our own choice of a white rambling rose would be 'Astra Desmond' which seems to be scarcely known. It is a vigorous rose, growing up to 5m (17ft) and capable of training up an apple tree or across a pergola. Its virtue is that its flowers are double, produced in heavy, opulent trusses, and that as they fade they tend to turn shades of grey rather than the more familiar pink. It is a ravishing rose.

CLIMBERS

In most white gardens climbers are of but limited use and most of the few spaces where they could be employed will be filled with roses or white wisteria. However, where white gardens are made in town gardens or courtyards or where they are enclosed by fencing or, as at The Little Cottage, by trellis work, climbers are indispensable.

Even in such situations matters may not be entirely straightforward. If trellis is to show, is it to be white, green or blue? And if it is white, then how will it look with white flowers growing over it; or white foliage? In fact if white trellis is used then it should peep through here and there, reinforcing the idea of whiteness. Green trellis would look better with white variegated foliage on it. Other problems arise where brick or stone walls form the setting to the white garden for they may be of an unsuitable colour. Stone is usually more sympathetic than brick, though at Barrington Court the Ham stone walls are too pale to afford a contrast with the whites planted within the garden. In such cases if the walls were to be more heavily clothed in greenery the overall effect would be better.

But there are other opportunities for using climbers. At The Little Cottage climbers are used not only to cover trellis work, but also the walls of the house, white iron arbors and to make arches over the entrances and exits. In other gardens white climbers could be trained up poles, up tripods of poles lashed together at the top with rope or along colonnades made by looping swags of rope between equidistant poles. At Folly Farm there is an arbor of white wisteria over a seat and the stems of the wisteria themselves afford support to a honeysuckle which passes unnoticed except for its fragrance.

It is also important to choose the right climber for the purpose for which it is intended. Climbers whose flowers hang down are always seen to best advantage when trained on an arch, arbor or pergola. Wisteria, for example, is ideal, with its pendent racemes of

(Opposite) Clematis montana *over trellis-work.*

flowers, but so too is *Wattakaka sinensis* with its hanging heads of flowers, just like those of a hoya. Most of the climbing hydrangeas, on the other hand, would be wasted for they carry their flowers above the foliage.

Next to roses and wisteria, clematis are the most effective climbers for white gardens. The earliest to flower is *C. cirrhosa balearica*. This has fern-like evergreen leaves which turn bronzy in winter and afford an attractive foil to the small, creamy-coloured flowers which are produced through January, February and March. The flowers are covered inside with a multitude of tiny purple spots. 'Wisley Cream' is a newer form, with leaves of a simpler shape and unspotted flowers. *C. cirrhosa* itself is less free-flowering. They grow up to 4m (13ft) and, being Mediterranean plants, like a warm, sunny spot. Annual or perennial sweet peas might be grown up them in summer. Next in season is *C. armandii*, an evergreen species with glossy dark green leaves and beautiful, wide open, starry flowers. 'Snowdrift' is a selection with pure white flowers. *C. armandii* is not notably hardy, needing the protection of a warm wall even in mild areas, and is not entirely to everyone's liking, in spite of its beauty in flower, for it tends to rush up to the top of whatever support is available and become bare at the base. Attempts at pruning usually kill it. *C. montana* follows in early May and is another rampant species, capable of reaching 6m (20ft) but when well grown over a suitable support it is one of the loveliest of all white climbers. The flowers are produced singly, are about 5cm (2in) across, always have four sepals and are typically white. 'Grandiflora' has larger white flowers, as has var. 'Wilsonii'. 'Alexander' is a new selection with large flowers of a stunning whiteness. It has larger leaves than other montanas, but is less rampant.

Flowering at much the same season are the white-flowered forms of *C. alpina* and *C.*

macropetala, both of which also always have four sepals. *C. alpina* is a lovely little clematis, growing to no more than 1.5m (5ft), and therefore very suitable for training up over a small shrub in the white garden – a philadelphus or deutzia perhaps. *C. macropetala* by contrast will climb up to 6m (20ft). There are two good white forms of *C. alpina*, 'Burford White' and 'White Columbine', both singles. *C.a.* 'Siberica' has sepals of a decidedly yellow tone. 'White Moth' is a double white form of *C. macropetala*, and is very beautiful; 'Snowbird' is a lovely, free-flowering, single white. In some gardens these clematis are, for reasons unknown, hard to establish.

'John Huxtable' is quite distinct among the large-flowered hybrids. Its sepals are pointed and pearly-white with a greyish-mauve bar on the bark, and it tends to hang its flowers, so it is better grown over an arch, arbor or pergola where you can look up into the flowers and appreciate them properly. It flowers from July till October.

'Marie Boisselot' (an old patens hybrid) has very large, pure white flowers with yellow stamens. As with so many clematis, the character of the flower changes with the advancing season. It is the first flowers of the season that are so enormous. Later ones are smaller but still lovely and produced in such abundance as to hide the foliage. It is often cut right back each year but will flower very freely if not pruned. It will reach 10m (32ft) or more. The newer 'Sylvia Denny' is a clear white semi-double that never needs pruning. 'Miss Bateman' has flowers only half the size, 15cm (6in) at most, but exquisite in detail and has the bonus of a fragrance. The shapely flowers open white with a cream bar, but this fades leaving the flower pure white, with a jewel-like centre of reddish-brown stamens surrounded by pink filaments. It flowers from May till September and is particularly useful in the white garden because it grows to only

2.5m (8ft), and so can be allowed to grow over quite small shrubs without risk of spoiling them.

Quite different from these is 'Henryi', which sounds like a species but is actually a *lanuginosa* hybrid. Oddly, it actually looks rather like a species, for it has pointed white sepals and dark stamens, like *C. fortunei*. It flowers in May and June. *C. viticella* 'Alba Luxurians' is relatively small-flowered and produces double, greeny-white flowers which, like those of 'Henryi', have dark centres, from June till September. 'Jackmanii Alba' has probably the largest flowers of all the doubles, a full 15cm (6in) across. They are pure white version of 'Jackmanii' itself, which was the clematis that started the clematis craze of the nineteenth century. 'Gillian Blades' has flowers of much the same size, and single, but distinct because it has wavy edges to the sepals. 'Huldine' is a vigorous grower, producing flowers 10cm (4in) across, the sepals having incurved margins but reflexed tips, the upper surface white, the under surface pale amethystine mauve with a deeper central bar and greenish stamens. It is a lovely clematis that needs to be grown so that you look up into the flowers. Not all forms are equally good; you have to grow it to find out whether yours is.

There are, in addition, two clematis whose flowers are not white but which can be useful in those white gardens that lean towards yellow. 'Wada's Primrose' has yellow anthers at the heart of a cream-coloured single. 'Moonlight' is yellower, and has flowers of a beautiful shape. Both flower in May and June.

Jasmines are as famed for their fragrance as clematis are for lacking it. The only one that has a place in the white garden is *Jasminum officinale*, the common white jasmine, which produces its sprays of long-tubed, intensely fragrant white flowers from June till October. It is most often seen making a tangle of growth on a cottage wall, for which purpose it is well suited. In the white garden it might be best employed on an arbor where its fragrance would be a particular pleasure to those sitting beneath.

Jasmine-like in flower and fragrance are the trachelospermums. Two species are grown. *T. asiaticum* is the hardier. It has small, oval, dark, glossy green leaves and when well grown will cover a sunny wall as densely as ivy, bearing sprays of small creamy-white flowers with yellow anthers in July and August. *T. jasminoides* is a larger, laxer, less dense plant, more tender, especially when young. Its flowers are just as fragrant, but much whiter. *T.j. wilsonii* is a form with very narrow leaves that turn reddish in winter, and 'Variegatum' is a most prettily variegated form with white, green and grey leaves that flush pink and crimson in winter. A plant that appears to be a more vigorous form of *T. jasminoides* was named *T.j.* var. *pubescens* by Makino. It is probably the same as the cv. 'Japonicum' of the Riviera, and the *T. majus* of Nakai. All are well worth a place in the white garden. Usually they need a little training to get them to climb but once started they will cling to a wall like ivy.

Wattakaka sinensis may best briefly be described as a deciduous hoya. Its flowers are almost identical, white with pink spots, and deliciously fragrant. Its leaves rather let it down, for they are like those of runner beans. It is a vigorous climber, best grown on an arch or arbour so that its pendent flowers may be seen from beneath. It is certainly hardy in a mild climate and perhaps a colder one. It is an interesting climber, and its fragrance is remarkable and yet it is not showy and has never become widely planted.

The other great family of hardy climbers is the *Hydrangeaceae*, some of which have flowers surrounded by showy sterile florets: none is famed for its fragrance. The climbing hydrangea itself is *H. petiolaris*, which may be grown in sun or shade, up a tree such as an oak, when it will clothe the whole trunk and cover itself in flowers or run up a wall becoming arborescent as ivy does when it reaches the top and there flowering. The flower heads are composed of fertile flowers surrounded by a ring of showy white florets, the whole head being about 25cm (10in) across. Its peeling bark is foxy-red in winter. *H. anomala* is similar but the heads are domed in shape, not flat and the leaves are more coarsely toothed. Both will reach 12m (40ft) or more. They are perhaps too vigorous for most white gardens. The first is grown to great advantage on the garden wall at Sissinghurst.

In addition there are two evergreen climbing hydrangeas which though less well known can both in their different ways be useful in white gardens. *H. serratifolia*, which is also known contradictorily as *H. integerrima*, has tough, leathery, dull dark green leaves and short, dense panicles of fertile flowers which differ in colour very little from the leaves. Its use is for clothing unsightly walls with a fabric of matt greenery. Since it flowers when it reaches the top of the wall, the lower the wall the sooner it flowers. It looks handsome on the wall between the cedar and the tea rooms at Hidcote. *H. seemannii* is similar but its fertile flowers are surrounded by showy white sterile florets making it much more useful. Both will reach 15m (49ft) in conditions that suit them.

The schizophragmas are in effect merely highly-refined versions of the climbing hydrangeas. They differ chiefly in that whereas in the hydrangeas the showy sterile florets are in fours, in schizophragma they are single. Each bract is creamy-white, beautifully shaped and rather larger than those of the hydrangeas. *S. integrifolia* is the finer of the two species, a most aristocratic and showy plant, capable of climbing a tree to 10m (32ft) or more. *S. hydrangeoides* is similar but smaller in all its parts.

The Passion flower is often considered by those who have never grown it to be among the most desirable and beautiful of all flowers; indeed, the flowers are beautiful but more beautiful than usual in the form 'Constance Elliott', which has pure ivory white flowers. On the negative side the Passion flower is a rampant climber with a stoloniferous root system throwing up new stems in all directions.

If one wants a plant whose leaves make a real contribution to whiteness then one needs to turn to the ivies. Though they are usually considered hardy the Canary Isles ivy, *H. canariensis*, can be killed outright in a severe winter and be badly defoliated in one that is not so bad. It is sometimes confused with the other large-leafed ivy, the Persian ivy, *H. colchica*, but that has much thicker, rather leathery leaves. The variegated Canary Isles ivy is known as 'Gloire de Marengo'. The leaves are variegated grey and white on green and although the individual leaves are nothing special the overall effect of an established plant is most pleasing. It both looks best and grows best in a sheltered corner or courtyard. *H.c.* 'Margino-maculata' is a form whose leaves are speckled white all over but most intensely at the margins. It is a little more tender than 'Gloire de Marengo'. *H. colchica* has leathery leaves as much as 20cm (8in) long and nearly as wide though they always appear narrower because they roll back on themselves. The variegated form, *H.c.* 'Dentata Variegata' has leaves that are dramatically variegated cream in spring, the colour fading to more nearly white later in the season. It is a very dominant plant, too dominant to be merely a background, so if it is used at all, it should be used as a feature. It is hopeless to expect anything else to compete with it. There is also an arborescent form, which is hard to propagate, but equally dramatically variegated, and equally dominant.

Of the small leafed ivies, *Hedera helix*, our own favourite is 'Marginata-Major' and the reason we like it is that it branches freely, making a dense, even covering. Its leaves are rather square as compared with other *H.h.* forms, and the creamy-white variegation is mainly marginal. 'Ardingly' and 'Adam' are very similar.

The solanums belong here, though they do not so much climb walls as lean against them. They need the support of wires or trellis-work around which they will twine their petioles. Given such support, *S. jasminoides* will reach 6m (20ft) high. It can be an asset in a white garden, grown over a wall or resting on the roof of a pergola or summer house. Its leaves and stems make no attempt at beauty but its flowers, which are just like those of the potato, tomato or deadly nightshade, are produced in large flattened heads of 20 or so and are of a good bright white. Coming from southern Brazil the solanum is not especially hardy, though once established it will usually grow again from the base if the top is frosted.

GREYS AND SILVERS

In the making of white gardens there are two extremes which need to be avoided. The first is too much contrast; the second is too little. While yew hedges are the classic material with which to enclose a white garden they are almost too extreme in their darkness. The means usually adopted to moderate this extremity is grey and silver foliage, for white flowers look best with light colours. The second extreme, therefore, to avoid is overdoing the greys and silvers, thereby making the white garden too bland. In the planning of colour schemes in the garden a useful rule is always to use more of the darkest colour, less of the middling colour and least of the lightest colour. Expressing this as a ratio one might aim for green, grey and white in the ratio of 3:2:1.

The classic grey plant for all formal gardens, whether white or not is *Pyrus salicifolia* 'Pendula' which is discussed on page 49. An alternative is the Caspian oleaster, *Elaeagnus angustifolia* var. *caspica*, whose slender willowy leaves are silver and whose thorny branches have the bonus of producing tiny but powerfully scented flowers in June. It is amenable to being trained up into a tree on a single stem and can quickly reach 4 or 5m (13 or 17ft) though when happy it will grow to twice this size. It is sometimes likened to the weeping silver pear but differs most of all in the shimmering silvery brightness of its leaves. It is perhaps too bright for many for its very brightness can destroy a whole effect.

Euphorbia characias *with variegated honesty.*

At Tintinhull, silvers are used in a most interesting way to create symmetry in the white garden. At each corner, in the angles of the yew hedges behind the rest of the planting, are four silver willows, *Salix helvetica*. Such symmetry is always effective. The same plant, *S. helvetica*, is used in its more usual shrubby form in the white garden at York Gate, with the rather similar *S. lanata* on the opposite side. Both form small, quite dense bushes, about 1.2m (4ft) tall and across, with silver-grey leaves, oblanceolate in *S. helvetica*, almost round in *S. lanata*. Both produce good catkins in early spring. At the other extreme is the silver white willow, *S. alba* 'Sericea'. The white willow is a native of water meadows and river sides, and 'Sericea' only grows a little less large than the wild *S. alba*, its leaves intensely silvery. It is one of those trees that might be best planted outside the white garden, where it can be enjoyed from within.

The buddleias, which are discussed on page 123, also provide bulk and some greyness of leaf. *B. fallowiana* 'Alba' is the best, with white flowers and silvery-white felted leaves. *Berberis temolaica* will provide a similar volume of greyness but is more glaucous. Its stems grow upright, and then arch, and in spring the leaves are a veritable symphony of blue and white, harmonising perfectly with the lemon-yellow flowers. It grows to 3m (10ft) and can be as wide as tall. *B. dictophylla* is similar but smaller, with rounder leaves. It grows to 1.8m (6ft).

If one is looking for greys to furnish the white garden then three of the best are the euphorbias, the senecios (now *Brachyglottis*) and *Melianthus major*. It is the most exotic-looking foliage shrub, its slender stems producing huge grey-green pinnate leaves which are deeply serrated and beautifully poised. It is naturally a shrub but in colder regions it can be treated as a perennial and cut to the ground each winter. To achieve density, plant three or five a yard apart. *Brachyglottis*

'Sunshine' is about the most reliable and useful grey shrub for furnishing a white garden, provided you do not mind their yellow flowers, which of course can always be removed (for in the white garden there is endless scope for artfulness and titivation). 'Sunshine' varies quite a lot in regard of leaf size and colour. *B. compactus* is effectively a dwarf version of 'Sunshine', but much less hardy. *B. monroi* is similar but hardier, with unattractively wavy margins to the leaves.

It is to the euphorbias that one turns for the finest of all furnishing shrubs, *E. characias* and *wulfenii* (which lacks the purple eye of *E. characias*). What is so arresting and satisfying is the balance between verticals and horizontals in the leaf and stem patterns. The first year stems arise stiff and straight or slightly leaning, clothed all round like a bottle brush with narrow, grey-green leaves. At the beginning of their second year the tops of these erupt into large heads of gaudy-green, saucer-shaped bracts enclosing tiny almost black flowers after which the stem dies and is replaced by others. In many gardens they seed themselves about, and the seedlings often come up in the most fortuitous places. 'Lambrook Yellow' is a Margery Fish selection with bigger heads of yellower flowers. *E. myrsinites* is a useful front-of-the-border relative, sprawling over paving. Its flowers are a bit gambodian. *E. rigida* is like an erect-growing *myrsinites*, and forms a useful visual link between the 1.2m (4ft) *characias* and *myrsinites*. Both *E. rigida* and *E. myrsinites* are most effective used in groups.

Several good greys are what might loosely be called herbs. Rue, *Ruta graveolens*, is a genuine herb, but it is more usually encountered in gardens in the form 'Jackman's Blue' which is very blue indeed. It is problematical as to whether the blue is really desirable or whether the grey of the typical *R. graveolens* is going to be more effective. If blue is needed one is better off using

Mertensia ciliata or *M. asiatica*, both of which are intensely blue. *Hosta* 'Hadspen Blue', almost as intense, is for shaded places, being merely grey in full sun. Such plants are quite acceptable in white gardens that lean towards pink, for the pink has an underlying blue tone. But in a white garden that leans towards the gaudy-green of feverfew and golden hop it would create cacophony among the colours.

One or two artemisias are true herbs though they are the ones least likely to be used in the white garden. The finest for white gardens is *A. canescens* which has extremely finely-cut leaves which create a filigree effect, of brightest silvery-greyness. It grows to 45cm (18in) and its flowers are greyish-yellow, most inoffensive. It is lovely with regal lilies poking through it, or at the feet of white roses. *A. stelleriana*, the dusty miller, has deeply divided grey-white leaves and forms clumps or patches of silver. *A. schmidtiana* 'Nana' is a useful dwarf, growing 5–10cm (2–4in) tall and making a low silvery carpet of soft finely-cut foliage. It is lovely spilling out across paving. *A.* 'Powys Castle' is a giant among artemisias, reaching 1.4m (3½ft) high and across, but most beautiful in its finely-cut silvery foliage. It never flowers which on the whole is a good thing but will need replacing after a few years. *A. ludoviciana* has slender stems and willow-like, silvery-grey-white leaves. It runs energetically at the root and forms thickets, giving one the winter chore of cutting it back to size.

The sages are also culinary herbs, though the culinary one is not especially grey, but valuable in its white-flowered form. Far more silvery is its diminutive relative *S. lavandulifolia*, a low-growing plant to 30cm (12in) or less, but spreading by rooting at its elbows and in time making good weed-proof mats. Its flowers, produced in May, are acceptable in a garden where you also admit blues and pinks, but need to be removed in a garden of white, grey and gaudy-green. Far more silver

and far more difficult to grow are *Salvia argentea* and the very similar *S. aethiopis*. In their first year they form a rosette of large leaves, like elephant's ears, of silvery-grey covered in fine white hairs. In their second year they throw up great candelabras 1m (3ft) tall of white flowers set in grey-white calyces. To grow these salvias you need perfect drainage.

Lavender and santolina are often lumped together as herbs, presumably because of their aromatic foliage. The brightest, most silvery-grey is that of *Lavendula spica* 'Seal'. It is a largish lavender making bushes of about 1m × 1m (3ft × 3ft) with long spikes of pale but very blue flowers. There are two white-flowered lavenders, of which 'Alba' is the larger, growing to 1m × 1m (3ft × 3ft). It flowers in late July. 'Nana Alba' grows to 30cm (12in) and flowers a fortnight earlier. Santolina, or lavender cotton, is grown for its densely-packed silvery foliage which is very pungent when bruised. Plants are variously called *S. chamaecyparissus*, *incana* or *neapolitana*. All are sadly let down by their flowers which are a frightful bright yellow. However, *S.n.* 'Sulphurea' has pale, primrose yellow flowers and 'Edward Bowles' has flowers that are cream and could pass for white if grown near enough to the gaudy-green of golden feverfew or something similar.

Phlomis is known as Jerusalem sage and like true sage it is a labiate; with the typical flowers of its family, but bright yellow, perhaps a little too bright for the white garden, though its triangular soft grey leaves are perfect for it. Usually ranked as a small shrub, in a favoured corner it will run up 2m (7ft) tall and as much across. *P. chrysophylla* differs in having yellowish foliage, which makes it useful in a white garden where one might otherwise use the lime-yellow of feverfew. *P. italica* is smaller in stature, reaching 60cm (2ft) or so. Its leaves are more

Onopordum acanthium *at Tintinhull.*

(Opposite) A white incident: Phlox 'Norah Leigh' *and the silken seed heads of honesty.* York Gate.

sage-like in shape, very silvery, and its flowers are mauvey, putting it very much in the pink-white garden. It is less hardy than the other two.

Two more edible plants with fine silvery foliage are the wild sea cabbage, *Crambe maritima*, and the globe artichoke, *Cynara scolymus*. The sea cabbage has thick and strangely-rubbery leaves, each about 30cm (12in) long, beautifully curved and lobed. In colour they are similar to those of rue, more blue than grey. It throws up large, diffuse heads of white flowers in June. The globe artichoke, and its sister the cardoon, are especially valuable silvers as they will thrive in heavy clay where most greys and silvers perish. Both have superbly architectural foliage and are so massive that they need to be used as feature plants, perhaps filling a corner. The globe artichoke is essentially a giant grey-leafed but very sophisticated thistle, as its flowers reveal. Its huge, finely-cut, arching leaves build up into a great pile as much as 1.8m (6ft) tall and 2m (7ft) across. The foliage stays in better heart longer if the flowers are removed. The cardoon is *Cynara cardunculus*, and it is more silver than grey. Its leaves can be 1.2m (4ft) long, making it 2.4m (8ft) across at ground level, too large for all but the very largest gardens. It sends up in thistle fashion tall leafy silver stems at the top of which are borne huge thistle heads of rich mauvey-purple. Both should be planted in spring in well-manured ground in a sunny site, and in the autumn their decaying leaves should be removed otherwise invasions of slugs will eat the growing shoots. For those who do not have enough space for these there is the Scots thistle, *Onopordum acanthium*, and the very similar *O. arabicum*. Both have intensely silver-grey leaves, and both are biennial and monocarpic, reliably producing abundant seed. The leaves are spine-tipped, and in their first year build up into a fine rosette from the midst of which, in the second

year, a tall leafy stem arises 2.4m (8ft) or more, topped with a typical mauve thistle-head. These huge thistles are so eye-catching they need to be used with care and not over done. Because of their sheer size, and also being midway between the extremes of dark green and white, they link them.

At the other extreme are the indispensable, diminutive silverlings that clothe the front edge of the white garden and spill over on to paving. The most universally used of these is lambs' lugs, *Stachys byzantina* (*S. lanata*), a plant whose sprawling stems produce mats of silver-furry ear-like leaves at ground level, and spikes of rather insipid mauve flowers in summer. It grows 30–45cm (12–18in) tall. 'Silver Carpet' is a clone that rarely flowers, and grows to only 20cm (8in). 'Primrose Heron' is a pale yellow-leafed version of *byzantina*, the colour fading to the usual grey by autumn. 'Variegata' is liked by some: its leaves are irregularly splashed creamy-white. There is also a giant silver-leafed form, with leaves three times as large as usual, that was known, until the Index Hortensis corrected the errors of our naming, as *S. olympica* but is now no longer differentiated nomenclaturally by any name at all. It grows to 60cm (2ft). It is a suitable carpet to set beneath large, coarse plants such as acanthus, veratrums, and the stronger-growing philadelphus. With all these grey carpeters it is helpful to the harmony of the garden to repeat them like a pattern, but not quite regularly. Thus in a long straight border there might be four clumps of lambs' lugs; the gap between the first clump and the second and the second and the third might be the same, x, but the gap between the third and the fourth only half x. The first, third and fourth clumps might each be 1m (3ft) long, but the second clump 2m (7ft) long. Clumps of irises could be placed to the right of the first lambs' lugs but to the left of the third and fourth, thereby weaving a recursive rhythm on one original theme. The

whole of this foreground pattern should relate to the planting behind it. There could perhaps be rose 'Francine' behind and to the right of the irises by the first clump of lambs' lugs, and behind and between the two iris clumps behind the third and fourth lambs' lugs, with three roses 'Iceberg' equally spaced behind them at the back of the border. Such repetitions are far more satisfying than trying one of everything all round the border. As with music, a theme needs to be stated and then variations on that theme played around the garden, using all a composer's skills of inversion and reversion and recombination.

There are other foreground silverlings that can be similarly used. *Artemisia schmidtiana* 'Nana', already mentioned, is one of the loveliest, but *Tanacetum densum* 'Amani' (*Chrysanthemum haradjanii*) is easier. It has tiny leaves, like short, almost round, feathers, of a clear, clean silver, and it grows to only 15cm (6in) at most. To make any impact with it at all several plants need to be set out at 10cm (4in) intervals. They will then grow together into a respectable carpet. It needs full sun and gritty, well-drained soil. Its flowers are yellow and just like groundsel. *Cerastium tomentosum*, on the other hand, is almost too easy to grow and too invasive. It is commonly known as snow-in-summer, and makes a carpet of small grey leaves over which showers of white flowers appear in May and June. It is an ideal plant to use to suppress weeds in a newly-planted white garden, and being only surface-rooting is easily pulled up when the need arises. *Anthemis cupaniana* is another easy carpeter, though on heavy soils it may succumb to winter wet. It has very finely divided silvery-grey leaves and masses of 2.5cm (½in) wide, white daisy flowers all through the summer. It grows to 30cm (12in), and spreads slowly but indefinitely.

Achillea 'Moonshine' is a cross between *A. taygeta* and *A. clypeolata*, and the result is a plant with lovely feathery silver foliage and pale ochrous yellow flowers that fit easily into a white garden. It grows to 60cm (2ft) tall and goes well with plants with glossy green leaves, crinums, for example, or the indispensable *Choisya ternata*.

The lamiums, though lower-growing, never seem to be foreground plants, but suitable rather for covering the ground under other plants, or for a dark corner in a courtyard. The typical *Lamium maculatum* (which has dark green leaves with a white central stripe) has mauvey-pink flowers; 'Album' has white flowers; 'Beedhams White' is a brighter white. 'Silver Beacon' has smaller leaves that are silver except for a green margin, but the typical puce flowers; 'Nancy's White', introduced by Nancy Lindsay in the early 60s, has the same leaves as 'Silver Beacon' but white flowers and is most desirable. The pulmonarias are another group of plants that by and large seem more suited to background than foreground. *P. saccharata* 'Argentea' has the typically scabrid, tongue-shaped leaves, about 20 × 10cm (8 × 4in), but silver-grey, with only the margin green. It is most pleasing in foliage but sadly let down by its flowers which are pink turning through mauves to blue and usually showing all three colours at the same time, making it difficult to use in a white garden. Several of the dicentras similarly let one down by having flowers of a difficult shade of pink, but *D. formosa* 'Alba' has lovely blue leaves and white flowers (see page 83). Most hostas suffer a similar defect in flower, and suitably glaucous grey varieties are discussed above.

The hebes are not to everybody's taste, but *H. pinguifolia* 'Pagei' is a useful carpet-forming shrublet of neat and controllable growth. It has tiny glaucous leaves arranged in four ranks on slender prostrate stems, and it produces in early summer short spikes of small whitish flowers. It is not in the first rank of plants, but easy and useful. *H. albicans* 'Prostrata' is similar but larger in all its parts.

The thymes are even smaller and neater, but though several have good grey foliage, their crimson-magenta flowers are difficult to handle in a white garden and so the genus is perhaps best passed over. *Anaphalis triplinervis* presents no such problems, having grey leaves and everlasting white flowers, in spite of which it fails to be attractive. It can however be useful between shrubs in the white garden as it will withstand some shade and actually likes to grow in fairly moist soil. It reaches 30–40cm (12–16in) in height and tends to get leggy if grown in too much shade and shelter.

There are several other suitable greys which we have discussed elsewhere; several potentillas have greyish leaves, as do most bearded irises and most pinks; the leptospermums are discussed under shrubs, as are the various cistus.

We have left the loveliest silverling till last; *Convolvulus cneorum*. It makes a dense but relaxed plant with silver willow-like leaves on slender stems and produces, throughout much of the summer, typical convolvulus flowers of purest whiteness within, stained pink on the outside, like a regal lily. It is one of those rare plants in which leaf, and flower and plant form seem to come together in perfect balance. It should be grown in every white garden that can give it sharp drainage and full sun.

TREES AND SHRUBS

Most white gardens are in themselves too small to contain trees of any size, though there will often be space enough for small, shrubby trees or, as at Tintinhull, formal representations of trees. Yet there is often scope to plant trees outside a white garden that can be seen and enjoyed from within the white garden, as is the case at Hazelby House.

For such a purpose flowering cherries

would be ideal, especially the great white cherry, 'Tai-haku' which produces its very large, pure white single flowers in staggering profusion in mid to late April, just as the leaves are beginning to unfurl. It is ultimately a big tree, up to 12m (40ft) with spreading branches making a rounded head. 'Washi-no-o' is similar but inferior, with smaller, slightly scented flowers. 'Jo-nioi' is similar but not quite so vigorous, its single flowers deliciously scented, contrasting well with purple-brown sepals. It flowers in mid to late April, and its new leaves are pale green. 'Taki-noi' is in effect a later-flowering version of the same thing, though its flowers are a little smaller, but strongly honey-scented, and the emerging leaves coppery-red. It is one of the last cherries to flower, its season being early to mid May, just when the white garden should be coming into its best.

All of the foregoing have flowers that tend towards pinkness but there are three cherries in which the flowers are decidedly yellowish. The best known of these is 'Ukon', quite distinct in its colour from other cherries, and also in its spreading, flat-topped habit. Its flowers are semi-double and are borne in late April, 'Asagi' has paler flowers, and might be more suitable for associating with a white garden. It flowers two weeks earlier than 'Ukon'. 'Gyoike' ('Gioike') flowers later than 'Ukon' and has more upright branches. Its flowers are semi-double, creamy-white, streaked green and tinged pink. It used to be called 'Tricolor' which speaks volumes, and is the least useful of the three.

There is a number of cherries which might be grown within the white garden itself. *P. serrula* is sometimes called the Chippendale cherry because it has the most beautiful bark in the world; it peels in horizontal bands to reveal a stem of purest, polished mahogany. It is also distinct on account of its narrow, willowy, greyish, finely-toothed leaves; its flowers are small, white and fortunately fleeting. *P. tibetica* is similar, or possibly the same. *P. mume* is the Japanese apricot, and the popular forms have very double flowers that look as though they are made of icing sugar. They are tightly buttoned on to long, straight whippy green stems and the combination of stems and flowers tends to look rather artificial (which can be fine in a formal white garden). 'Alba' has usually single white flowers; 'Alboplena' has longer-lasting double white flowers; 'O-moi-no-wae' has mostly double white flowers, but the occasional flower – or occasional petals – may be pink, which can make the white seem even whiter. *P. tenella* is the dwarf Russian almond, and it makes a low, slowly suckering bush seldom more than 1m (3ft) high. The form 'Alba' produces pure white, starry flowers on the bare stems in March or April. Sadly it now seems rare.

The cherries, for all their legendary loveliness, are only briefly beautiful. In leaf and habit of growth they are mostly utterly undistinguished. The magnolias, by comparison, are aristocrats, of some interest at most seasons, having usually bold leaves, and interesting winter buds. Several of the precocious sorts would be excellent for growing outside the white garden. *Magnolia* x *soulangiana* is the name given to a group of hybrids originally raised at Fromont near Paris by M. Soulange-Bodin a high-ranking army officer who, sick of the Napoleonic wars, decided to retire and spend the rest of his days breeding these beautiful plants. They produce narrowly cup-shaped flowers on their bare branches, usually in April, and they tend to grow into huge bushes, rather than real trees, though if the lower branches are gradually removed they will become arborescent in time, as at Sissinghurst. *M.* x *s.* 'Alba Superba' is white, with highly-scented flowers which are produced a fortnight later than those of *M. denudata*, which was one of its parents. It is quite upright in growth.

Borrowed scenery at Knightshayes. White flowering cherries might be used in this way beyond the boundary of the white garden.

M. x s. 'Lennei Alba' has larger, fatter flowers, like enormous goblets, produced in March and April. It is the most vigorous of the white *soulangiana*, making a very large, multi-stemmed bush. *M. denudata* is a superb magnolia with pure white flowers similar to those of the *soulangiana* but produced two weeks earlier in consequence of which they are usually ruined by frost. *M. kobus* becomes in time, a real tree with a single trunk. It opens its flowers wider than the *soulangiana*, and also appears to have more petals; it is regarded by botanists as merely a tree-like form of the familiar star magnolia, *M. stellata*. It has neat, small leaves. *M. salicifolia*, the willow-leafed magnolia, is similar in its small leaves, but its flowers are a little smaller though produced in the most enormous quantities in April, on leafless boughs. The flowers (and wood) are lemon-scented.

M. x loebneri is another group of hybrid magnolias created by crossing *M. stellata* with *M. kobus*. They grow with good speed when young and at first make narrow, upright trees, but spread with age, becoming as wide as tall. Several clones are available: 'Snowdrift' is one of the original seedlings, but 'Merrill' may be better with larger more fragrant white flowers. Finest of all is 'Wada's Memory' (which looks similar but may in fact be an *M. kobus* x *salicifolia* hybrid). Its flowers are larger and more fragrant than those of 'Snow-drift' or 'Merrill', pure white and produced unfailingly in great abundance.

119

By contrast there are three lovely magnolias which are really suitable for inclusion in the white garden itself. The first of these is *M. stellata*, a low-growing, compact rounded shrub that completely covers itself in March and April with pure white flowers composed of many strap-shaped petals. 'Water Lily' is a form that was selected in Japan and which has larger flowers with more petals. 'Royal Star' is more compact and has even larger flowers. The second is *M. wilsonii* which is not precocious but flowers with its leaves in May and June. The flowers are saucer shaped, with conspicuous rosy-crimson anthers and pink sepals and a fragrance that with fill an entire white garden, which is the main reason for growing it. It makes a thin shrub, narrow when young, more spreading with age. *M. sinensis* is similar but larger in all its parts and on the whole rather coarser. The third is *M. virginiana* which is a variable plant and makes a small tree or large, leggy shrub evergreen or semi-evergreen, the leaves glossy sea-green above and glaucous or almost white beneath. The flowers are smaller than those of most magnolias, creamy-white and intensely fragrant, produced from June till September. The glaucous overall appearance of some clones makes it eminently suitable for a far corner of a white garden, in the angle where dark yew hedges meet. It needs full sun to flower freely. 'Havener' is a selected clone with double flowers, and 'Hensel' has large flowers and fruits freely.

M. virginiana has been crossed with the swamp bay, *M. grandiflora*, to produce *M.* x 'Freeman' and *M.* x 'Maryland'. Both have the glossy evergreen leaves of the swamp bay, though smaller, and flowers like the swamp bay. Of the two, 'Maryland' is free-flowering and forms a rounded bush. Like *M. grandiflora* itself it can gradually be trained up into a small round-headed tree. *M.* x 'Freeman' forms a narrow columnar tree so that it would fit into a relatively small space, but it suffers

the defect that its flowers never open properly so that even a large plant appears to be covered with buds but never with flowers. Of the *M. grandiflora*s the new 'Samuel Sommer' is reputed to have the largest flowers of all; 'Goliath' also has very large flowers and big, rounded leaves with a distinct twist to them; 'Exmouth' and 'Ferruginea' both have leaves with rusty-red felt beneath them. All are suitable for growing outside a white garden where in time they will make rounded domes appearing above the hedge tops, though they would take time to reach the necessary height. *M.* 'Little Gem' is entirely different and suitable for growing inside the white garden. It is narrowly upright, almost formal in outline, and has small leaves and flowers like the typical swamp bays.

Given the free run of an uncluttered site, the ideal tree with which to surround a white garden would be catalpas, for their large, limp, pale green heart-shaped leaves and their rounded heads make them the perfect complement to the straight lines of formal yew hedges. The best species is *C. bignonioides*, the Indian bean tree. It is always one of the last plants in the garden to put on its leaves, usually as late as May and then in July and August it produces its flowers, in upright spikes like those of the horse chestnut, but more refined for the individual flowers are shaped like those of the foxglove, pure white with purple spots and delicately scented. These are followed by long bean-like pods which remain on the tree long after the leaves have fallen. *C.b.* 'Aurea' is a slow-growing form with lovely golden leaves that could be ideal beyond the hedges of a white garden with a lot of limey-green.

Halesia carolina is known as the snowdrop tree from the fancied resemblance of its flowers to those of galanthus. It is merely an overgrown shrub. The only species which is really tree-like is *H. monticola* which forms a clean stem and gets its branches up high enough for its snowdrop-like flowers to be seen from below. The variety *H.m. vestita* is reputed to have larger flowers. The genus *Styrax* is closely related and produces very similar flowers. Both *S. hemsleyana* and *S. obassia* are sufficiently treelike to use beyond the hedges of a white garden.

There are surprisingly few shrubs that are actually floriferous enough for inclusion in the white garden, bearing in mind that the aim is effectiveness: shrubs that are merely charming may not contribute enough. In the first rank of free-flowering white shrubs are the mock oranges, philadelphus, all of which are white-flowered, deciduous and extremely hardy. Our own favourite is 'Belle Etoile' partly because the crimson blotch at the base of each petal is more interesting than the unrelieved whiteness of some mock orange flowers, and partly because the flowers are rather bell-shaped, later opening more nearly flat, and partly because it has the finest fragrance in the genus. It grows at most to 1.8m (6ft) 'Beauclerk', which was raised by the Hon Lewis Palmer at Headbourne Worthy (the home of hardy agapanthus) from a cross between 'Burfordensis' and 'Sybille', attains similar dimensions but has flowers that are flushed pink at the base, with lovely yellow anthers at the centre. The fragrance is almost as good. It won an FCC in 1951, as well as an AM in 1947 and an AGM in 1957. 'Sybille', one of its parents is often rated the best mock orange for small gardens. It grows to 1.2m (4ft) but is of spreading habit, reaching as much as 2m (7ft) across. It has a graceful habit of growth and is notably free-flowering. The individual flowers are as much as 5cm (2in) across, very fragrant, the petals fringed and stained purplish-rose at the base. 'Bouquet Blanc' and 'Alabastie' both grow to much the same height, but are less spreading. 'Alabastie' has fragrant double flowers in July, and 'Bouquet Blanc' has semi-double to almost single flowers with far less scent. 'Manteau

d'Hermine' is a true drawf, attaining only 75–90cm (30–35in), and very compact. Its flowers are creamy-white and fragrant, and it is useful towards the front of a border. The twigs are of a reddish-brown that can be attractive in winter. The reason for the French names is that most of the mock oranges grown in gardens were bred by Victor Lemoine of Nancy in the early years of this century. All these will grow in any fertile soil, preferably in sun, and flower most freely if pruned annually. Pruning consists of removing the shoots which have flowered, cutting them off right down at the base of the plant. This leaves the whippy unbranched young growth to flower the following season.

The genus deutzia is closely related to philadelphus from which it is separated by some small but crucial botanical details. From a garden point of view it flowers earlier, in June and July. Most deutzias are fairly upright in habit, though spreading when in flower. They need the same general conditions and treatment as philadelphus. One of the best is *D. compacta* which makes a densely compact shrub up to 1.8m (6ft) with peeling bark on its main stems. Its flowers are creamy-white, borne in large, flat heads. The clone now called 'Magnifica' was the original cross of the deutzias known as *D. x magnifica*, and it is the best of the group. It has double white flowers. *D. x M.* 'Latiflora' has the largest flowers in the genus, some 2.5cm (1 in) across, single, white, borne in very large clusters. Both grow to about 2.8m (9ft). There are two dwarf deutzias, both useful at the front of the border. 'Boule de Neige' one of the *D.* x *lemoinei* group, grows to 90cm (3ft) and has large, pure white flowers in dense clusters. 'Dwarf Nikko' is almost prostrate growing no more than 30cm (12in) tall, its branches lying flat on the ground and rooting where they lie, gradually making a ground cover. The starry white flowers are produced in clusters.

Carpentaria californica when happy is as

showy and lovely as the mock oranges to which it is very closely related, but it needs a hot, sunny site at the south foot of a good hedge or wall to flower really freely and is seldom successful in the open garden.

The genus cistus contains very many of the finest and most suitable plants for the white garden, the species and hybrids being in the very first rank of white plants. Their flowers are somewhat rose-like, usually white, though in some sorts there is a yellow stain to the petal which together with the abundance of stamens at the centre of the flower can give it from a distance a yellowish appearance. Others have a crimson blotch at the bottom of the petal and such varieties are more suitable in white gardens that lean towards pink. All produce their flowers in June and July at which season they cover themselves in blossom. Yet each flower opens for only a few hours in the morning, making it unsuitable for gardens which open their gates to visitors only in the afternoon. Few are wholly hardy. They all do best in light, dry soil in full sun and they never suffer from drought. There seems to be little agreement as to which species are hardy, which probably shows how critical cultural conditions are. There are surprisingly few species, but they all interbreed, so there are many hybrids. Among the hardiest are *C. laurifolius* and *C. ladanifer*. The first makes a rounded shrub about 2m (7ft) high with leathery, dark green leaves, lighter beneath, and white flowers with a yellow centre. The second is a taller, narrow plant with lance-shaped leaves and 10cm (4in) flowers with crinkled petals with a chocolate stain at the base. 'Elma' is a hardy and floriferous hybrid raised by 'Cherry' Ingram at Benenden. It has 8cm (3in) pure white flowers produced with great freedom. *C. creticus*, a pink-flowered species, is another

(Opposite) Cistus and helianthemum at Hazelby House.

generally regarded as hardy. It has a lovely white form, 'Albus' which is just as hardy. *C. canescens* 'Albus' is a hybrid between this and *C. albidus* with grey leaves and white flowers, a lovely combination for a white garden. *C. hirsutus* and *C. libanotis* are both dwarf, compact species. The first has white flowers with yellow stamens, the second small plain white flowers. *C. populifolius* is another hardy species. It is of dense, erect growth, ideal for a small white garden, and has small, hairy leaves and white flowers stained yellow at the base. *C.p. lasiocalyx* is a subform with larger, wavy flowers and a showy inflated calyx. It may be even hardier.

One of the most effective and enchanting shrubby combinations in the white garden is achieved by growing cistuses with helianthemums at their feet, for the flowers of the latter are perfect miniatures of the former. They are in fact botanically very close and are separated merely by the differing numbers of valves on the capsules. They both enjoy the same cultural conditions. There are two well-known white helianthemums. The first is 'The Bride', which is a low, compact, small-growing variety with grey leaves and flowers that are white with a yellow blotch, perfectly imitating, but in miniature, such cistuses as *hirsutus*, *laurifolius* and *laxus*, at whose feet it should be grown. The other is 'Wisely White' a vigorous variety forming large patches. It has silver-grey leaves and rather bland, plain white flowers; it is better used with plain white cistuses than those with a dark blotch on the petal.

One of the great features of the gardens at Chenies Manor near Amersham in Buckinghamshire is a show of white buddleias grown up as standards. The effect is dramatic. There are several buddleias with which one could do this, all forms of the familiar *B. davidii*. The least interesting is *B.d. alba* which occurs in the wild: it is rather small-flowered. *B.d.* 'White Profusion' has large spikes of yellow-eyed flowers; 'White Bouquet' is exceptionally fragrant, but again has flowers with yellow eyes; 'White Cloud' has pure white flowers in very dense spikes. *B.d. nanhoensis* is a dwarf form introduced by Farrer from Kansu. It grows 1 to 1.5m (3 to 5ft). There is a most desirable white form. All need to be grown in sun, in good soil, and pruned really hard in winter, almost down to ground level.

The plant originally called *Syringa sempervirens* forms an evergreen shrub about 2m (7ft) high, usually dense and rounded with rounded, polished, dark green leaves which are larger in warmer localities, smaller in colder ones but usually about 5cm (2in) long. Its fragrant flowers are creamy-white, produced in spikes just like those of the lilac but smaller, though if grown in sun they are produced most plentifully. This particular combination of white flowers and dark evergreen foliage at this time of year is most effective. The plant is now called *Parasyringa sempervirens*, though it is in fact almost certainly a privet – ligustrum – a very closely related genus of which at least one other member makes a pretty white garden plant. This is *Ligustrum henryi*, a dainty bush with small, dark evergreen leaves, no more than 2.5cm (½ in) long and highly polished. It produces scented white, lilac-like flowers in August, on spikes as much as 15cm (6in) long. It makes a dense shrub, prettiest when young. Its leaves are as dark as those of yew. *L. quihoui* is one of the last hardy shrubs to flower, producing panicles of white flowers in October, at the same time as *Leucanthamella serotina* and *Aster tradescantii* and suitable for grouping with them. Its panicles can be as much as 50cm (20in) long and in its season it is the prettiest shrub there is. Its leaves are narrow, dull green and not very distinguished.

Escallonia is another useful genus of glossy-leafed evergreens, several of which could be effective in the white garden. The best known is *E*. 'Iveyi', which originated as chance seedlings at Caerhays Castle in Cornwall where they were found growing between plants of *E*. x *exoniensis* and *E. bifida* by one of the gardeners, a Mr Ivey. It has large, glossy, toothed leaves and big rounded clusters of white flowers, the clusters as much as 15cm (6in) long, produced mainly in July and August but intermittently both earlier and later. The hybrid 'Donard White' is much hardier, and grows to only 1.5 to 1.8m (5 to 6ft) tall. Its white flowers have very conspicuous golden-yellow anthers, giving the flower a distinct yellowish tang. *E. virgata* is the deciduous escallonia. It bears very small leaves on arching branches and produces its clusters of flowers on short spurs. In many ways it resembles *Leptospermum scoparium*. It is very hardy.

The hardiest of the white flowered leptospermums is *L. humifusum*, a Tasmanian species, with slender snaking stems and tiny, round-tipped leaves and flowers 1.3cm (¼ in) across. It forms low, rounded hummocks, with its outer branches spreading over the ground. It is useful where it can be allowed to tumble over a wall or spread out across paving. *Leptospermum cunninghamii* and *L. lanigerum* are particularly useful in the white garden for in addition to crowds of white flowers in May and June they have intensely silver leaves. They are shrubs of upright habit, but in summer the sheer weight of the flowers causes the branches to splay open. *L. grandiflorum* has the largest flowers of any species, as much as 7.5cm (3in) across. It is a tall, fast-growing species, with grey but not intensely grey leaves. These three species are certainly hardy in the mild areas. *L. scoparium* is much more tender, but contains two named double white forms, 'Leonard Wilson' and 'Album Flore-pleno', and these are so beautiful that they would be worth growing in pots under glass to stand out in the white garden in summer, especially if the white garden is a courtyard.

Equally suitable for growing in pots to stand out in summer are the tender scented white rhododendrons. These were beloved of the Victorians who raised them in great quantities and regularly exhibited them at the shows of the Royal Horticultural Society. They were frequently awarded First Class Certificates but sadly, the details of these award winners were so inadequately recorded that at this distance in time it is scarcely possible to sort one from another. The other problem is that in those days FCCs were given to grexes, not clones, so that the quality of some of the plants offered quite legitimately as the FCC form is very indifferent. They all have large, lily-like flowers, usually tinged yellow in the throat with a faint pink stripe on the outside, like a regal lily, but their greatest glory is their scent, perhaps more powerful and pervasive than that of any other plant we grow. Their problem is that they are all lanky, leggy, straggly shrubs, epiphytes in the wild and they need to be pinched out severely to make them bushy. If this is done, and they are pinched out rather than being allowed to flower for their first five years, the plant will then be much more floriferous than if left to its own devices. They should be grown in a freely-draining compost, and should be watered freely and given weekly liquid feeds from March till August, after which watering should be drastically reduced. They should be given no water at all from November till March. Of the species both *Rhs. edgeworthii* and *bullatum* have been awarded FCCs. *Rh. maddenii*, which is more powerfully scented, only won an AM, as did *Rhs. crassum* and *polyandrum* and *formosum*. *Rh. crassum* has the bonus of large thick leaves, and flowers later than the others, in June. *Rh. rhabdotum* is the flashiest of the group, with large trumpet-shaped white flowers striped like pyjamas on the outside. *Rh. dalhousie* is exquisite, with buds of a curiously unripe green, the flowers opening warm white, stained at

the throat with iced mint. It has produced two hybrids, which should be avoided: 'Henryanum' with inferior flowers, and 'Countess of Haddington' is too bud-tender to bother with.

The deciduous azaleas are merely rhododendrons that lose their leaves in winter. Oddly, they can be used quite successfully in formal gardens and settings, especially the smaller flowered species and their hybrids. For the white garden one is better off with, for example, *Rh. viscosum* and its forms, known in America as the swamp honeysuckle. Typically it has small white tubular flowers and a heavy and pervasive fragrance; var. *nitidum* has shiny instead of matt leaves, and var. *glaucophyllum* has intensely grey leaves; var. *aemulans* will grow in much drier ground than the other forms, which are all natives of swampy places. *Rh. arborescens* has an intense heliotrope scent, perhaps even more pervasive than that of *Rh. viscosum*. It can grow to as much as 5m (17ft), but takes time to get there. White-flowered forms usually have crimson anthers protruding from the mouth of the flower. The *viscosum* forms and *arborescens* flower in July and August, and they, together with some of the later flowering *atlanticum* forms, make lovely companions for the old gallica roses, Pemberton's hybrid musks and the New English roses from David Austin. 'Whitethroat' has dainty, double, pure white flowers, but no scent.

The evergreen azaleas present other problems. Normally they are thrown together in undisciplined howls of colour (when they are ravishingly effective if used in schemes of for example only pink and white). The secret is to use the azaleas with restraint; only one variety in one white garden. 'Palestrina' is unique, with its white flowers flushed green at the centre: it grows about 1.2m (4ft) tall, and flowers in May. 'Kure-no-yuki', which is sometimes called 'Snowflake' is one of the original Wilson 50. Its flowers are white,

Pleached limes at Sissinghurst: initial training.

Pleached lime walk at Mottisfont in Hampshire. The squares at the feet of the trees are filled in spring with chionodoxa.

slightly tinged green, and its habit of growth is very dwarf and compact. The Gumpos are hardy forms of *Rh. simsii* (the houseplant azalea). 'Gumpo White' has very large flowers produced in July. Some of the newer Glen Dale hybrids are also excellent and very hardy: 'Polar Sea', which has frilled petals, is outstanding. 'Gardenia' is fully double, low-growing and only suitable for a very formal white garden.

The plants most often used to provide colour in rhododendron gardens once the rhododendrons are over are the hydrangeas, though the best whites are to be found among the lesser known sorts. A first choice for a white garden is a form of *H. quercifolia* called 'Snowflake'. *H. quercifolia* itself is the oak-leaf hydrangea, so called for its large leaves which have a fancied resemblance to those of the oak. 'Snowflake' has huge heads of very long lasting, double flowers, also white with green shadows. It likes rich, moist soil, and is usually grown in shade, though it would probably flower more freely in sun. It has the best autumn colour of all hydrangeas. Another singularly good hydrangea for the white garden is *H. arborescens* 'Annabelle' which has toothed, plain green, almost round leaves and produces in July and August huge, almost spherical heads of showy sterile flowers that are individually quite small but which together are highly effective. It needs to be pruned hard every winter to produce these huge flower heads, and if so pruned remains a small shrub 1 or 1.5m (3–5ft) tall at most. Left to its own devices it will struggle up to 3m (10ft) and produce ever smaller flower heads. *H. paniculata*, if treated in the same way, will produce the showiest flower heads of all hydrangeas. The finest form is *H.p.* 'Grandiflora', and if this is planted in a prepared hole to which liberal quantities of farmyard manure have been added, and the number of shoots is reduced in spring, when they are about 60cm (2ft) tall, to six or eight, then the pyramidal flower heads may be 45cm (18in) long. The best effects are achieved with several plants grown together.

The lacecap hydrangeas have heads composed of fertile flowers surrounded by a ring of showy sterile flowers and while in some varieties these sterile flowers may be of a good whiteness, the fertile ones are always coloured, either palest blue or palest pink, depending on the acidity of the soil. Only one is really white enough for the white garden and this is 'Whitewave'. Its flower head is rather flat, the centre typically palest blue or pink, surrounded by about eight very large sterile flowers of a pearly white: the overall effect is white. It grows to about 1.5m (5ft), and makes a rounded and well-furnished shrub. The only other contender, 'Lanarth White', also has white sterile flowers – a very pure white at that – but the fertile flowers are more strongly coloured, so that the overall

effect is of blue and white or pink and white heads, and this could still be acceptable in the white garden. It seldom grows to more than 1m (3ft), which makes it most useful in small white gardens. 'Veitchii' grows to 2m (7ft) and its white flowers go quite a strong pink in sunlight, or bright green in shade, making it much less suitable.

The mop-head hydrangeas, properly called hortensias to celebrate a lady whose identity has now been lost, were originally bred for use in the conservatory or as houseplants, which is how they should really be used even now, for most of them are tender except in the mildest areas. They are perhaps acceptable in town gardens, preferably in tubs or large terracotta pots, or beside the sea where they flourish as nowhere else. The best white is 'Mme E. Mouilliere' which was bred by Messrs Mouilliere of Vendome out of 'Whitewave' and *H. rosea*. It grows best and is whitest in shade. It will reach 2m (7ft) in time.

Carl Peter Thunberg, the Swedish botanist who was one of the first Europeans to botanise in Japan and certainly the first to record a hydrangea, mistook it for viburnum, and named the Japanese forerunner of our hortensia *Viburnum macrophyllum*. The whitest-flowered viburnum is *V. furcatum*, which has, like the lacecap hydrangeas, a mass of fertile flowers at the centre of the head surrounded by showy sterile florets of the most glistening white. It is a tall, thin plant, growing to 4m (15ft), but only 1m (3ft) or so across. More useful in most gardens is *V. tomentosum* (properly *V. plicatum* forma *tomentosum*), which has similar but more showy flowers presented most effectively on a bush whose branches grow almost horizontal. 'Mariesii' is the form most usually grown, and 'Lanarth' is indistinguishable. Both produce their branches in tabulated layers, and then present their flowers as though dancing along the tops of the branches. Both eventually make small trees. 'Rowallane' is much smaller, usually under 1.2m (4ft): the flower heads are a little smaller and more neatly symmetrical than those of the foregoing. 'Cascade' is another low-growing form raised in Holland from seed of 'Rowallane'. These flower in May and June. 'Nana Semperflorens' is useful because if cut to the ground each spring it will produce its flowers in the autumn. Left to its own devices it will grow to 2m (7ft).

The potentillas flower from early May till well into October. Most are shrubs of neat, tidy habit and, although deciduous, attractive in winter on account of their reddish twigs and bark. They will grow in any fertile soil in full sun. The most useful species for white gardens is *P. dahurica*, a hardy species coming from such inclement climates as Siberia, Tibet and northern China. Typically it grows into a well-furnished bush about 1.2m (4ft) high with peeling stems. It has bright green leaves and white flowers which, as in all potentillas, are like miniaturised dog-roses. 'Farrer's White' is a selected form with plenty of white flowers all summer. *P.d.* var *veitchii* has leaves that are silky-hairy on both sides, giving them a greyish effect; it is also more robust than *P. dahurica* itself, growing to 1.5m (5ft). It is debatable whether or not white flowers are effective against silver or grey leaves. Plainly they are less conspicuous than they would be against green leaves, but in a white garden the subtlety of white against grey is just on the right wavelength of refinement – so long as the effect is not overdone. 'Abbotswood' is a clone or possibly a hybrid with abundant and beautiful white flowers; it grows to 60cm (2ft). 'Abbotswood Silver' is a variegated form greatly to be desired in the white garden, for the leaves are edged with white and the effect of this together with the flowers, is exquisite, making it one of the most useful white garden shrubs. 'Vilmoriniana' has the silveriest leaves in the genus and grows taller than most, to 1.2m (4ft), but

its flowers are palest primrose not white, though this would make it highly desirable in some white gardens where it could pick up the yellows of background golden catalpas, and little foreground limy feverfews and nicotianas.

Exochorda is also a genus in Rosaceae, and also has flowers which resemble a dog-rose but there the similarity ends. In exochorda the leaves are simple, obovate, and the white flowers quite large. There are four or more species but the best sort for white gardens is a hybrid raised (as by now no doubt you have come to expect) by Messrs Lemoine of Nancy. It is called *E. macrantha*, and the finest clone is called 'The Bride'. It grows about 1.2m (4ft) tall and has a pendulous habit, the branches weeping and spreading out over the ground. In April and May it is covered with pure white flowers nearly 4cm (1½ in) across carried on racemes 11cm (4½ in) long. The sheer quantity of flowers can be judged from the fact that it produces a raceme from literally every bud of the previous season's growth. For sheer effectiveness there is nothing to compete with it in its season.

SHRUBS – FOLIAGE

White-foliaged shrubs can, if used in moderation, effectively increase the intensity of whiteness in the white garden. Used to excess, they can kill the whiteness of neighbouring white flowers. But this tends to be true anyway, of white-variegated, white-flowered shrubs. There is, for example, a form of *Philadelphus coronarius* known as 'Bowles Variegated' (which is supposed to have a showier and whiter variegation than ordinary *P.c.* 'Variegatus'). Its leaves are conspicuously margined and blotched white. Its white flowers would pass unnoticed but one is arrested by their fragrance. The flowers are of silken smoothness in contrast to the rather coarse leaves. 'Innocence' on the other hand, has leaves that are irregularly splashed a quite yellowish cream, sometimes scarcely splashed at all, so its white flowers show up rather better. It is unfortunately a gawky and ungainly shrub, throwing up its arms at all angles.

There are four araliad shrubs that are useful for furnishing the white garden. The daintiest and most desirable is *Acanthopanax sieboldianus* 'Variegatus', a shrub which grows to about 1.5m (5ft), with all its branches upright and bearing clusters of prettily cream-variegated three to five parted leaves, each cluster with a curved prickle at the base. The flowers usually pass unnoticed. It is quite hardy but needs shelter from north and east winds. The bulkiest araliad is the variegated form of *Fatsia japonica* which makes a dense, rounded bush sometimes as much as 3m (10ft) tall and across, though its size can be controlled by pruning. The handsome palmate leaves are edged and splashed creamy white often with further grey splashes at the centre of the leaf. It produces its large umbels of white flowers in October, when most white flowers are over. These are sometimes followed by round black fruits. x *Fatshedera* is a putative hybrid between *Fatsia* and *Hedera*, and two white variegated forms exist. One is simply a white-margined form with leaves virtually the same size, but the other, which is much more intensely white variegated mainly at the margin, has leaves only half the size and is also far less vigorous. Both are called x *F.l.* 'Variegata'. Their stems are neither stiff enough to make them shrubs nor flexible enough for them to be climbers. If the tips of the shoots are pinched out to make them branch they will make low mounds of attractive foliage. The most difficult to use of the araliad shrubs is the variegated aralia itself, *A. elata* 'Variegata', which is grown for its huge, doubly pinnate leaves, the leaflets margined creamy-white. The problem arises because it

is neither truly tree nor truly shrub. It starts branching from ground level so that it makes in time an inconveniently flat-topped plant which is wider than it is high. It looks best with smooth green leaves beneath it, a white-flowered bergenia for example, which would be in flower before the aralia puts on its leaves, or *Alchemilla mollis* whose leaves and flowers would make a lovely contrast. Another possibility would be *Pachysandra terminalis* which again would be most effective in winter. *P.t.* 'Variegata' would be a distraction with its white-splashed leaves. The leaves of the aralia have a lot of pink in them at first, and the mid rib and lesser ribs retain this colour throughout the season, the pink returning in autumn. The flowers, which are tiny, are produced in huge open heads in August and September, when they are most conspicuous. They are not pure white but creamy and once past their best start to look as though they are going rusty.

The dogwoods are another group of white-flowered, white-variegated shrubs, though how useful they are in the white garden is less obvious. Probably the most useful is the ubiquitous *Cornus alba* 'Elegantissima'. This is one of those plants which first-time gardeners quite understandably purchase with great delight and then throw out a few years later when they find it has swamped everything else. The first rule is to keep control of it by pruning it judiciously (but not too hard) in winter; the second is not to give it the rich damp soil it so much enjoys but rather to grow it in poor, dry soil, which will reduce its vigour. The leaves are irregularly white margined grey-green in the centre. It has an osier-like habit. Where space permits it can be most effective in front of dark yews. It is perhaps best used next to plain green shrubs, or as a backing to lime-green nicotianas, or with *Alchemilla mollis* at its feet.

Of the other dogwoods most are more arborescent than shrubby. *C. controversa*

Cornus controversa *'Variegata'*, *a large specimen at Bath Botanic Gardens.*

'Variegata' has attained more than 16m (52ft) at Bath Botanic Garden, where there are two plants, side by side (still labelled *Thelycrania controversa* 'Variegata', a name so antique it is seldom even cited in the synonymy), and where it is obviously very much at home. Bearing in mind these ultimate dimensions, it is obviously a tree to put outside the encircling hedge, rather than in the white garden proper. There is also a problem with its reliability, for there are very few specimens of any real size, and most of the trees known to us seem to suffer more or less severely with die-back. Far more reliable, and far more suitable for planting within the white garden itself is *C. alternifolia*

'Argentea', usually called 'Variegata' which used to be known as the wedding-cake tree on account of its overall whiteness and the horizontal layers in which the branches grow, but the name has been purloined for the aforementioned cornus. The leaves are much smaller than those of *C. controversa* 'Variegata', widest in the middle, tapering at both ends, margined and splashed white, often with a decidedly pink tinge, especially early and late in the season. It is not really tree-like and is best grown as a tall 5m (17ft) multi-stemmed shrub, producing its close-layered densely leafed branches from ground level right up to the top, which at maturity is always flat. It is so dense that nothing grows beneath it, except perhaps a few cool snowdrops to flower before it puts on its leaves. There is a school of thought which maintains that this tree should only ever be grown as a specimen on a lawn, which not only affords a contrast between the uniform smoothness of the lawn and the complexity of the branching, the leaves and the variegation, but also offers the re-enforcement of the horizontals, the level line of the lawn marrying in the mind with horizontal tiers of the branches. But it looks just as good in front of a yew hedge (also of a uniform greenness and also offering the horizontal line of its no doubt neatly clipped top) so long as nothing is planted nearby to detract from these associations. The complexity of the variegation and the force of the horizontals can be further reinforced by juxtaposing plants with upright, sword-shaped leaves, tall bearded irises, for example, or better still *Sisyrinchium striatum* which not only has the upward-pointing leaves (of a complementarily plain grey) but also bears its flowers in distinct and well-spaced whorls up the stems, echoing the branching pattern of the dogwoods. One might, perhaps, have a bold drift of sisyrinchium to one side of the cornus, and a drift of Lady's mantle the other side, or perhaps in part in front of the cornus. Anything of a competing complexity of variegation should be kept well away.

The variegated Cornelian cherry raises an interesting problem, for while in leaf it is in the first-rank of white-variegated shrubs, its marginal variegation being a very pure white, its flowers, which are produced in February and into March are bright yellow. If one is creating a white garden that is to be enjoyed only in June, then the colours the plants assume for the other eleven months do not matter. But if one is likely to stray into one's white garden in February or March, might one not make, if not a white winter garden, at least a white winter corner? Besides the

variegated *Cornus mas* one could also grow *Abeliophylium distichum* (which is in effect a white forsythia), *Lonicera* x *purpusii*, several sarcococcas, *Viburnum farreri* 'Candidissium', *Prunus subhirtella*, *Clematis cirrhosa* (with creamy-lemony-greeny flowers), *Chimonanthus praecox*, with flowers of much the same colour, the white *Iris unguicularis*, *Helleborus niger*, *Bergenia stracheyi* 'Alba', all with a carpet of white snowdrops and crocuses.

The common elder is usually regarded as a coarse and unlovely plant to be weeded out whenever it appears, but there are two forms which may be of use in the white garden. The first is *Sambucus nigra* 'Albovariegata' which differs from the wild plant only in its white-edged leaves and slightly reduced vigour. It is perhaps too lacking in refinement to admit to the inner sanctum of the white garden, but it would make a useful round-topped tree beyond the boundary. Far more lovely is *S.n.* 'Pulverulenta', whose leaves are so heavily speckled white as to appear grey all over; they are, in addition, streaked with white. It grows to half the height of the wild plant, 2m (7ft) at the very most and is most apt for the white garden. 'Pulverulenta' means very beautiful and it is a fitting epithet for this plant. There is a deutzia with a similar variegation, *D. scabra* 'Punctata' but it is an inconstant thing.

A favourite of our own is the *Buddleia davidii* known as 'White Harlequin'. It has typically long, narrow leaves edged creamy-white at first, becoming pure white later, a showy and conspicuous variegation. The tiny white flowers are produced in the usual long pyramidal spikes, and are pleasant but not brilliant. It is the combination of leaf and flower that is so good. It is still a newish plant and inclined to revert but so too did 'Harlequin' itself when it was first introduced. Constant propagation from well-variegated shoots will eventually stabilise it.

131

Like other buddleias, it needs to be grown in sun, in good soil, and to be pruned almost to the base each winter. Such heavy pruning, however, leaves an ugly lump in the border over winter and, though the young shoots as they arise may be attractive enough, as they lengthen they become bare at the base and one needs to plant something to hide this, preferably something low, rounded and green-leafed. *Daphne mezereum* 'Album' would be ideal, its flowers being long over and its leaves exceedingly uninteresting in themselves, thereby accentuating the attractions of the leaves of the buddleia.

There are two acers which may be useful just outside the white garden, beyond the hedge. The first is the variegated box elder, *Acer negundo* 'Variegata', and the second is *A. platanoides* 'Drummondii'. The latter has sycamore-like leaves, though more refined, broadly edged white and ultimately makes a large tree; the former has pinnate leaves with five, seven or even nine lobes, the lobes conspicuously white-edged. It makes a tree of no more than 10m (30ft). Both are much inclined to revert and are only worth growing in gardens where care will be taken to remove any green-leafed shoots.

There are two variegated lacecap hydrangeas that are highly suitable for the white garden, in spite of their flowers being palest pastel blue and/or pink. The first is *H. macrophylla* 'Variegata', whose leaves are edged with clean, clear white. The other, usually considered the more desirable, is 'Quadricolour' whose leaves are edged with white and marked both grey and white as well as yellow. It is an odd and messy variegation and yet its effect is highly pleasing.

The variegated weigela that is usually seen is *W. florida* 'Variegata' and it is a multi-coloured variegation, red/pink/cream/white/green – just what is not wanted in the white garden. *W. praecox* 'Variegata' has broader, nearly round leaves, margined white, and a clean and attractive variegation. Its flowers are rose pink which could be acceptable in white gardens that lean towards the pink tones. The same goes for the variegated *Cotoneaster horizontalis*, whose leaves are edged white but flush crimson towards autumn.

This tendency to pink crops up in many of the white-variegated evergreens. *Rhamnus alaternus* 'Argentea Variegatus', which is in general effect one of the whitest of variegated shrubs, can be seen on closer examination to have not only red petioles and reddish stems, but even a certain amount of red in the leaves themselves, which are basically white margined. It is one of the most beautiful of all variegated shrubs and worthy of a place in any white garden large enough to accommodate it. Its symmetry is pleasing; its leaves are oval, the variegation marginal and constant, the plant itself assuming a dense oval outline. Its flowers are tiny and yellowish and usually pass unnoticed, but are followed by small scarlet berries which soon disappear. As with most plants whose leaves make an intricate pattern, it looks best next to something with big, bold, plain leaves: *Fatsia japonica* for example; or *Magnolia* x 'Maryland'; or a loquat, *Eriobotrya japonica*; or *Ilex latifolia*, preferably the male which has conspicuous white flowers, with bergenia at its feet; or the white-flowered *Crinum* x *powellii*. *Azara microphylla* 'Variegata' has even tinier leaves, set on tenuously thin twigs, and an upright habit of growth and, though just as lovely as the rhammus, is far more tender, making it suitable not only for sheltered gardens in the south and west, but also for town gardens and courtyards, where it can benefit from the extra warmth. It looks lovely next to lance-leafed aucubas and backed by green-leafed, green-stemmed bamboos. *Buxus sempervirens* 'Elegantissima' is another shrub with small, white variegated leaves, which similarly benefits from association with larger leafed plants.

With the hollies one has fewer problems of association, for being natives we are more in harmony with them anyway. The most apt for a white garden is the Silver Hedgehog holly, *Ilex aquifolium* 'Ferox Argentea' whose leaves are not only edged with spines but whose entire upper surface is covered with an array of fine spines, as well as being marked and margined creamy-white. It is slow-growing and ideal for a white garden. Most of the argenteo-marginate sorts can be used, but particularly good are 'Silver Sentinel', (which is an x *altaclarensis*) whose leaves are almost flat and scarcely spined, edged creamy-white with pale green and grey markings on a dark green ground. It forms an erect pyramidal shrub. 'Handsworth New Silver' is also very fine, with leaves rather longer than those of most hollies, margined creamy-white, with greyish markings in the centre. 'Silver Queen' is an old variety with good white edges to the typical holly leaves. It was named before the sexes of plants were understood and is actually male (just as its contemporary 'Golden King' is female). On the whole one tends to avoid hollies with centrally variegated leaves because they revert far more than the marginally variegated ones. Indeed the only one good enough to justify its space is *I.a.* 'Silver Milkboy' the centre of whose leaves is splashed with white. These hollies look best grown with shrubs with small, round leaves, like box or the Japanese holly, *Ilex crenata*. In the white garden at Little Bowden near Pangbourne Mr and Mrs Verey use symmetrically placed argento-marginate hollies clipped into balls on short stems to re-inforce formality.

Finally there is the genus euonymus of which there are several useful white-variegated sorts. *E. japonicus* 'Macrophyllus Albus' is the brightest and whitest, with quite large oval leaves, as much as 8cm (3in) long. One of its merits is that it will grow well in even quite heavy shade and that it will endure quite dry conditions at the root. More familiar perhaps are the various forms of *E. fortunei*. *E. fortunei* is a climbing shrub which in its juvenile phase climbs by clinging to a vertical surface by aerial roots, just like ivy, and just like ivy, the adult phase is arborescent (shrubby and non-climbing). The original variegated form was *E.j. radicans* 'Variegatus' with larger leaves than the typical *E. fortunei*, edged white, marked grey in the centre, often flushed pink or crimson in winter. The arborescent form of *E.f. radicans* 'Variegatus' is 'Carrierei', which is propagated from the adult growths of *radicans* 'Variegatus' (like arborescent ivies). It will not go back to the climbing phase. Its variegation is a good white at first, becoming yellower as winter approaches. Neither of these seems to be sold much now, having been ousted by flashier newcomers of which the best for white gardens are 'Silver Queen' and 'Silver Pillar', both sports from 'Carrierei'. Both have a whiter variegation than 'Carrierei', but whereas 'Silver Queen' is a spreader, 'Silver Pillar' is quite upright in growth. 'Emerald Gaiety' is another, its leaves variegated white and grey and though a cleaner white, a rather frigid plant. Like most small-leafed plants, these associate best with larger leaves, though not excessively large, and with plain green plants. Alternatively they make the perfect foil to the tall biennial thistle *Onopordum acanthium* and also look good all year round next to *Choisya ternata*.

WATER PLANTS

Water in the white garden can be thought of in two completely different ways. It can either be seen as a medium in which to grow yet more white plants, or it can be regarded as a complementary void, valued for its still, calm surface. In practice most people settle for a compromise, and a compromise in which the planting is restrained will be most effective.

The white garden at Folly Farm, originally designed by Lutyens as a lily pool. Where once the water was is now a sea of hosta leaves.

In the pool in the white garden at Tintinhull only three plants are used: a white Japanese iris (*I. ensata*), a white water-lily (*Nymphaea* 'Odorata Alba') and the Falkland Isles daisy, *Senecio smithii*, and they are planted asymmetrically. In the pool in the white garden at The Little Cottage ethereal white goldfish drift dreamily beneath the pads of a dwarf white lily. Such studied effects are strictly for formal pools in formal white gardens. In less formal settings the plants can be indulged in more freely.

Water-lilies are of course the finest flowers that can be grown actually in the water, but most are far too large for the sorts of pools likely to be created or encountered in white gardens. Of the medium growers, which need 45–60cm (18–24in) of water above them and which cover a surface area of 0.46–0.65m^2 'Virginalis' is one of the loveliest, purest white and in flower all summer; 'Gloire de Temple sur Lot' is double and creamy white, and *N. odorata* is a North American species with sweetly scented white flowers and a creeping rootstock. It can colonise quite large areas if allowed to. Of the small water-lilies, that cover a surface area of 0.27m^2 or less and grow in 30–45cm (12–18in) of water, 'Albatross' is remarkable for its proportionately very large flowers and golden anthers; *N. caroliniana* has notably fragrant flowers, and *N. candida* is notably hardy, but very variable. True miniatures that can be grown in tubs or pools of less than 1m (3ft) across include *N. pygmaea alba* and *N. tetragona* which are indistinguishable from each other, and *N. odorata* 'Minor' with tiny flowers and soft green leaves. The only plant that one can use to echo the water-lily is *Hydrocharis morsus-ranae*, the frog-bit. It looks just like a miniature water-lily, with small round leaves 4cm (1½in) across, and white, three-petalled flowers with golden-yellow anthers. It needs sun and prefers acid water.

Of the other plants that can be grown actu-ally standing in the water, the arum family provides the most showy sorts. The hardy arum, *Zantedeschia aethiopica*, with its arrow-shaped leaves and large white spathes, is perfectly hardy if covered by 10cm (4in) of water in winter. 'Crowborough' is even hardier. 'Apple Court' is a dwarf form growing to 30cm (12in) at most. 'Green Goddess' is a form with green spathes which is hardy with us when grown in this way. *Calla palustris* produces remarkably similar flowers, but is really a floating plant. It needs to anchor itself in solid ground somewhere, and then floats out across the surface of the water, making a dense carpet of broad arrow-shaped leaves above which the white spathes float.

The arrow arums also belong here. There are two species, both North American and both with broad upward-pointing arrow-shaped leaves on 45cm (18in) stems. The showier of the two is *Peltandra undulata* 'Alba', which has white arum-like flowers. *P. undulata* itself has curious green spathes, which could also be useful in a white garden, especially if used to echo the flowers of *Zantedeschia aethiopica* 'Green Goddess'. One could indeed create a ravishingly disciplined effect, especially in a white garden that is paved and has no lawn, by confining the planting in the pond and its environs to things with green flowers including not only the arum and arrow arum mentioned above but also *Moluccella laevis* beside the pond and the green rose, *R. chinensis* 'Vividiflora', though such a departure would only be advisable in a white garden where there were already gaudy-greens.

Orontium aquaticum, golden-club, a non-showy aroid (that is, one that lacks the showy spathe, the spadix being pure white), is tipped gold and most attractive in a gaudy-green white garden. It has waxy, glaucous leaves with silver undersides and it will grow anchored to mud or floating freely. It picks up and plays a theme on the leaves of the glaucous hostas, especially the tardiana group.

Carex riparia 'Variegata' produces 60–90cm (2–3ft) long leaves only 0.5cm (¼in) wide or less, and is strikingly white variegated right through till the end of August. The problem is that it is a great runner, and let loose in open ground it will run in all directions, sending up tufts of leaves here and there but never concentrating itself enough in one place to make a show. Two other grass-like plants worth growing in the same way in white gardens are *Scirpus lacustris tabernaemontana* 'Albescens' and *S.l.t.* 'Zebrinus'. Both are rushes with tubular stems and occasional small leaves, and both can grow up to 3m (10ft) tall though they usually reach less than 2m (7ft). 'Albescens' is technically longitudinally white-variegated, but often whole stems are so white variegated as to appear entirely white, while others are merely streaked or striped. Its overall effect is dramatically white. Sometimes the plant produces a high proportion of green stems, and these will usually be found to be all springing from the same piece of rhizome, which should be cut off and discarded. 'Zebrinus' is transversely banded creamy-white. It is particularly useful for echoing the banding on *Miscanthus sinensis* 'Strictus' or 'Zebrinus'.

The sagittarias, with their upward-pointing heart-shaped leaves, look as though they ought to be aroids but are not. The typical plant, *S. sagittifolia*, has scented single white flowers with dark centres 5cm

(2in) across in early summer. The double form, now known as *S.s.* var. *leucopetala* 'Florepleno', is much showier, much whiter and stays in flower all summer. It grows from tubers which are slow to multiply and is best planted in groups of five or seven. It needs 10cm (4in) of water over the tuber.

The water hawthorn, *Aponogeton distachyos* is grown for its fragrant white flowers. The fragrance is sweet, and rather like vanilla. The flowers are white with black marks inside them, borne in short spikes. The leaves are elliptical. It is not the showiest of plants, but its fragrance is pleasant on a still, warm day.

Several irises will grow with their roots covered by an inch or two of water (5cm). A first choice would be *I. laevigata* 'Alba' which has huge, floppy white flowers. It grows 60cm (2ft) or more, and is similar to *I. ensata* (*kaempferi*). It is a striking plant that should be used on its own in a white garden pool, in big groups. *I. ensata*, the clematis-flowered iris, has even larger flowers than *I. laevigata*, and is the most sumptuous of all irises. There are several lovely whites: 'Alba', 'White Swan' and 'White Heron' are all good.

There are many marginals that could be used in a white garden such as astilbes and primulas, but formal ponds in formal gardens usually provide no opportunities for growing marginals, since they have vertical sides and are paved right up to the edge. Most of these marginals can be grown successfully enough in ordinary garden soil so long as plenty of humus is added and the plants are well watered in summer.

Part 4
Garden Plans and Planning

There are as many ways of planning a garden as there are gardens to plan, but it helps if you make plans in a particular sequence.

1. The first step is a consideration of the general topography of the area. It is important to take account not only of the garden itself but also its environs, both near and distance. Occasionally there is a view or some feature beyond the garden that needs to be allowed for. Most white gardens however are self-contained and inward-looking. More often account has to be taken of near features that stand just outside the boundaries of the white garden; the huge holm oak at Tintinhull or the flowering cherries that can be seen over the hedge at Hazelby House.

Other factors which need to be noted at this stage are whether the ground is level or sloping, whether there is water on the site, pond or stream. Most of all it is important to notice whether or not the site has any particular feel or character. Very often it is such elusive feelings that are the starting point of the design. On other sites it is the sheer flatness of the ground that dictates the planting of strong verticals; *Chamaecyparis lawsoniana* 'Kilmacurragh' for example, or *Thuja occidentalis* 'Malonyana', the English garden equivalents of the pencil cedars of Italy. It is also important to consider the degree of formality appropriate. The general rule is that formality belongs nearest the house and diminishes the further from the house one goes. But then formality is also appropriate to white gardens which are essentially formal in concept. Certainly formality, because it presents the mind with rhythms and patterns that are easily grasped, seems to hold a white garden together.

Very often it helps at this stage to make a rough sketch in a notebook of the general topography of the site.

2. The next step is to try to determine what will and will not grow in the proposed garden. The two main limiting factors are the nature of the soil and the severity of the climate. The nature of a soil sample can be determined with considerable accuracy by sending it to ADAS or to the RHS. Analysis will reveal not only the pH of the soil, but also any peculiarities, like massive magnesium defects or some unexpected toxicity. Experienced gardeners can tell by looking at the wild flowers and at what the neighbours grow whether acid-loving plants will grow or not. Assessing climate is more difficult. It can be measured with instruments but it takes years to accumulate a meaningful amount of data. Many gardening books contain maps that give some broad guidance as to climate. The short cut is to see what grows in neighbouring gardens. Generally in the making of white gardens greatest reliance is placed on wholly dependable plants and plants of dubious hardiness really do not belong here.

Any such data as to soil and climate should be added as a footnote to the site sketch.

3. The third stage is to consider the white garden in relation to the rest of the site.

White gardens are usually compartments within larger gardens and it is easiest to make a white compartment if there are already other compartments or others are planned. Single compartments do occur. In some gardens there may be a variety of places where the white garden might be placed though more often there is, for all sorts of reasons, only one possible place for it. Interestingly it is often the case that the white garden served some other function first. The white garden at Barrington Court was originally a rose garden and the one at Chenies Manor was designed as a herb garden. The one at Hidcote was originally the Phlox Garden while the one at Sissinghurst started out as a rose garden in mauves and pinks, with wide lavender hedges and an avenue of almond trees.

In considering the relationship of the white garden to the rest of the garden it is important to consider the function of the white garden in terms of flow. The White Garden at Hazelby House appears to be a secret garden insomuch as that you turn aside into it from a main thoroughfare; but once there you turn out to be en route for a yet further compartment, in this case the even more secluded swimming pool. The white garden at Tintinhull lies almost in a corner of the garden, where two main paths meet; whichever way you go round the garden you are led to the white garden, as though it were the culmination of everything else in the garden. Our own white garden by contrast is to be a secret garden, enclosed by yew hedges and unseen from without. The entrance is also the exit, and an elliptical path takes you round the garden and returns you to where you entered.

Another consideration is the approach to the white garden. One of Miss Jekyll's tenets is that gardens of limited colour should be self-contained and that the approaches to them should be of a complementary colour to prepare one, and that they should also be utterly different in character. At Lytes Cary

the approach to the white garden is along a garden corridor at one side of which is a border of brilliantly coloured plants. At Tintinhull one is lured down a smoothly paved path towards the white garden by a white seat set against a dark yew hedge that lies not in but beyond the white garden. At Barrington Court one goes through a solid garden door in a stone wall to find oneself walking through a pergola, with blue-leafed hostas at ground level and the golden hop climbing the pillars, with a rose garden lying beyond the pergola. One turns off this path into the white garden which is a complete contrast. At Hazelby House one also turns off a major path, flanked by tall hedges and brightly coloured borders, into the White Garden. At Apple Court the white garden lies across a lawn and is guarded by knots of brightly coloured flowers. The simplicity of a white garden requires the contrast of complexity of colour or form or both in the approaches.

4. The next stage is to make a small plan not only of the white garden but also of its approaches and environs. This plan should show the main existing features such as trees, as well as the area designated for the white garden. It should also indicate the points of the compass. This makes it possible to see where shadows fall.

5. The next step is to produce a measured plan, which can be derived in part from the sketch plan. It sometimes helps to make a list on a scrap of paper of the measurements needed and then to go outside to take the measurements. These can then be incorporated into a plan drawn to scale, perhaps on squared or graph paper. Again it is sometimes useful to make more than one plan, an overall plan to work out the general themes and then larger scale plans of different areas for the detailed planting plans. Polaroid photographs can also help.

6. At some point it is necessary if there is ever

to be a white garden to move beyond merely recording the existing topography and proposed boundaries. This is the creative moment. Any garden that is to rise above the mundane is about an idea, or several ideas. The basic idea in any white garden is its whiteness. But whiteness can be diffuse and amorphous, and it needs a stronger framework than most gardens to hold it together. The enclosing hedges contain the white garden, but they are not its structure. The structure is produced by rhythm, pattern and repetition. In coloured gardens this can be achieved by repeating a colour (or a combination of colours) at regular intervals along a border. In a white garden it is more likely to be achieved by the repetition of a grey plant or a dark green one, or both together. Or, as at Barrington Court, the unity may come from the pattern of the beds. Sometimes the central idea of a white garden may be an artefact, a statue, a sundial, a pavilion, a rose arbor. Whatever it is, the idea must be over and above the white flowers.

It is usually easier to work out these ideas in a sequence of quick, rough scribbles than in polished drawings. One way is to make eight or ten (or more) photocopies of the rough plans made at stage 4, and to scribble over those. Some people find that actually having to re-draw the plan in rough each time helps to focus the mind on just what it is that one is drawing. It is important that the plan should show the approaches to the white garden as the two must relate either complementing or contrasting with each other. Where the white garden is approached down a broad corridor some pattern of clipped box pompons in terracotta pots could be carried through into the white garden unifying both. Equally well one might mark the approaches with clipped balls of copper beech and use the same clipped balls but in green beech within the white garden, these both unifying and distinguishing the white garden from its approaches.

7. Once the basic idea or theme of the white garden has been conceived it should be worked out and measured to scale. The sequence of drawings of the white garden at Apple Court (on pages 140–6) start at this stage. It is sometimes helpful to make several photocopies in which to work out further stages.

This is also the time to decide whether the white garden is going to lean towards pinks, yellows or towards lime-greens: it cannot do all three. A decision to lean towards pinks is also a decision to exclude creams, yellow and lime-greens. A decision to lean towards lime green excludes pink tones, cream and ivory. Glaucous blue-toned foliage fits in beautifully with pink tones, and the garden that picks up the gaudy green tints, but does not look right in association with cream, yellow and ivory-whites.

8. The next step is to indicate the positions of what Vita Sackville-West called the 'untroublesome shrubs'. They are the bones of the white planting scheme. This corresponds to the second Apple Court drawing.

9. The next step is to draw in the marker plants, if these are needed here. They may be obviated by some more fundamental pattern established at Stage 6 or, as at Apple Court, both may be needed. By marker plants we mean those that create a recurring pattern and rhythm. The third Apple Court drawing shows how this may be done. It is not necessary to use exactly the same plant every time. In the Apple Court white garden one sub-theme is to use clumps of *Hosta* 'Halcyon' to create in the shaded parts the same component of the rhythm as is created in the sunny parts by the garden pink 'Haytor', for both have leaves of the same colour. The eye recognises colour well before it identifies shape.

10. The next step is to decide when the garden is to be at its peak, and also any months when there will be no one to see the

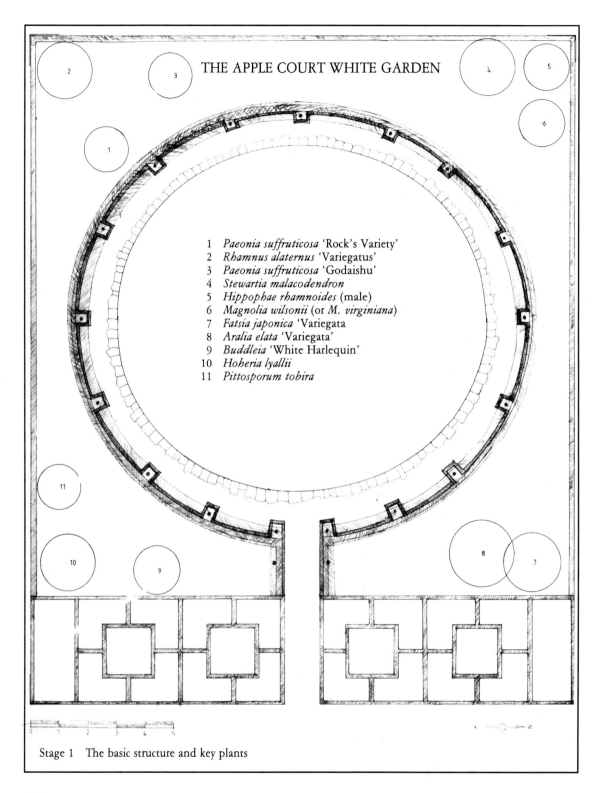

THE APPLE COURT WHITE GARDEN

1 *Paeonia suffruticosa* 'Rock's Variety'
2 *Rhamnus alaternus* 'Variegatus'
3 *Paeonia suffruticosa* 'Godaishu'
4 *Stewartia malacodendron*
5 *Hippophae rhamnoides* (male)
6 *Magnolia wilsonii* (or *M. virginiana*)
7 *Fatsia japonica* 'Variegata
8 *Aralia elata* 'Variegata'
9 *Buddleia* 'White Harlequin'
10 *Hoheria lyallii*
11 *Pittosporum tobira*

Stage 1   The basic structure and key plants

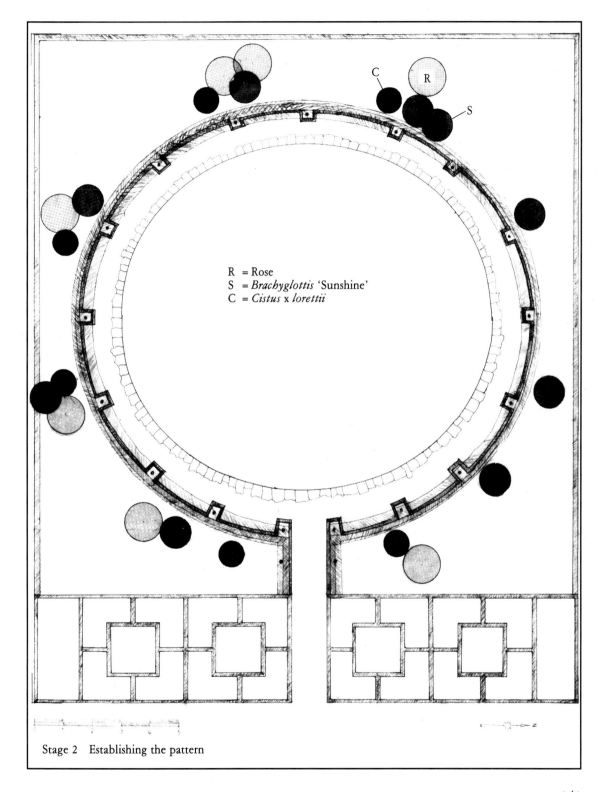

R = Rose
S = *Brachyglottis* 'Sunshine'
C = *Cistus* x *lorettii*

Stage 2 Establishing the pattern

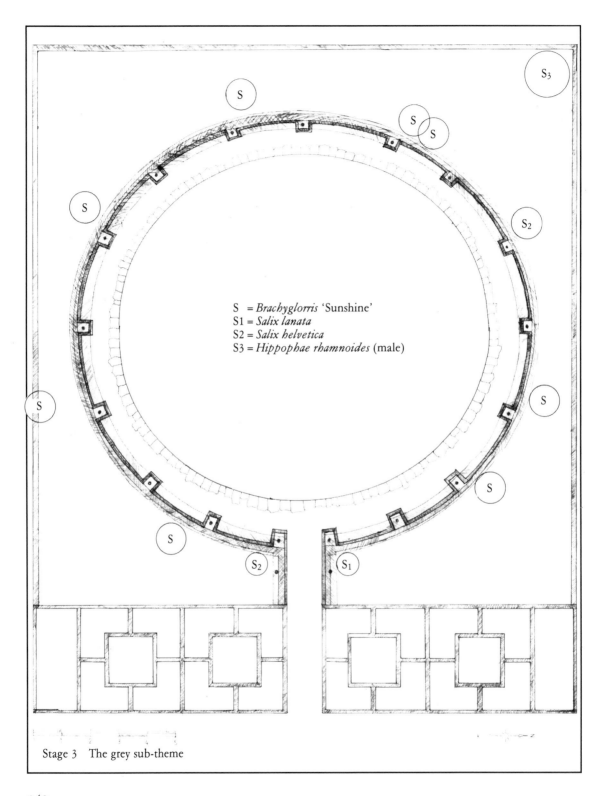

S = *Brachyglorris* 'Sunshine'
S1 = *Salix lanata*
S2 = *Salix helvetica*
S3 = *Hippophae rhamnoides* (male)

Stage 3   The grey sub-theme

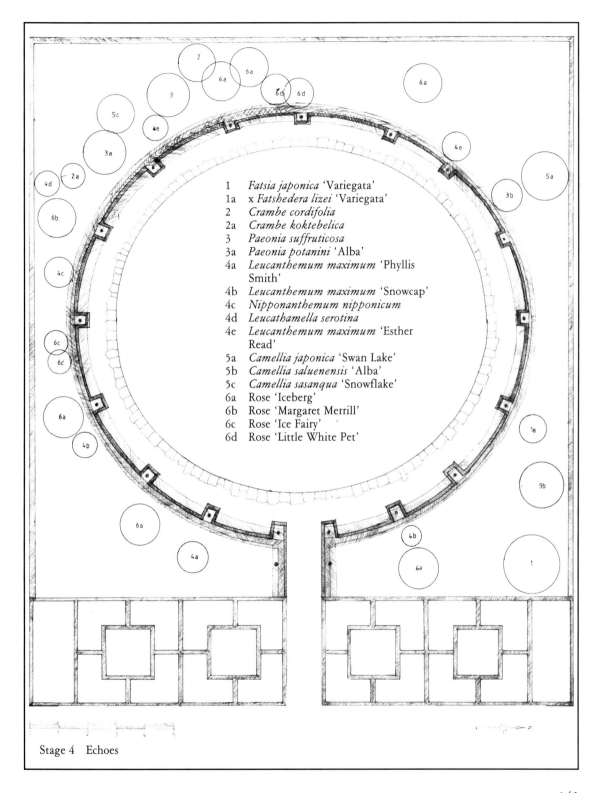

1   *Fatsia japonica* 'Variegata'
1a   x *Fatshedera lizei* 'Variegata'
2   *Crambe cordifolia*
2a   *Crambe koktebelica*
3   *Paeonia suffruticosa*
3a   *Paeonia potanini* 'Alba'
4a   *Leucanthemum maximum* 'Phyllis Smith'
4b   *Leucanthemum maximum* 'Snowcap'
4c   *Nipponanthemum nipponicum*
4d   *Leucathamella serotina*
4e   *Leucanthemum maximum* 'Esther Read'
5a   *Camellia japonica* 'Swan Lake'
5b   *Camellia saluenensis* 'Alba'
5c   *Camellia sasanqua* 'Snowflake'
6a   Rose 'Iceberg'
6b   Rose 'Margaret Merrill'
6c   Rose 'Ice Fairy'
6d   Rose 'Little White Pet'

Stage 4   Echoes

143

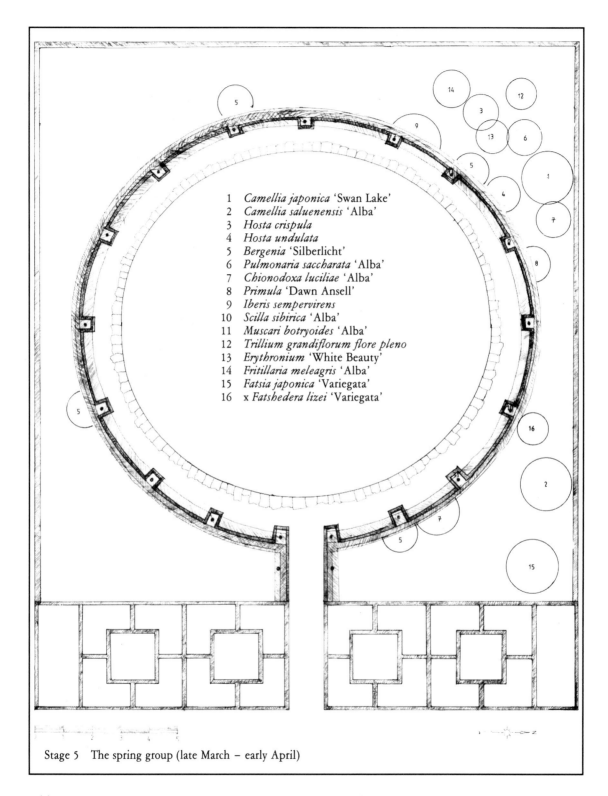

1 *Camellia japonica* 'Swan Lake'
2 *Camellia saluenensis* 'Alba'
3 *Hosta crispula*
4 *Hosta undulata*
5 *Bergenia* 'Silberlicht'
6 *Pulmonaria saccharata* 'Alba'
7 *Chionodoxa luciliae* 'Alba'
8 *Primula* 'Dawn Ansell'
9 *Iberis sempervirens*
10 *Scilla sibirica* 'Alba'
11 *Muscari botryoides* 'Alba'
12 *Trillium grandiflorum flore pleno*
13 *Erythronium* 'White Beauty'
14 *Fritillaria meleagris* 'Alba'
15 *Fatsia japonica* 'Variegata'
16 x *Fatshedera lizei* 'Variegata'

Stage 5   The spring group (late March – early April)

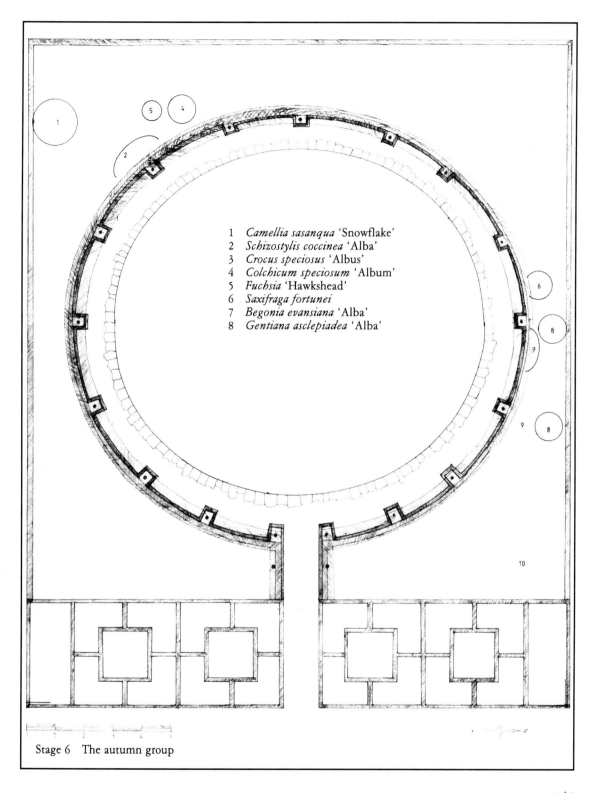

1 *Camellia sasanqua* 'Snowflake'
2 *Schizostylis coccinea* 'Alba'
3 *Crocus speciosus* 'Albus'
4 *Colchicum speciosum* 'Album'
5 *Fuchsia* 'Hawkshead'
6 *Saxifraga fortunei*
7 *Begonia evansiana* 'Alba'
8 *Gentiana asclepiadea* 'Alba'

Stage 6   The autumn group

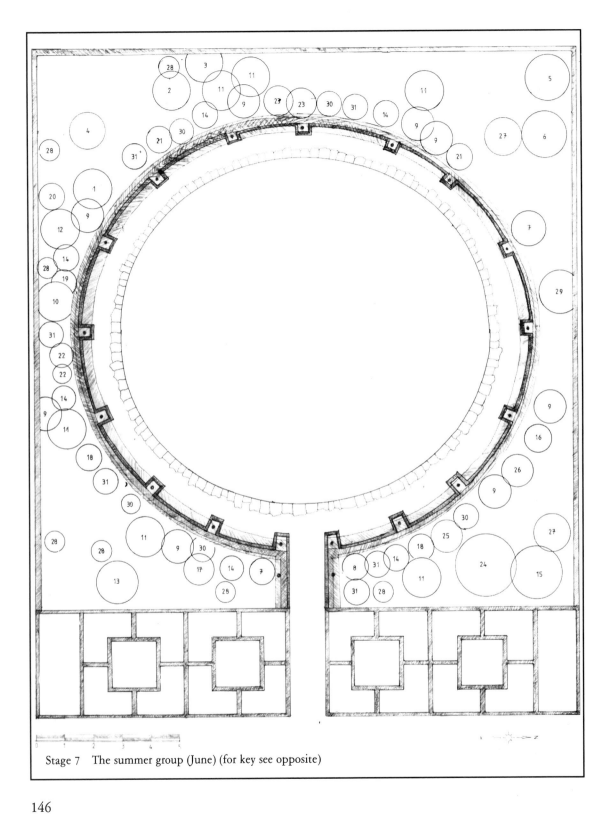

Stage 7   The summer group (June) (for key see opposite)

<table>
<tr><td>1</td><td>*Paeonia suffruticosa* 'Rock's Variety' (last flowers)</td></tr>
<tr><td>2</td><td>*Paeonia suffruticosa* 'Godaishu' (last flowers)</td></tr>
<tr><td>3</td><td>*Crambe cordifolia*</td></tr>
<tr><td>4</td><td>*Crambe koktebelica*</td></tr>
<tr><td>5</td><td>*Hippophae rhamnoides* (male)</td></tr>
<tr><td>6</td><td>*Magnolia wilsonii*</td></tr>
<tr><td>7</td><td>*Salix helvetica*</td></tr>
<tr><td>8</td><td>*Salix lanata*</td></tr>
<tr><td>9</td><td>*Brachyglottis* 'Sunshine'</td></tr>
<tr><td>10</td><td>*Potentilla* 'Abbotswood Silver'</td></tr>
<tr><td>11</td><td>Rose 'Iceberg'</td></tr>
<tr><td>12</td><td>Rose 'Margaret Merrill'</td></tr>
<tr><td>13</td><td>*Philadelphus* 'Innocence'</td></tr>
<tr><td>14</td><td>*Cistus lorettii*</td></tr>
<tr><td>15</td><td>*Fatsia japonica* 'Variegata'</td></tr>
<tr><td>16</td><td>x *Fatshedera lizei* 'Variegata'</td></tr>
<tr><td>17</td><td>*Leucanthemum maximum* 'Phyllis Smith'</td></tr>
<tr><td>18</td><td>*Leucanthemum maximum* 'Snowcap'</td></tr>
<tr><td>19</td><td>*Nipponanthemum nipponicum*</td></tr>
<tr><td>20</td><td>*Leucanthamella serotina*</td></tr>
<tr><td>21</td><td>*Leucanthemum maximum* 'Esther Read'</td></tr>
<tr><td>22</td><td>Rose 'Ice Fairy'</td></tr>
<tr><td>23</td><td>Rose 'Little White Pet'</td></tr>
<tr><td>24</td><td>*Aralia elata* 'Variegata'</td></tr>
<tr><td>25</td><td>*Paeonia* 'Duchesse de Nemours'</td></tr>
<tr><td>26</td><td>*Paeonia obovata*</td></tr>
<tr><td>27</td><td>*Rhododendron viscosum* var. *aemulans*</td></tr>
<tr><td>28</td><td>*Onopordum acanthium*</td></tr>
<tr><td>29</td><td>*Rhododendron simsii* 'Gumpo White'</td></tr>
<tr><td>30</td><td>Iris 'Henry Shaw'</td></tr>
<tr><td>31</td><td>*Malva moschata* 'Alba'</td></tr>
</table>

flower at different seasons. In the white garden at Apple Court the peak comes in June (page 146). There is also a concentrated corner of autumn interest (page 145) and a period of spring interest (page 144). Finally all the schemes need to be brought together on a single scale plan.

11. Stage 11 is to take out one-third of the plants proposed in the plan. This was Russell Page's invariable rule. We tend to throw into our white gardens all the white flowers we can think of. White gardens invariably look better with half as many different sorts of plants. And each sort should be used in drifts of three, four, five, seven or nine, rarely as a singleton. Gardens planned and planted in this way are far more pleasurable to be in: they have harmony and serenity of a kind that can never be achieved in gardens created by planting one of everything.

It helps to major on one plant. The majority plant in most white gardens seems to be the rose 'Iceberg'. In the Apple Court plan, stage two, the frequency of the 'Icebergs' can be seen. It also helps to echo one plant with another one being a smaller form of the other, see Apple Court Stage 4. *Fatsia japonica* 'Variegata' is echoed by the white-edged x *Fatshedera lizei* 'Variegata', *Brachyglottis* 'Sunshine' by *B. compactus* which is similar but smaller. Such replications form patterns in the mind, and together with rhythm and harmony produce a sense of peace and security.

12. The final step is to check that there is enough green in the white garden to balance the whiteness. A surfeit of whiteness is bewildering, indigestible. Green is the background colour of the natural world, midway between the darkness of yew and the lightness of white. White flowers may gleam and glisten against a background of green, but white on white merely dazzles. Grey is also midway between the darkness of yews and the brightness of white, but used in excess it

garden: precious space need not be wasted growing plants no one will see. The best white gardens are designed to peak in June, July or August (for example), but not for all three. The least satisfactory are designed to be white all year round. The maxim is to concentrate one's effects. If more than one season of interest is wanted then everything that flowers at the same season should be concentrated in the same place. It helps to use a separate photocopy to draw in the plants that will detracts from the whites. The eye perceives the greys and misses the whites.

In the plans that follow the points made above can be variously discerned. The town garden has a very strong structural shape to hold the scheme together, as well as creating interest through the winter. The courtyard also has deliberate elements of winter interest, but the white border is completely without interest in the winter and for good reasons. The border is viewed most often from the conservatory, where the family take their meals from spring through summer till autumn. In winter the conservatory's only use is to house a few tender greens. There is thus no point in providing winter interest in the white garden. Besides, there is a winter garden elsewhere.

An analysis of the evolution of the white garden at Apple Court may help to fill out the planning process. The garden is contained by four walls, the house occupying a section of the south-west wall. It was once a vegetable garden, and so is completely flat. It is without mature planting of any sort, though ancient oaks may be seen beyond the walls. When we took it over it was derelict, and we could create what we like. Its squareness, levelness and the fact that it was walled coincided with our predilection for formality. The basic plan divides the garden into four approximately equal quarters, though their equality will be less apparent once the planting matures. The compartments are separated by broad walks which are themselves lesser compartments. The white garden occupies the south-east quarter. It measures 21 × 21m (69 × 69ft) and is approached across an open lawn though at the foot of the yew hedges by the entrance to the white garden there will be parterres the detail of which has not yet been worked out, though the essence is that they should be colourful.

The first and basic concept was to square a circle. The square inevitably had to be the enclosing yew hedge, the circle a path enclosing the lawn, the area between the circle and the square to be the beds containing the white plants. The white garden goes nowhere. Once you have reached it you have arrived.

It was always part of the concept of our white garden that it should be cloistered. We achieve this cloistered effect by planting round the outside of the circular path a ring of pleached hornbeams. The hedge is set on 1.5m (5ft) stilts, the stilts corresponding to the pillars of a cloister. The hornbeams are actually set into the path, in brick-edged squares, and behind them, following the line of the brick edging of the path, is a low hedge of box edging. Thus the white flowers will be framed by the box edging below and the hornbeam above, and thus will concentrate the mind and focus the attention on the white flowers. A further deliberate effect is that the flowers will appear to be lit from above, making them look more luminous than they really are. See page 140. There is only one entrance, which is also the exit.

At the eleventh hour, the central circle of lawn was changed to an ellipse, and with it the path and the hornbeam stilt hedge. This creates far more interesting shapes, and more scope to use the borders in different ways.

There is a danger in any garden where the borders are what remains when a circular lawn is set in a square garden, that there will be four separate gardens in the corners, rather than one cohesive garden. At Apple Court the garden is given a basic unity by the elliptical lawn, path and stilt hedge set in its recursive brick squares. The stilts are a particularly powerful unifying force because, being vertical, they present themselves very strongly to the eye. None the less it has been felt necessary to reinforce the unity of the garden by the planting of a repetitive but varied group of plants (Apple Court Stage 2). This sort of planting is useful in most white gardens to establish rhythm, pattern and unity.

At this stage we also decided where the key plants were to go (Stage 1). Each of us had particular favourites and they, together with the pattern plants, determine how the planting will develop. If a garden starts with roses and cistus, then lavenders, santolinas, helianthemums and so on are likely to follow, but if it starts with a camellia then rhododendrons and azaleas will probably follow. If, as at Apple Court, part of the garden is in sun and part in shade, then there are problems of unifying this diversity. The very strong repetitive theme of the hornbeam stilt ellipse is one unifying ingredient, and the pattern plants is another.

In any white garden the rule is to concentrate the effects with all the plants that flower at the same season in the same place. At Apple Court we want the main effect to be in June/July (Apple Court Stage 7), but we also want a little spring effect and some autumn effects. It helps to draw each season out on a separate plan (see Apple Court Stages 5 and 6). The main plan (Stage 7) is largely produced simply by bringing together in one plan all the elements already planned, and then adding a few more. It is planned knowing that there are several specific sorts of campanula and geranium we shall use as fillers, as well as underplantings of *Viola cornuta* and *Holcus mollis* 'Variegata', and that about a quarter of the total border area will be bedding. The tree squares will have the first flowers of the year in them, the white forms of *Cyclamen coum*, *Ipheion uniflorum*, *Scilla sibirica*, *Puschkinia libanotica* and so on. No one ever gets a white garden quite right first time and no doubt we shall be fiddling with it almost for ever.

Of the other gardens whose plans we include, the town garden (page 151) is strictly formal. In formality symmetry is all-important. The garden is viewed from a terrace (6) which itself is paved and unplanted, such plants as are used being contained in

pots. The white garden proper is composed of five box-edged beds. The one at the centre contains a non-directional sculptural object, a carved bowl of fruits or armillary rings (a sculpted figure would tend to look this way or that). The bed is filled with *Scilla sibirica* 'Alba' to flower in early spring; these are followed in late summer and into autumn by the hardy fuchsia 'Hawkshead'. The main season is taken up by the roses in the other four beds, 'Margaret Merrill' and climbing 'Iceberg' contained in trellis pyramids which, being painted Brunswick green, become a feature in the winter. The roses are underplanted with a white form of *Viola cornuta*, but white-flowered pinks would do as well. The garden is partitioned by yew hedges, the end compartment being almost empty – just pea-grit, a pavilion and two terracotta pots containing clipped bay trees.

The white border (page 152) by contrast is completely informal. It is set in front of a leylandii hedge, closed at its south end by a group of trees that pre-date the border. Beyond them is a vast expanse of lawn. To the north the border is closed by a brick wall, in which is a pair of gates. It is viewed most often from the conservatory which backs on to, and may be entered from, the house. Its front edge is defined by a mowing strip of stone slabs over which some of the plants sprawl. As befits a garden within sight of the sea, there is a lot of grey, perhaps more than would be right further inland. Although informal, pattern, rhythm and repetition are still important. Standard white French daisies stand out distinctively as a pattern (14). In winter they are housed in the conservatory. Santolina is used similarly at roughly equal intervals along the front edge. The Arabian thistles (*Onopordum*) are used symmetrically at the back of the border (12). The whole border makes a harmonious garden, enchanting when seen from any angle, at any time through the summer.

The terrace at Hazelby House, with argyranthemums and white furniture. Many a town garden could look as good.

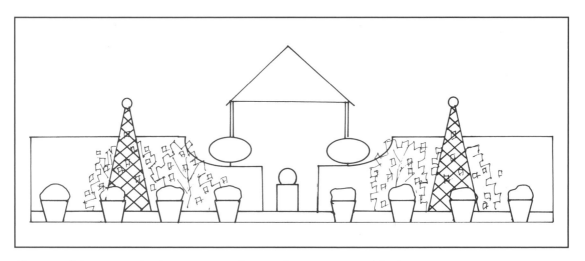

The view of the town garden from its terrace, showing the juxtaposition of the features (see opposite).

THE TOWN GARDEN

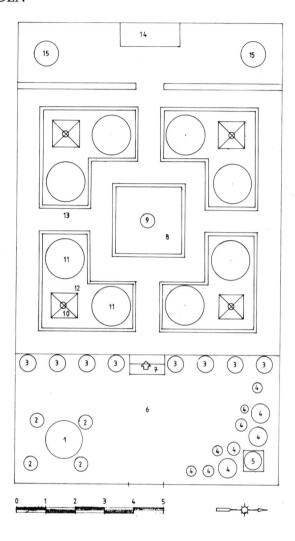

1 White iron table
2 White iron seats
3 Terracotta pots with white busy Lizzies
4 A collection of interesting pots of various sizes with a selection of white-flowered plants.
5 Statue: in white stone
6 Terrace, paved with slabs
7 Steps down
8 Box-edged bed filled with *Scilla sibirica* 'Alba' for spring display and hardy *Fuchsia* 'Hawkshead' for late summer display

9 Non-figurative, non-directional sculpture
10 Trellis pyramid painted Brunswick green with climbing rose 'Iceberg' growing up inside
11 Rose 'Margaret Merrill'
12 Box-edged bed containing underplanting of *Viola cornuta* 'Alba'
13 Paving
14 Pavilion
15 Terracotta pots containing clipped bay trees

THE WHITE BORDER

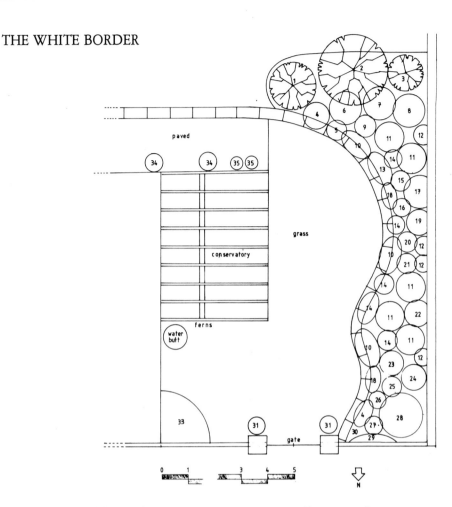

1   *Pyrus salicifolia* 'Pendula'
2   Wild hawthorn
3   Wild holly
4   *Alchemilla mollis*
5   *Dianthus* 'Haytor'
6   *Philadelphus coronarius* 'Aureus'
7   *Choisya ternata*
8   *Pittosporum* 'Garnettii'
9   *Paeonia obovata*
10 *Santolina incana* 'Nana'
11 Rose 'Iceberg'
12 *Onopordum acanthium*
13 *Anthemis cupaniana*
14 Standard argyranthemums
15 *Artemisia* 'Powys Castle'
16 *Paeonia* 'White Wings'
17 *Romney x hybrida*
18 *Tanacetum densum*
19 *Nicotiana sylvestris*
20 *Penstemon* 'Snowflake'
21 *Leucanthemum maximum* 'Esther Read'
22 *Hoheria glabrata*
23 *Lysimachia ephemera*
24 *Rosmarinus* 'Miss Jessop's Upright'
25 *Anaphalis triplinervis*
26 *Leucanthemum maximum* 'Phyllis Smith'
27 *Helictotrichon sempervirens*
28 *Garrya elliptica* 'James Roof'
29 *Hedera canariensis* 'Variegata'
30 *Zephyranthes candida*
31 *Fatsia japonica* 'Variegata'
32 Water butt
33 Tubs of *Agapanthus orientalis* 'Alba'
34 *Argyranthemum* 'Powder Puff'

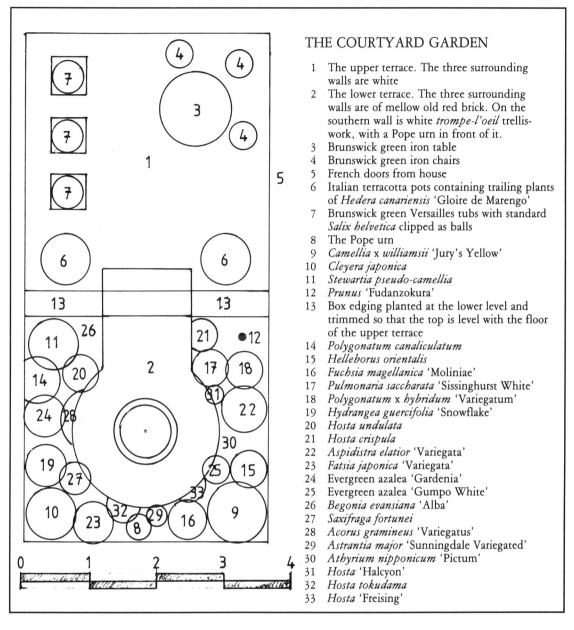

THE COURTYARD GARDEN

1 The upper terrace. The three surrounding walls are white
2 The lower terrace. The three surrounding walls are of mellow old red brick. On the southern wall is white *trompe-l'oeil* trellis-work, with a Pope urn in front of it.
3 Brunswick green iron table
4 Brunswick green iron chairs
5 French doors from house
6 Italian terracotta pots containing trailing plants of *Hedera canariensis* 'Gloire de Marengo'
7 Brunswick green Versailles tubs with standard *Salix helvetica* clipped as balls
8 The Pope urn
9 *Camellia* x *williamsii* 'Jury's Yellow'
10 *Cleyera japonica*
11 *Stewartia pseudo-camellia*
12 *Prunus* 'Fudanzokura'
13 Box edging planted at the lower level and trimmed so that the top is level with the floor of the upper terrace
14 *Polygonatum canaliculatum*
15 *Helleborus orientalis*
16 *Fuchsia magellanica* 'Moliniae'
17 *Pulmonaria saccharata* 'Sissinghurst White'
18 *Polygonatum* x *hybridum* 'Variegatum'
19 *Hydrangea quercifolia* 'Snowflake'
20 *Hosta undulata*
21 *Hosta crispula*
22 *Aspidistra elatior* 'Variegata'
23 *Fatsia japonica* 'Variegata'
24 Evergreen azalea 'Gardenia'
25 Evergreen azalea 'Gumpo White'
26 *Begonia evansiana* 'Alba'
27 *Saxifraga fortunei*
28 *Acorus gramineus* 'Variegatus'
29 *Astrantia major* 'Sunningdale Variegated'
30 *Athyrium nipponicum* 'Pictum'
31 *Hosta* 'Halcyon'
32 *Hosta tokudama*
33 *Hosta* 'Freising'

The last plan (above) is of a minute town courtyard so surrounded by larger buildings that it never gets any sun. Because the green leaves of plants absorb light, making a dark courtyard darker, the yard has been split into two halves by a change of level, and the plants consigned to the lower level. The walls surrounding the upper level are painted white.

Set against one of the white walls, opposite the French windows, are three Versailles tubs, painted Brunswick green and each containing a standard *Salix helvetica* (7). Plainly white tubs with white flowers would be of no avail against a white wall. Green roses (*Rosa chinensis* 'Viridiflora') could also be interesting here. A white iron table (3) and chairs

The approach to the white garden at Folly Farm, designed by Lutyens.

(4) also help to lighten and brighten the yard. Two giant terracotta pots with variegated Canary Isles ivy (*Hedera canariensis* 'Gloire de Marengo') trailing out of them (6) guard the change in level, which is also strongly defined by the dark band of box edging clipped to the same height as the floor of the higher level. At the centre of the lower level is a small round pond and a small fountain. The walls are old red brick, but the south wall has on it *trompe-l'oeil* trellis-work in front of which is an ornamental urn. Each corner is occupied by a single large plant, *Camellia japonica*, *Cleyera japonica* (which has

creamy-white edged leaves), the deciduous azalea *viscosum*, grown more for its scent than its flowers, and *Stewartia pseudo-camellia* to give height, autumn colour, winter bark interest and flowers in mid-summer. The rest of the planting amounts to little more than fillers among these, but there is some emphasis on contrasts of foliage. Large-growing plants such as *Fatsia japonica* are contained in pots and discarded when they grow too large. A courtyard, because of its smallness, needs more titivating than larger gardens and needs in its own way to be more perfect.

(Opposite) Artemisias recline across a brick path at the Manor House, Birlingham.

Index

Note: Page numbers referring to illustrations are indicated in *italics*.

Abeliophyllum distichum 81
Abutilon 'Tennants White' 87; *A. vitifolium* 'Album' 21
Acanthopanax sieboldianum 'Variegatus' 129
Acer negundo 'Variegata' 132; *A. platanoides* 'Drummondii' 132
Achillea 'Moonshine' 92, 116; *A.* 'The Pearl' 42; *A.* 'Perry's White' 42; *A.* 'Snowball' 42; *A. ptarmica* 42
Aconitum cammarum 'Grandiflorum Album' 92; *A. napellus* 'Album' 92; *A. septentionale* 'Ivorine' 92
Acorus gramineus 'Variegatus' 153
Adiantum venustum 100
Aegopodium podagraria 'Variegatum' 97
Agapanthus 'Alice Gloucester' 92; *A.* 'Ardernei Hybrid' 92; *A.* 'Victoria' 92; *A. africanus* 'Univittata' 24; *A. campanulatus albus* 15; *A. inapertus* 92; *A. orientalis* 'Alba' 152; *A. orientalis albus* 'Lady Moore' 92
Alchemilla mollis 20, 41, 129, 152; variegated 24,52
Allium beesianum 77; *A. neapolitanum* 77; *A. nigrum* 77; *A. schoenoprasum* 'Album' 77; *A. triquetrum* 77; *A. tuberosum* 77
almonds 12
Anaphalis triplinervis 117, 152
Anemone blanda 76; *A.b.* 'White Beauty' 76; *A. coronaria* 'De Caen' 76; *A.c.* 'French Giant' 76; *A.c.* 'St Brigid' 76; *A.c.* 'The Bride' 76; *A.x hybrida* 'Whirlwind' 93; *A.x h.* 'White Giant' 93; *A. japonica* 'Honorine Jobert' 93; *A. nemorosa* Flore-pleno 76; *A.n.* 'Leeds Variety' 76; *A.n.* 'Vestal' 76
annuals 65–74
Anthemis cretica ssp. *carpatica* (camomile) 64, 89; *A. cupaniana* 13, 89, 116, 152; *A. tinctoria* 'Powys Castle' 89
Anthericum algeriense 79; *A. liliago* 79
Antirrhinum majus 'Taff's Pride' 69; *A.m.* 'White Spire' 69; *A.m.* 'White Wonder' 69
Aponogeton distachyos 136
aquilegias 13, 16, 98; *Aquilegia flabellata* 84; *A.f.* 'Nana Alba' 84; *A. vulgaris* 83; *A.v. nivea* 83
arabis 16, 20, 24
Arachnoides aristata 'Variegata' 99
Aralia elata 'Variegata' 129, 140, 147

argyranthemums 16, 66, *150*; *Argyranthemum frutescens* 72–3; *A.* 'Powder Puff' 152
Arrhenatherum elatius bulbosum 'Variegatum' 101
artemisias 86, 98, 113, 116, *154*; *Artemisia* 'Lambrook Silver' 24; *A.* 'Powys Castle' *98*, 113, 124, 152; *A. canescens* 64, 113; *A. ludoviciana* 113; *A. schmidtiana* 'Nana' 24, 60, 113, 116; *A. stelleriana* 113; *A. tridentata* 13,
Arum italicum 'Pictum' 75,77,98; *A.i.* 'Tiny' 77
arum lily 78,135
Aruncus dioicus 90
Aspidistra elatior 'Variegata' 153
astilbes 89–90, 136; *Astilbe* x *arendsii* 89; *A.x a.* 'Avalanche' 89; *A.x a.* 'Bergkrystall' 89; *A.x a.* 'Bridal Veil' 89; *A.x a.* 'Irrlicht' 89; *A.x a.* 'Praecox' 89; *A.x a.* 'Professor van de Wielen' 89; *A.x a.* 'White Gloria' 89; *A. grandis* 89; *A. japonica* 89; *A. rivularis* 89; *A. thunbergii* 89
Aster corymbosus 94; *A. divaricatus* 94; *A. novaeangliae* 94; *A.n.* 'Snow Queen' 95; *A. umbellatus* 94
asters, New York, 'Alaska' 95; 'Chorister' 95; 'Niobe' 95; 'Snow Sprite' 95; 'White Ladies' 95; 'White Swan' 95
Astrantia major 'Shaggy' 90, 91; *A.m.* 'Sunningdale Variegated' 97, 153
Athyrium nipponicum 'Pictum' 99, 153; *A. otophorum* 'Okonum' 99
azaleas, deciduous 125; evergreen 125; 'Gardenia' 126, 153; 'Gumpo White' 126, 147, 153; 'Kure-no-yuki' 125; 'Palestrina' 125; 'Snowflake' 125; *viscosum* 155
Azara microphylla 'Variegata' 132
Ballota pseudodictamnus 60
Bampton Manor, Oxon 157
Barrington Court *11*, *30*, 40, 68, 106, 138, 139, 157
Bath Botanic Gardens *130*
bedding 65–74
beech hedging 17, 28
Begonia evansiana 'Alba' 145, 153; *B. semperflorens* 'Viva' 68
Berberis atropurpurea 'Nana' 45; *B. dictyophylla*; *B. temolaica* 112
bergenias 81, 101, 131, 144, 145; *Bergenia* 'Apple Court White' 81; *B.* 'Bressingham White' 81; *B.* 'Silberlicht' 81, 144; *B. cordata* 81; *B. ligulata* 81; *B. stracheyi* 'Alba' 81, 131
biennials 65–74

birches, white-stemmed 24
Birlingham Manor House *34*, *74*, *154*, 157
border, white 149, *152*
box 12, 17
box edging 36, 132, 153
bleeding heart 17
Brachyglottis 'Sunshine' 13, 16, 49, 112, 141, 147; *B. compactus* 112, 147; *B. munroi* 50, 112
Brompton stocks 13
Brunnera macrophylla 96; *B.m.* 'Dawson's White' 96; *B.m.* 'Langtrees' 96; *B.m.* 'Variegata' 96
buddleias 112, 123–4, 131–2; *Buddleia davidii* 123, 131; *B.d.* 'Alba' 123; *B.d.* 'White Bouquet' 124; *B.d.* 'White Cloud' 124; *B.d.* 'White Harlequin' 131, 140; *B.d.* 'White Profusion' 123; *B.d. nanhoensis* 124
bulbs 24, 74–80
Buxus balearica 28; *B. sempervirens* 'Suffruticosa' 28; *B.s.* 'Elegantissima' 132
Calla palustris 135
Camassia leichtlinii 79; *C. quamash* 80
Camellia japonica 52, 53, 155; *C.j.* 'Alba Simplex' 53; *C.j.* 'Charlotte de Rothschild' 53; *C.j.* 'Gauntletti' 53; *C.j.* 'Haku-rakuten' 53; *C.j.* 'Henry Turnbull' 53; *C.j.* 'Lily Pons' 53; *C.j.* 'Lotus' 53; *C.j.* 'Matterhorn' 53; *C.j.* 'Sode-gashuki' 53; *C.j.* 'Swan Lake' 53, 143, 144; *C.j.* 'White Swan' 46, 53; *C. oleifera* 56; *C. salvensis* 56; *C.s.* 'Alba' 143,144; *C.s.* 'China Clay' 56; *C.s.* 'Francis Hangar' 56; *C. sasanqua* 56, 145; *C.s.* 'Blanchette' 56; *C.s.* 'Duff Alan' 56; *C.s.* 'Fuji-no-mine' 56; *C.s.* 'Mine-no-juki' 56; *C.s.* 'Snowflake' 56, 143, 145; *C. x williamsii* 155; *C.x w.* 'Jury's Yellow' 153
Campanula alliariifolia 44; *C.a.* 'Ivory Bells' 44; *C. glomerata* 'Crown of Snow' 45; *C. latifolium album* 13,44; *C. persicifolia* 45; *C.p.* 'Boule de Neige' 45; *C.p.* 'Fleur de Neige' 45; *C.p.* 'Hampstead White' 45; *C.p.* 'Hetty' 45; *C.p.* 'Moorheimii' 45; *C. takeshimana* 45; *C. trachelium* 'Alba Flore Plena' 45; *C.p. alba* 45; *C.p. alba flore pleno* 45
candytuft 41, 60
Carex riparia 'Variegata' 136
Carpentaria californica 123
Carpinus betulus 29
catalpas 120; *Catalpa bignonioides* 120; *C.b.* 'Aurea' 120

Centaurea candidissima 73; *C. gymnocarpa* 73
Cerastium tomentosum 116
chaenomeles 20,76
Chamaecyparis lawsoniana 'Kilmacurragh' 137
Chamaenerion angustifolium 'Album' 90
Chenies Manor 12, 66, *98*, 123, 138, 157
cherries, flowering 17
Chimonanthus praecox 131
Chionodoxa luciliae 29, 75; *C.l.* 'Alba' 144
Choisya ternata 24, *50*, 116, 133, 152; *C.t.*
   'Sundance' 20
Chrysanthemum coccineum 88; *C.c.* 'Avalanche'
   88; *C.c.* 'Carl Vogt' 88; *C.c.* 'Mont Blanc' 88;
   C.c. 'Silver Challenger' 88; *C. maximum* 48;
   C. nipponicum 48; *C. uliginosum* 48
Chrysanthemopsis hosmariense 88, 89
Cimicifuga ramosa 89; *C.r. simplex* 24, 89
Cistus 122, 149; *C. albidus* 123;
   C. canescens 'Albus' 123; *C. creticus* 123;
   C.c. 'Albus' 123; *C. hirsutus* 123;
   C. ladanifer 123; *C.l.* 'Cherry' 123;
   C.l. 'Elma' 123; *C. laurifolius* 123; *C. laxus*
   123; *C. libanotis* 123; *C.* x *lorettii* 141, 147;
   C. populifolius 123; *C.p. lasiocalyx* 123
Clarkia elegans 'Albatross' 69
Clematis 16, *107*, 108–9, 131; *C.* 'Duchess of
   Edinburgh' 20; *C.* 'Gillian Blades' 109;
   C. 'Huldine' 20, 109; *C.* 'Mrs. George
   Jackson' 20; *C.* 'John 'Huxtable' 20, 108;
   C. 'Jackmanii Alba' 20; *C.* 'Marie
   Boisselot' 21, 108; *C.* 'Miss Bateman' 108;
   C. 'Moonlight' 109; *C.* 'Sylvia Denny' 20,
   108; *C.* 'Wada's Primrose' 109; *C.* 'White
   Moth' 21; *C.* 'White Swan' 21; *C. alpina*
   'Burford White' 108; *C.a.* 'White
   Columbine' 108; *C.a. sibirica* 108;
   C. armandii 20, 108; *C.a.* 'Snowdrift' 108;
   C. cirrhosa 131; *C.c balearica* 108;
   C.c.b. 'Wisley Cream' 108; *C. florida* 'Belle
   of Woking' 64; *C.f.* 'Duchess of Edinburgh'
   64; *C.f.* 'Fortunei' 64, 108; *C.f.* 'Plena' *63*,
   64; *C. lanuginosa* 'Henryi' 109;
   C. macropetala 108; *C.m.* 'Snowbird' 108;
   C.m. 'White Moth' 108; *C. montana* 20;
   C.m. 'Alexander' 108; *C.m.* 'Grandiflora'
   108; *C.m.* 'Wilsonii' 108; *C. sieboldii* 'Alba
   Plena' 21; *C. spooneri* 20; *C. viticella* 109;
   C.v. 'Alba Luxurians' 109
Cleyera japonica 153, 155
Clianthus puniceus 'Albus' 21
climate 137
climbers 106–11
Cobaea scandens 68; *C.s.* 'Alba' 21
Colchicum speciosum 'Album' 65, *71*, 145
colonnades 28–9, *31*
columbines 25
container plants 74
Convallaria majalis 84; *C.m.* 'Fortin's Giant'
   84; *C.m.* 'Lineata' 84; *C.m.* 'Prolificans' 84;
   C.m. 'Variegata' 84
Convolvulus cneorum 16, 117
Cordyline australis 24
Cornelian cherry 131
Cornus alba 'Elegantissima' 129; *C. alternifolia*
   130; *C.a.* 'Argentea' 130; *C.a.* 'Variegata'
   130; *C. controversa* 'Variegata' 129, *130*, 130
Cosmos bipinnatus 'Purity' 66

Cotoneaster horizontalis 132
courtyard gardens 24,153
Crambe cordifolia 17, 40–1, *43*, 68, 102, 143,
   147; *C. koktebelica* 143, 147; *C. maritima* 114
Cranborne Manor, Dorset 157
Crathes Castle, Scotland 157
Crinum x *powellii* 132; *C.* x *p.* 'Album' 65, *70*
Crocus chrysanthus 'Snow Bunting' 74; *C.c.*
   'Warley White' 75; *C. niveus* 75; *C.*
   ochroleucus 75; *C. sieberi* 'Bowles White' 75;
   C.s. 'Joan of Arc' 75; *C.s.* 'Kathleen
   Parlow' 75; *C.s.* 'Snowstorm' 75; *C. speciosus*
   75; *C.s.* 'Albus' 145; *C. vallicola* 75
x *Cupressocyparis leylandii* 24,28
Cyclamen coum 78, 149; *C. europaeum* 77;
   C. neapolitanum 77; *C. repandum* 78
Cynara cardunculus 114; *C. scolymus* 114
Cyrtomium falcatum 56
Cytisus praecox 76
Daffodils; *see Narcissus*
dahlias, white 66; *D.* 'Nicola' 68; *D.* 'Peace
   Pact' 68; *D.* 'White Moonlight' 68
Daphne mezereum 'Album' 132
Datura cornigera 'Knightii' 73; *D. suaveolens* 73
design of white gardens 22–8, 137–55
delphiniums 15, 82; *Delphinium* 'Damavand'
   90; *D.* 'Mary Loake' 90; *D.* 'Rona' 90
deutzia 41; *Deutzia compacta* 121; *D.* x
   lemoinei 'Boule de Neige' 121; *D.* x *l.*
   'Dwarf Nikko' 121; *D.* x *magnifica* 121;
   D. x *m.* 'Latiflora' 121; *D.* x *m.* 'Magnifica'
   121; *D. scabra* 'Punctata' 131
Dianthus 'Alan Titchmarsh' 44; *D.* 'Ballerina'
   44; *D.* 'Haytor' 44, 139, 152; *D.* 'Joy
   Sinkins' 44; *D.* 'Mrs Sinkins' 42, 44; *D.*
   'Nan Bailey' 44; *D.* 'White Ladies' 44
dicentras 117; *Dicentra formosa* 'Langtrees' 83;
   D.f. 'Alba' 117; *D. spectabilis* 'Alba' 13,
   17, 83
Dictamnus albus 92
Digitalis purpurea 'Alba' 13,25,69
dogwoods; *see Cornus*
Dryopteris affinis cristata 'The King' 83
Echinops 'Nivalis' 95; *Echinops tournefortii* 95
Elaeagnus angustifolia 'Caspica' 111
Elymus arenarius 101–2; *E. hispidus* 101;
   E. magellanicum 101
Epilobium glabellum 13; *E. hirsutum* 90
epimediums 84–5; *Epimedium grandiflorum*
   'White Queen' 84; *E. pubigerum* 84; *E.* x
   youngianum 'Niveum' 84
enclosure, of white gardens 27–8, 30
Eremurus elwesii 80; *E. himalayicus* 80
Eriobotrya japonica 132
Erythronium californicum 76; *E. oregonum* 76;
   E.o. 'White Beauty' 76, 144
escallonias 124; *Escallonia* 'Donard White'
   124; *E. iveyi* 24, 124; *E. bifida* 124; *E.* x
   exoniensis 124; *E. virgata* 124
Euonymus 133; *E.* 'Emerald Gaiety' 49; *E. fortunei*
   133; *E.f. radicans* 'Variegatus' 133; *E.f.r.*
   'Carrieri' 133; *E.f.r.* 'Silver Pillar' *133*; *E.f.r.*
   'Silver Queen' 133; *E. japonicus* 'Macrophyllus
   Albus' 133; *E.j. radicans* 'Variegatus' 133
Eupatorium cannabinum 'Album' 89;
   E. purpureum 93; *E. weinmannianum* 93

Euphorbia 'Lambrook Yellow' 112; *E.*
   characias 17, 111, 112; *E. marginata* 74; *E.*
   mysinites 112; *E. rigida* 112; *E. wylfenii* 112
Exochorda 127; *E. giraldii* 24; *E. macrantha*
   128; *E.m.* 'The Bride' 128
Fatsia 129; *F.* x *fatshedera* 129; *F. hedera* 129;
   F. japonica 41, 101, 129, 132, 143, 153, 155;
   F. japonica 'Variegata' 24, 129, 140, 144,
   147, 152; *F. lizzei* 'Variegata' 143, 144, 147
fences, use of 28
ferns 98–102
Folly Farm 12, 32, *34*, 106, *134*, 157;
   approach to 155; 'Iceberg' 42; wisterias 60
formality, of white garden 137
foxgloves, *see Digitalis*
Fragraria vesca 'Variegata' 97
Fritillaria meleagris 'Alba' 144
fuchsias 73; *Fuchsia* 'Annabelle' 73;
   F. 'Constellation' 73; *F.* 'F M Abbott' 73; *F.*
   'Hawkshead' 145, 149, 151; *F. magellanica*
   'Moliniae' 153; *F.* 'This England' 73;
   F. 'Ting-a-ling' 73; *F.* 'White Fairy' 73
Galactites tomentosum 73
Galanthus elwesii 75; *G. ikariae* 75; *G. latifolius*
   75; *G. nivalis* 'Arnottii' 75; *G.n.* 'Atkinsii' 75;
   G.n. 'Flore-pleno' 75; *G. whittallii* 'Merlin' 75
Galtonia candicans 13, 56, 61, 80, 86
gardens, concept of 8–12; discipline in 10–11;
   unity in 9, 139, 148; to visit 160
Garrya elliptica 'James Roof' 152
Gentiana asclepiadea 'Alba' 145
geraniums 16, 17, 95, 149; *Geranium clarkei*
   'Kashmir White' 24; *G. renardii* 41;
   G. sanguineum 'Album' 60, 95
gladioli 61, 78; *Gladiolus cardinalis* 78;
   G. nanus 78; *G. tristis* 78; *G. tubergenii* 78;
   G. 'Antarctic' 78; *G.* 'Antoinette' 78; *G.*
   'The Blushing Bride' 78; *G.* 'The Bride' 78;
   G. 'Green Bird' 78; *G.* 'Green Woodpecker'
   78; *G.* 'Nymph' 78; *G.* 'Snow Princess' 78;
   G. 'White Friendship' 78
Glechoma hederacea 'Variegata' 97
grasses 13, 98–102
green, use in white gardens 147
grey plants 111–17
gypsophila 40, 41, 42; *Gypsophila* 'Bristol
   Fairy' 86; *G.* 'Compacta Plena' 86; *G. nana
   alba* 86; *G. paniculata* 80, 86
Halesia carolina 120–1; *H. monticola* 120;
   H.m. vestita 121
Hazelby House *10*, 12, 16–17, *18*, *31*, 40,
   101, *122*, 138, 157; roses *103*, 105; terrace
   150; trees 117
Heale House 30
hebes 117; *Hebe albicans* 'Prostrata' 24, 117;
   H. andersonii 'Variegata' 24; *H. pinguifolia*
   'Pagei' 24, 117
Hedera canariensis 110; *H.c.* 'Gloire de Marengo'
   110, 153, 155; *H.c.* 'Margino-maculata' 110;
   H.c. 'Variegata' 152; *H.c. colchica* 'Dentata
   Variegata' 110; *H.c.* 'Paddy's Pride' ('Sulphur
   Heart') 20, 110; *H. helix* 111; *H.h.* 'Adam'
   111; *H.h.* 'Ardingly' 111; *H.h.* 'Marginata-
   major' 111
hedging, types of 27–8, 36
helianthemums 23, *122*, 123, 149; *Helianthemum*
   'The Bride' 17, 123; *H.* 'Wisley White' 24, 123

Helichrysum microphyllum 73; *H. petiolatum* 7, 69, 73

Helictotrichon sempervirens 13, 101, 152

hellebores 98; *Helleborus* 'Bowles White' 81; *H.* 'Ladham's Variety' 81; *H. corsicus* 81; *H.* 'Potters Wheel' 81; *H.* 'Prince Rupert' 81; *H. niger* 80–1, 131; *H. orientalis* 153

hemerocallis (day lilies) 85, 86; *Hemerocallis* 'Irongate Iceberg' 85; *H.* 'Joan Senior' 85; *H.* 'Loving Memories' 85; *H.* 'Serene Madonna' 85

Heuchera brizoides 'Taff's Joy' 98

Hidcote Manor 12, 27, 29, 138, 157; topiary *38;* tulips at 79

Hippophae rhamnoides 140, 142, 147

Hoheria glabrata 152; *H. lyallii* 140

Holcus mollis 'Albovariegatus' 100, 101, 148

holly 36

honeysuckle 106

hop, golden 20

hornbeam, hedging 25

horse chestnut 120

hostas 17, 57, 64–5, 92–3, 95–6, 101, 113, 117, *134*, 135; *Hosta* 'Blue Skies' 52; *H.* 'Dorset Charm' 52; *H.* 'Freising' 56; *H.* 'Halcyon' 139, 153; *H.* 'Honeybells' 93; *H.* 'Louisa' 93, 95; *H.* 'Royal Standard' 93; *H.* 'Thomas Hogg' 25; *H.* 'Wiehenstephan' 56, 93; *H. crispula* 84, 153; *H. fortunei* 'Albo Marginata' 96; *H.f.* 'Freising' 93, 153; *H. hyacinthina* 17; *H. hypophyllum* 52; *H. minor alba* 93; *H. plantaginea* 24; *H. sieboldiana* 'Big Daddy' 52; *H.s.* 'Elegans Alba' 52;, *H.s.* 'Snowden' 52; *H. sieboldii* 'Ginko Craig' 95; *H.s. alba* 93; *H. tardiflora* 52; *H. tardiana* 17; *H. tokudama* 52; *H. undulata* 98, 144, 153; *H.u.* 'Univittata' 25, 96, *98;* *H.u.* 'See-saw' 96; *H.u.* 'Albo Marginata' 96

Humulus lupulus 'Aureus' 20

hydrangeas 15, 126–7, 132, 153; climbers 109–10; 'lacecap' 127; 'mop-heads' 127; *Hydrangea* 'Lanarth White' 127; *H.* 'Mme E Mouillère' 127; *H.* 'Veitchii' 127; *H.* 'Whitewave' 127; *H. anomala* 110; *H. arborescens* 'Annabelle' 127; *H.m. macrophylla* 'Variegata' 132; *H.m.* 'Quadricolour' 127; *H. paniculata* 127; *H.p.* 'Grandiflora' 127; *H. querifolia* 'Snowflake' 126, 153; *H. petiolaris* 109–10; *H. rosea* 127; *H. seemannii* 110; *H. serratifolia* 110

Hydrocharis morsus-ranae 135

Hypolepis millefolium 100

Iberis sempervirens 144; *I.s.* 'Little Gem' 41

Ilex (holly) 133; *I. aquifolium* 'Ferox Argentea' 133; *I.a.* 'Golden King' 133; *I.a.* 'Handsworth New Silver' 133; *I.a.* 'Silver Milkboy' 133; *I.a.* 'Silver Queen' 133; *I.a.* 'Silver Sentinel' 133; *I. crenata* 133; *I. latifolia* 132

Impatiens hybrida 'Futura White' 66; *I.h.* 'Super Elfin White' 66

Ipheion uniflorum 75–6, 149

ipomoeas 18

irises 85, 116; intermediate bearded 60; miniature bearded 60; variegated 96–7; water 136; *Iris* 'Cliffs of Dover' *54*, 57;

I. 'Cup Race' 57; *I.* 'Henry Shaw' 57, 147; *I.* 'L'Innocence' 80; *I.* 'Jeanne d'Arc' 80; *I.* 'Irish Doll' 60; *I.* 'Just Jennifer' 60; *I.* 'Lilli White' 60; *I.* 'Mont Blanc' 80; *I.* 'Moonlight' 60; *I.* 'Princess Irene' 80; *I.* 'Queen Wilhelmina' 80; *I.* 'White Pearl' 80; *I. ensata* 135, 136; *I.e.* 'Alba' 85; *I.e.* 'Moonlight Waves' 85; *I.e.* 'White Heron' 136; *I.e.* 'White Swan' 85, 136; *I. florentina* 57; *I.f.* 'Albicans' 57; *I. germanica* 57; *I. kaempferi* 90; *I. laevigata* 'Alba' 85, 136; *I.l.* 'Snowdrift' 85; *I. orientalis* 13, 85; *I. pallida* 97; *I.p.* 'Argenta Variegata' 97; *I.p.* 'Variegata' 97; *I. tingitana* 80; *I. unguicularis* 131; *I. xiphiodes* 80; *I. xiphium* 80

ivies, 'Little Diamond' 20; variegated 90, 110–11, 152, 153, 155

Japanese anemone 17

jasmine 21, 109; *J. officinale* 109

Jekyll, Miss Gertrude 12, 16, 32, 138

juniper 23

Knightshayes Court 56, *119*

Lady's mantle 20

lamb's lugs 116

Lamium 'Album' 117; *L.* 'Beedhams White' 117; *L.* 'Nancy's White' 117; *L.* 'Silver Beacon' 117; *L. maculatum* 117

Lathyrus 'White Pearl' 20; *L. odoratus* 68; *L.o.* 'Jilly' 68; *L.o.* 'Royal Wedding' 68; *L.o.* 'Snowdonia Park' 68; *L.o.* 'White Leamington' 68

Lavatera 'Mont Blanc' 68; *L. olbia* 'Ice Cool' 87–8

lavender 12, 23, 149

Lavandula spica 'Alba' 60, 113; *L.s.* 'Seal' 113; *L.s.* 'Nana Alba' 113

lenten roses 81

Leptospermum cunninghamii 124; *L. grandiflorum* 13, 124; *L. humifusum* 124; *L. lanigerum* 124; *L. scoparium* 124; *L.s.* 'Album Flore-pleno' 124; *L.s.* 'Leonard Wilson' 124

Leucanthamella serotina 48, 89, 93, 94, 124, 143, 147

Leucanthemum maximum 48, *50*; *L.* 'Aglaia' 48; *L.* 'Bishopstone' 48; *L.* 'Esther Read' 48, 143, 147, 152; *L.* 'Fiona Coghill' 48; *L.* 'Phyllis Smith' 48, 143, 147, 152; *L.* 'September Snow' 48; *L.* 'Snowcap' 48, 143, 147; *L.* 'Wirrall Supreme' 48; *L.* 'W L Harkness' 48

Ligustrum (privet) 124; *L. henryi* 124; *L. quihoui* 124

lilies, Madonna 17; varieties 64; *Lilium pricei* 64; *L. regale* 40, 42, 61, 62, 64

lily of the valley (Mugget) 25, 84

limes 29; pleached *126*

Little Cottage, The, Lymington 18, *19*, 20–1, 106, 157

Lobelia erinus 'Snowball' 69; *L.e.* 'White Cascade' 69

Lonicera nitida 28, 36; *L. x purpusii* 81

Lunaria alba 'Alba' 69; *L.a.* 'Alba Variegata' 72; *L.a.* 'Variegata' 72

lupins 17, 88; *Lupinus polyphyllus* 88; *L.p.* 'Blushing Bride' *L.P.* 'Noble Maiden' 88

Lychnis coronaria 'Alba' 13, 41; *L.c.* 'Oculata' 41; *L. viscaria* 24

Lysimachia clethroides 93; *L. ephemera* 24, 152; *L. ephemerum* 90, 101

Lytes Cary 12, *15*, 16, *50*, 138, 157; entrance *26*

Mandevilla suaveolens 21

magnolias 118–20; *Magnolia x* 'Freeman' 120; *M. x* 'Maryland' 120, 132; *M. denudata* 118, 119; *M. grandiflora* 'Exmouth' 21, 120; *M.g.* 'Ferruginea' 120; *M.g.* 'Goliath' 120; *M.g.* 'Samuel Sommer' 120; *M. kobus* 119; *M.k.* 'Little Gem' 120; *M. x loebneri* 'Merrill' 119; *M. x l.* 'Snowdrift' 119; *M. x l.* 'Wada's Memory' 119; *M. salicifolia* 119; *M. sinensis* 120; *M. x soulangeana* 'Alba Superba' 118; *M. x s.* 'Lennei Alba' 119; *M. stellata* 119; *M.s.* 'Royal Star' 120; *M.s.* 'Water Lily' 120; *M. virginiana* 120, 140; *M. wilsonii* 120, 140, 147

Malva moschata 'Alba' 16, 41, 87, 147

marguerites, 'Powder Puff' 73; 'Snowflake' 73

marker plants 139

Melianthus major 112

Mertensia asiatica 113; *M. ciliata* 113

Mexican orange blossom 24

Miscanthus sinensis 'Cabaret' 101; *M.s.* 'Strictus' 136; *M.s.* 'Variegatus' 24; *M.s.* 'Zebrinus' 136

Molucella laevis 135

Mottisfont, Hants *126*

Muscari botryoides 'Alba' 75

Narcissus cyclamineus 57; *N.c.* 'Dove Wings' 57; *N.c.* 'February Silver' 57; *N.c.* 'Jenny' 57; *N. poeticus flore-pleno* 57; *N. tazetta* 56; *N.t.* 'Thalia' 47, 56–7; *N. triandrus* 'Silver Chimes' 56–7

Nepeta faassenii 'Alba' 95

Newby Hall, Yorks 157

Nicotiana affinis 68; *N. alata* 41, 52, 68; *N.a.* 'Dwarf White Bedder' 68; *N. langsdorfii* 41, 52, 68; *N.l.* 'Lime Green' 68; *N. sylvestris* 68, 152

Nigella damascena 68; *N.d.* 'Miss Jekyll Alba' 68

Nipponanthemum nipponicum 48, 89, 143, 147

Nymphaea 'Odorata Alba' 15, 135; *N. candida* 135; *N. caroliniana* 135; *N. odorata* 135; *N.o.* 'Minor' 135; *N. pygmaea alba* 135; *N. tetragona* 135

Oleander 'Alba' 73; *O.* 'Alba Plena' 73; *O.* 'Soeur Agnes' 73

Omphalodes linifolia 69; *O. verna* 81

Onopordum acanthium 13, *14*, *82*, 88, 114, *114*, 133, 147, 149, 152; *O. arabicum* 114

Orontium aquaticum 135

Osmanthus armatus 106; *O. delavayi* 24

Osteospermum 'Blue Streak' 72; *O. ecklonis* 'Prostrata' 72; *O.e.* 'Tauranga' ('Whirligig') 72; *O.e.* 'Weetwood' 72

ox-eye daisies 16

Oxford Botanic Garden 27

Pachysandra terminalis 129; *P.t.* 'Variegata' 129

Paeonia 'Duchesse de Nemours' 61, 147; *P.* 'Kelways Glorious' 61; *P. lactiflora* 'Whitley Major' 60; *P. obovata* 'Alba' 61, 147, 152; *P. potaninii* 'Alba' 24, 143; *P. suffruticosa* 143, 147; *P.s.* 'Godaishu' 140, 147; *P.s.* 'Rock's Variety' 140, 147; *P.s.* 'White Wings' *58*, 60, 152

pansies 20; 'Little David' 24

Papaver orientale 85, 87; *P.o.* 'Black and White' 85; *P.o.* 'Perry's White' 85; *P.* 'somniferum* 'White Cloud' 69

Paradisea liliastrum 24, 79

Passiflora caerulea 'Constance Elliott' 21, 110

paths 32, *34*

pelargoniums, zonal, 'Avalon' 72; 'Hermione' 72; 'Snow Queen' 72; 'White Century' 72; 'White Orbit' 72; *Pelargonium* x *domesticum* 'Nomad' 72; *P.* x *d.* 'White Glory' 72; *P. peltatum* 'L'elegante' 72; *P.p.* 'Snowdrift' 72

Peltandra undulata 135; *P.u.* 'Alba' 135

Penstemon 'Garnet' 16; *P.* 'Snowflake' 152

perennials 80–95; foliage 95–8

pergolas 28–9

petunias 7, 20; *Petunia hybrida grandiflora* 'White Magic' 65; *P.h.g.* 'White Swan' 65; *P. hybrida multiflora* 'Prio White' 65; *P.h.m.* 'White Cloud' 65

Phalaris arundinacea 'Picta' 100

philadelphus (mock orange) 16, 41, 116, 121, 128–9; *Philadelphus* 'Alabastre' 121; *P.* 'Beauclerk' 24, 121; *P.* 'Belle Etoile' 121; *P.* 'Bouquet Blanc' 121; *P.* 'Burfordensis' 121; *P.* 'Manteau d'Hermine' 121; *P.* 'Sybille' 121; *P. coronarius* 'Aureus' 152; *P.c.* 'Bowles Variegated' 128; *P.c.* 'Variegatus' 128; *P.c.* 'Innocence' 129, 147

phlomis 113–4; *Phlomis chrysophylla* 113; *P. italica* 113

phlox 12, 17, 20, 45, 48, *115*; *Phlox maculata* 'Alpha' 48; *P.m.* 'Nora Leigh' 95; *P.m.* 'Omega' 48; *P. paniculata* 'Alba Grandiflora' 48; *P.p.* 'Iceberg' 48; *P.p.* 'Mia Ruys' 48; *P.p.* 'September Schnee' 48; *P.p.* 'White Admiral' 48

phormiums 24, 101

phillyrea 36

pinks 16, 17, 18, 24, 117; *see also* Dianthus

Pittosporum 'Garnettii' 152; *P. tobira* 140

planning 137–55

planting, basic 40–52; pattern and rhythm 9

Platycodon grandiflorum 'Alba' 45; *P.g.* 'Flore Pleno' 45; *P.g.* 'Mariesii' 45; *P.g.* 'Mariesii Albus' 45

pleached walks 29, *126*

Plumbago capensis 90

Polemonium caeruleum Alba' 92; *P. foliosissimum* 'Album' 92

polyanthus 25

Polygonatum canaliculatum 153; *P. commutatum* 84; *P. falcatum* 'Variegatum' 95; *P.* x *hybridum* 'Variegatum' 84, 95, 153; *P. multiflorum* 84; *P. odoratum* 84

Polystichum aculeatum 'Pulcherrimum' 84; *P.a.* 'Pulcherrimum Bevis' 100; *P.a.* 'Pulcherrimum Druery' 100; *P.a.*

'Pulcherrimum Druery Superbum' 100; *P. setiferum* 56, 81, 83, 90; *P.s.* 'Acutilobum' 100; *P.s.* 'Divisilobum Mrs Goffrey' 100; *P.s.* 'Proliferum' 100

potentillas 117, 128; *Potentilla* 'Vilmoriniana' 128; *P. dahurica* 128; *P.d.* 'Abbotswood' 128; *P.d.* 'Abbotswood Silver' 128, 147; *P.d.* 'Farrer's White' 128; *P. veitchii* 128

Poterium magnificum 24

primroses 25

primulas 83, 136; *Primula denticulata* 83; *P.d.* 'Alba' 83; *P. sieboldii* 'Alba' 83 ; *P. vulgaris* 83; *P.v.* 'Dawn Ansell' 83, 144; *P.v.* 'Kiss of Snow' 83; *P.v.* 'Kiss of Snow Improved' 83

privet 28, 36

Prunus 'Asagi' 118; *P.* 'Fudanzokura' 153; *P.* 'Gyoike' 118; *P.* 'Jo-nioi' 118; *P.* 'Tai-haku' 76, 118; *P.* 'Taki-noi' 118; *P.* 'Trivolor' 118; *P.* 'Ukon' 118; *P.* 'Washino-o' 118; *P. mume* 118; *P.m.* 'Alba' 118; *P.m.* 'Albaplena' 118; *P.m.* 'O-moi-no-wae' 118; *P. serrula* 118; *P. subhirtella* 131; *P. tenella* 118; *P.t.* 'Alba' 118

pulmonarias 117; *Pulmonaria augustifolia* 83; *P.a.* 'Alba' 83; *P. officinalis* 83; *P.o.* 'Sissinghurst White' 81, 83, 153; *P.o.* 'White Wings' 83; *P. rubra* 83; *P.r.* 'Albocorollata' 83; *P. saccharata* 117; *P.s.* 'Alba' 144; *P.s.* 'Argentea' 117

puschkinias 29, 61, 76; *Puschkinia libanotica* 149

Pyrus x *canescens* 49; *P. eleagrifolia* 49; *P. nivalis* 49; *P. salicifolia* 'Pendula' 49, 111, 153

Queen Anne's lace 24

Rhamnus alaternus 'Argentea Variegatus' 132

rhododendrons 23, 125, 149; *Rhododendron* 'Whitethroat' 125; *R. arborescens* 125; *R. atlanticum* 125; *R. bullatum* 125; *R. crassum* 125; *R. dalhousie* 125; *R.d.* 'Countess of Haddington' 125; *R.d.* 'Henryanum' 125; *R. edgeworthii* 125; *R. formosum* 125; *R. maddenii* 125; *R. polyandrum* 125; *R. rhabdotum* 125; *R. schlippenbachii* 125; *R. simsii* 126; *R.s.* 'Gumpo White' 126, 147, 153; *R.s.* 'Gardenia White' 126, 153; *R.s.* 'Polar Sea' 126; *R. viscosum* 125; *R.v. aemulans* 125, 147; *R.v. glaucophyllum* 125; *R.v. nitidum* 125

Robinia pseudoacacia 'Frisia' *19*, 20

Romneya x *hybrida* 152

Rosmarinus 'Miss Jessop's Upright' 152

rosemary, white, 60

roses 12, 20–3, 23, *82*, 102, *103*, 104–6, 141, 149; climbing 105; English 104; hybrid musk 104; miniature 104; *R.* 'Aimee Vibert' 20; *R.* 'Anna Zinkeisen' 104; *R.* 'Astra Desmond' 106; *R.* 'Ballerina' 104; *R.* 'Blanc Double de Coubert' 17; *R.* 'Bobbie James' 106; *R.* 'Dedication' 61; *R.* 'Fair Bianca' 103; *R.* 'Felicite et Perpetue' 20; *R.* 'Francine' 116; *R.* 'Francine Austin' 104; *R.* 'Heather Muir' 106; *R.* 'Iceberg' 13, 16, 17, 20, 24, 25, 40, *42, 50*, 61, 88, 102–5, 116,

143, 147, 149, 151, 152; *R.* 'Ice Fairy' 104, 143, 147; *R.* 'Kiftsgate' 105–6; *R.* 'Little White Pet' 13, 17, 24, 40, 104, 143, 147; *R.* 'Margaret Merrill' 13, *59*, 44, 61, 66, 103, 104, 143, 147, 149, 151; *R.* 'Mary Rose' 103; *R.* 'Mme Alfred Carrière' 20; *R.* 'Mme Hardy' 61; *R.* 'Moonlight' 104; *R.* 'Mrs Herbert Stevens' 105; *R.* 'Noisette' 104; *R.* 'Pascali' 44, 66, 103, 104; *R.* 'Pax' 104; *R.* 'Polar Star' 103–4; *R.* 'Pristine' 103; *R.* 'Prosperity' 104; *R.* 'Proud Titania' 103; *R.* 'Purity' 21, 105; *R.* 'Rudolph Timm' 61; *R.* 'Sanders White' 20; *R.* 'Snow Carpet' 13; *R.* 'Swany' 104; *R.* 'The Fairy' 104; *R.* 'The New Dawn' 17; *R.* 'White Cockade' 105; *R.* 'White Spray' 103; *R.* 'Winchester Cathedral' 103; *R. chinensis* 135, 153; *R. synstylae* 105; *R.s. brunonii* 105; *R.s. filipes* 105; *R.s. longicuspis* 105,106; *R.s. moschata* 105

Ruta graveolens 'Jackman's Blue' 52, 112

Sagina glabra 'Aurea' 20

Sagittaria sagittifolia 136; *S. leucopetala* 'Florepleno' 136

salix *14, 82*, 112; *Salix alba* 'Sericea' 112; *S. helvetica* 13, 112, 142, 147; *S. lanata* 17, 112, 142, 147

Salvia aethiopis 113; *S. argentea* 113; *S. lavandulifolia* 113

Sambucus nigra 'Albovariegata' (elder) 131; *S.n.* 'Pulverulenta' 131

Santolina chamaecyparissus 113; *S. incana* 113; *S.i.* 'Nana' 152; *S.n.* 'Edward Bowles' 113; *S. neapolitana* 'Sulphurea' 113; *S. pinnata neapolitana* 13

Sarcococca confusa 81

Saxifraga fortunei 81, 98, 145, 153

Schizophragma hydrangeoides 110; *S. integrifolium* 110

Schizostylis coccinea 'Alba' 93–4, 145

scillas 29, 61; *Scilla peruviana* 76; *S. sibirica* 'Alba' 76, 144, 149, 151

Scirpus lacustris tabernaemontana 'Albescens' 136; *S.l.t.* 'Zebrinus' 136

Scrophularia aquatica 'Variegata' 97

sculptures and statues 33, 34, *35*

seats 33, *34, 35*

sedge 101

Sedum spectabile 'Iceberg' 94

Senecio 'Sunshine' 49, 142; *Senecio grayi* 49; *S. laxifolius* 49; *S. smithii* 15, 135

Seriphidium tridentatum 13

Shasta daisy 'Wirral Supreme' 17

shrubs 121–8; foliage 128–33

silver plants 111–17

Silybum marianum 73

Sissinghurst Castle, Kent *11*, 12, 32, 34, 69, *102*, 138, 157; pleached limes *126*; in winter *39*

Sisyrinchium striatum 92, 131; *S.s.* 'Apple Court' 78; *S.s.* 'Aunt May' 97

snowdrops 75, 98, 131

solanums 111; *Solanum crispum* 'Album' 21

Solomon's seal 25, 84, 95

space, boundaries of *27;* organisation of 25–6

Spiraea arguta 24

159

Stachys byzantina 116; *S.b.* 'Primrose Heron' 116; *S. lanata* 'Silver Carpet' 45, 116; *S. olympica* 116; *S.o.* 'Variegata' 116
steps 32–3, *34*
Stewartia malacodendron 140; *S, pseudo-camellia* 153, 155
stilt hedges 29, 149
Styrax hemslyana 121; *S. obassia* 121
sweet pea, perennial white 18, 20, 68; *see also Lathyrus odoratus*
Symphytum x *uplandicum* 96
Syringa sempervirens 124
Tanacetum densum 45, 116, 152; *T. partheneum* 'Aureum' 88; *T.p.* 'Plenum' 88; *T.p.* 'Sissinghurst' 88; *T.p.* Snowball' 88; *T.p.* 'White Bonnet' 88; *T. roseum* 88
Thelycrania controversa 'Variegata' 130
Thunbergia alata 69
Thuja plicata 28; *T. occidentalis* 'Malonyana' 137
thyme 117
Tintinhull, Fountain Garden 12–13, *14*, 15, 40, *82*, 112, 138, 157; pool *39*, 135; trees 117
topiary 36, *38*
town gardens 148–50, *151*
Trachelospemum asiaticum 21, 109; *T. jasminoides* 21, 109; *T.j.* 'Variegatum' 21,

109; *T.j.* 'Wilsonii' 109; *T.j. japonicum* 109; *T.j.* var *pubescens'* 109; *T. majus* 109
Trachycarpus fortunei 24
trees for white gardens 117–21
Trillium grandiflorum 51, 57; *T.g. flore pleno* 144
tulips 25, 76–7; *Tulipa* 'White Parrot' 77; *T.* 'White Triumphator' 77; *T. biflora* 77; *T. polychroma* 77; *T. tarda* 77; *T. turkestanica* 76; *T. viridiflora* 'Angel' 77
tunnels 20; apple *30*
Valerian, white 13, 17
veratrums 116
Verbascum hybridum 'Mont Blanc' 69
Verbena x *hybrida* 'Marbella' 72
veronicas 86–7; *Veronica gentianoides* 'Variegata' 87; *V. spicata* 87; *V.s.* 'Alba' 87; *V.s.* 'Icicle' 87; *V. virginica* 'Alba' 24, 86
viburnums 9, 127–8; *Viburnum davidii* 49; *V. farreri* 'Candidissium' 131; *V. furcatum* 127; *V. macrophyllum* 127; *V. tinus* 'French White' 81; *V. tomentosum* 9, 127; *V.t.* 'Nana' 9; *V.t.* 'Mariesii' 9, 127; *V.t.* 'Cascade' 9, 128; *V.t.* 'Lanarth' 127; *V.t.* 'Rowallane' 127; *V.t.* 'Nana Semperflorens' 128
Vinca major 97; *V.m.* 'Elegantissima' 97; *V. minor* 'Argentea Variegata' 97

Viola cornuta 16, 149; *V.c.* 'Alba' 24, 49, 151; *V.c.* 'Alba Minor' 49; *V. septentrionalis* 49
Wallflowers, 'Ivory White' 69; 'White Dove' 69
walls, use of 28, *30*
water, plants 133–6; use of 36–7, *39*
water-lily (*Nymphaea*) 15, 20, 37, 135; 'Albatross' 135; 'Gloire de Temple sur Lot' 135; 'Virginalis' 135
Wattakaka sinensis 21, 108, 109
Weigela florida 'Variegata' 132; *W. praecox* 'Variegata' 132
wisteria 20, *30*, 60, 106; *Wisteria floribunda* 20; *W.f.* 'Alba' 60; *W. japonica* 20; *W. sinensis* 'Alba' 29, *55*, 60; *W. venusta* 'Alba Plena' 29
woodruff 13, 25
Yew hedging 12, 13, 15, 16, 27–8, 111, 149
York Gate, Adel *23*, 72, 101, *115*, 157
yuccas 101; *Yucca filamentosa* 94; *Y. flaccida* 94; *Y.f.* 'Ivory' 94; *Y. floriosa* 94; *Y. recurvifolia* 94
Zantedeschia aethiopica (arum lily) 78, 135; *Z.a.* 'Apple Court' 135; *Z.a.* 'Crowborough' 78, 135; *Z.a.* 'Green Goddess' 135
Zephyranthes candida 80, 152
zinnias, 'Envy' 72; 'Carved Ivory' 72; 'Big Snowman' 72

WHITE GARDENS TO VISIT

Apple Court, Lymington, Hampshire
(National Gardens Scheme)

Bampton Manor, Witney, Oxfordshire
(National Gardens Scheme)

Barrington Court, Ilminster, Somerset
(National Trust)

The Manor House, Birlingham, Worcestershire
(By invitation only)

Chenies Manor, Amersham, Bucks

Cranborne Manor, Dorset

Crathes Castle
(National Trust for Scotland)

Folly Farm, Sulhampstead, Berkshire
(National Gardens Scheme)

Hazelby House, Newbury, Berkshire
(National Gardens Scheme)

Hidcote Manor, Mickleton, Gloucestershire
(National Trust)

Lytes Cary Manor, Somerton, Somerset
(National Trust)

Newby Hall, Ripon, Yorkshire

Sissinghurst Castle, Cranbrook, Kent
(National Trust)

The Little Cottage, Lymington, Hampshire
(National Gardens Scheme)

Tintinhull House, Ilchester, Somerset
(National Trust)

York Gate, Leeds, Yorkshire
(National Gardens Scheme)